ADOPTION
PARENTHOOD WITHOUT PREGNANCY

ADOPTION
PARENTHOOD WITHOUT PREGNANCY

CHARLENE CANAPE

HENRY HOLT AND COMPANY

NEW YORK

To Joseph

Library of Congress Cataloging in Publication Data
Canape, Charlene.
Adoption : parenthood without pregnancy.
Includes index.
1. Adoption—United States.   2. Adoption—United
States—Directories.   I. Title.
HV875.55.C36   1986   362.7'34'0973   85-24753
ISBN: 0-03-001594-4

First Edition
Designed by Katy Susan Riegel-Hood
Printed in the United States of America
10 9 8 7 6 5 4 3 2 1

ISBN 0-03-001594-4

362.734
C

CONTENTS

ACKNOWLEDGMENTS

When people ask me how long I spent working on this adoption book I am always tempted to say, "Seven years." That was the amount of time it took me to become a mother. Along the way, I cried a lot, made mistakes, and nearly gave up several times.

Now that I am an adoptive parent, I have been able to put those years behind me. Joseph has brought me and my husband more happiness than we ever thought possible. It is my hope that others will persevere so that they may discover those joys for themselves. In some small way, I hope that this book will aid them in their endeavors.

I would like to thank all of the adoptive parents who gave so generously of their time for talking with me so that others could benefit from their experiences. I would also like to thank the many adoption professionals who shared with me their knowledge, insights, and advice.

A special thanks to my agent, Denise Marcil, who first suggested to me that I write this book. I owe a debt of gratitude to my editors at Holt, Rinehart and Winston, Rachel Christmas and Yvonne Torstensson, for their many suggestions and skillful editing.

I am grateful to my sister, Lorraine Sorrell, for her tireless efforts in putting together the lists of adoption agencies and adoptive-parent support groups.

My own personal appreciation goes to all those who helped me and my husband during our own efforts to adopt. Our experience was so positive that it set a very high standard against which to judge other adoptions.

It would be impossible to thank all the friends and relatives who have been so supportive throughout the years. Without their love and understanding we would have been lost.

To my husband, Tom, who is my source of inspiration and strength. Most of all, to Joseph, who continues to light up our lives.

ADOPTION
PARENTHOOD WITHOUT PREGNANCY

INTRODUCTION

My husband and I were vacationing in Florida when we received the call from the adoption agency. "You have a son," the social worker told us. The event we had anticipated for years was finally happening. We were going to be parents.

We flew back to New York and spent the next four days preparing for Joseph's arrival. Those four days now seem to melt into one blur. I remember that one day was spent at the local baby store stocking up on supplies. A good friend who had adopted a baby girl two years before understood my daze and took charge, making up the list of essentials. As I wheeled the cart up and down the aisles she tossed in undershirts, blankets, bottles, and a soft stuffed white bear.

The room we planned to use for Joseph had been serving as my sewing room. Did I have an early vision of Joseph's arrival? How else could I explain the baby blue and white flowered wallpaper that I had selected for the room three years ago? It was now the perfect room for a baby boy. We borrowed a wooden cradle and outfitted it with blue gingham bumpers. Down from the walls came my sewing charts to make way for pictures of teddy bears and a soft-sculpture yellow balloon.

Word of Joseph's imminent arrival began to spread. The telephone rang incessantly. Each buzz of the doorbell brought a neighbor with another piece of baby equipment we didn't know we needed. Before too long our entry hall was filled with a carriage, two Snuglis, a travel bed, a baby seat, baby blankets, and bags of clothing. Baby gifts were stuffed into our mailbox. A good friend from the suburbs messengered a copy of the book *Your Baby and*

Child by Penelope Leach. "You'll have just enough time to read the first hundred pages before Joseph arrives," her note read.

All our family and close friends knew how much we had longed for a baby. Some of them cried quite openly when we told them about Joseph.

Four days after receiving the phone call from the social worker, we went to the agency to pick up Joseph. "He is the most perfect baby we have seen," our social worker told us. When we peeked in the crib at our son we had to agree.

We brought Joseph home and placed him in the cradle. He slept for two hours and we sat nearby watching his every move. He was the most beautiful baby in the world and he was our son.

Years ago when I thought about becoming a mother, I had envisioned a much different scenario. I had anticipated a nine-month pregnancy, during which I would gradually prepare for the baby's arrival. Then, of course, I had thought about those moments in the delivery room and the feeling of actually giving birth to another human being.

Yet I cannot imagine that experience being any more thrilling than the moment I saw Joseph. That glimpse into his crib has been printed indelibly in my mind. I can still recall his angelic expression and how soft and small he felt when I held him.

Those first few months I was so excited about Joseph that I fairly glowed. Even sleepless nights couldn't diminish my enthusiasm. I found I didn't need to take naps. I got by on pure adrenaline. Even people I didn't know well commented on my appearance. When I told them about Joseph, they peppered me with questions. I soon realized that these people were interested in more than my specific situation; they were interested in adoption themselves.

That fact was driven home several weeks after the adoption when I went to interview a woman executive for an article I was writing. I was late for the interview and because I knew I had only been allotted a half hour of her time, I launched right into my first question. Instead of responding, this woman walked over and closed the door to her office. She then sat opposite me and said, "I understand that you recently have had something wonderful happen to you." I was surprised that she had heard about Joseph but was glad to fill her in on the details. She then said, "I'm interested in adopting, too. Tell me what to do."

She was not the last person to approach me. Over the next few months I received calls from friends, acquaintances, business associates, and total strangers. Some were still grappling with infertility and wanted to know how my husband and I had reached the decision to adopt. Others had made the decision to adopt but didn't know what to do next. Still others had made some initial attempts and had been discouraged. They all sought my advice.

Before too long I found myself regularly dispensing information and advice on adoption. I began to realize that there was a desperate need for a book that could help other couples benefit not only from all the data I had collected over the years but also from my own personal experience.

I still had many questions about adoption. Why did the agencies have so few healthy infants available for adoption? How did these agencies decide which couples would be accepted? Since my own experience was through an adoption agency, I wondered about independent adoptions. Were they as risky as some people said? What about foreign adoptions? Were they as costly as the newspaper stories have led us to believe? I felt I could put my skills as a reporter and writer to good use by shedding light on many of these issues.

I tell everyone who seeks my advice the same thing: It is possible to adopt. You just have to be organized, aggressive, persistent, and patient. You must realize that the entire process—first dealing with infertility and then pursuing adoption—extracts a huge physical and emotional toll. There will be times when you are the strong one as your partner succumbs to depression. There will be other times when he or she is there to console you. Not everyone you deal with will be sympathetic to your cause.

My hope is that this book will help others through the adoption process. I am mainly concerned about those couples who choose to adopt because of infertility. These are the people who need help the most.

Few disappointments in life are as painful as being unable to bear children. The couple who find they are having trouble conceiving are apt to feel persecuted. Suddenly it seems as if everyone they know is having children. A sunny morning can be spoiled by the day's mail, which brings a birth announcement or invitation to a baby shower. Even a trip to the supermarket can be depressing. Every other shopping cart seems to be pushed by a pregnant woman. The other women checking out have their carts heaped high with diapers and baby food.

Relaxing in front of the TV set, particularly during the day, can be an exercise in masochism. Every commercial appears to feature a gurgling baby or giggling children.

Those who suffer from infertility often suffer in silence, in part because, to many people, infertility still carries with it a social stigma. Men feel a loss of their masculinity and even sexual potency.

Women feel less feminine and inadequate. Down through history, woman's main role was to provide future heirs. Who can forget that King Henry VIII had Anne Boleyn beheaded partly because she failed to give him a son? (And in Anne's case, she didn't do too bad a job. She did give birth to the future Queen Elizabeth I.) Can anyone imagine how the British people would feel about Princess Di if she hadn't been able to produce a future king of England?

Even terms like *barren*, once used to describe women who were infertile, make them sound like human deserts—dry, lifeless, devoid of emotion, almost as if they are missing a part of their souls.

There is added pressure on women today to have children. After years of being forced to choose between a career and motherhood, more women today are finding that they can successfully combine the two. While this is a positive development, it puts the infertile woman in a particularly stressful position. How can she be excited about the new freedoms for women when she can't take advantage of them?

Under the circumstances, who can blame the infertile couple for hiding their secret from family and friends? The most common reaction is for the couple to seek medical help while still trying to conceive. Inquiries from well-meaning parents about when they can expect grandchildren may be turned back with a noncommittal, "When we're ready." To friends, they can say that they are too busy with their careers to worry about children.

A couple can get so caught up in seeking medical remedies that they soon begin to live their lives around the wife's monthly cycle. It is akin to living life on a roller coaster with a couple's hopes rising and falling with the woman's temperature.

No one can fault a couple for trying to do everything they can to have a child. The problem occurs when conception becomes the central goal in their lives at the expense of everything else—their jobs, their friends, possibly even their marriage.

I have interviewed many couples who have coped with infertility. Some managed well, others made mistakes. Their comments, which are included throughout this book, should help anyone going through this trauma. To protect the privacy of those involved, fictitious names have been used.

Once the couple come to grips with their inability to have children, does the decision to adopt follow naturally? For some it is the most obvious alternative and one that they take to wholeheartedly. Others have trouble accepting the idea. I talked with couples who reached the decision to adopt as well as to professionals who counsel prospective adoptive parents. The views shared by these two groups should prove useful to anyone thinking about adoption.

Infertility is just one reason for adoption, of course. Aware that there are many children in need of families, some fertile couples choose to adopt instead of bringing more children into the world.

This book will help all prospective adoptive parents choose the best method of adoption and get through the process. Again, much of this advice comes not only from the people who have been through the system, but also from the professionals working within it.

For various reasons, more white Americans than Americans of other races adopt, and most people want to adopt children who appear to be theirs biologically. Most people also want to adopt healthy infants. There are currently more prospective parents looking for healthy white infants than there are healthy white infants available. This has led to increased interest in adopting foreign children; however, foreign adoption is an area in which a couple must really do their homework. I have included interviews with several couples who have adopted foreign children. The comments from these couples will prove useful for anyone wishing to pursue foreign adoption.

More people are also choosing to adopt American children of different races and "special-needs children"—those who are older or have physical or emotional handicaps. Taking such a child into your home can be as rewarding as it is challenging. A separate chapter will deal with adopting older or handicapped children.

Many single people decide to adopt, whether or not they are infertile. In the past, agency officials discouraged them from adopting, but this situation is changing. Single people are often considered top candidates for adopting non-white infants and older or handicapped children of all races, since so many of these children are waiting for homes. One chapter deals with single-parent adoption and includes interviews with single parents and with professionals who place children with them.

The adoptive family will face many future challenges. In fact, the thought that these problems may lurk in the days ahead has discouraged many couples from adopting. When and how do you tell the child he is adopted? What do you do if the child wants to look for this birthparents? (With more states passing legislation allowing adopted children and birthparents access to adoption records, this situation will become more common.) If a couple adopt a foreign child, how do they teach him about his native land? How do you handle problems the child may encounter at school because he is different?

Many adoption agencies have ongoing counseling services to help adoptive families tackle these problems. There are special independent counseling groups in different parts of the country that specialize in helping adoptive families. In addition, adoptive-parents groups around the country serve as tremendous support mechanisms for adoptive parents. A separate section tells about all these groups and what a couple can do to benefit from their services.

Now that I am an adoptive parent I am interested in the way adoption is perceived by the population in general. There is much that needs to be done to change our society's views on adoption. Recently there have been many articles in newspapers and magazines about the nationwide problem of teenage pregnancies, but seldom do these articles mention adoption. To many people today there are only two choices when a young unmarried girl gets pregnant—abortion or raising the child alone. There is a great need to publicize adoption as an alternative.

There is also a need to get corporations and other employers to regard adoption seriously. An adoptive couple may pay more than five thousand dollars in medical and legal fees to adopt a child, but rarely will the husband's or wife's employer or medical insurance cover part or any of the expenses. Most employers will not grant maternity leave. Many adoptive-parent groups around the country have been formed to address these issues. Encouraging adoptive parents to join and become active in these groups is an important task.

It is possible to adopt. More than that, it is a wonderful experience. My hope is that this book will help many other people toward that goal.

1

THE HEARTBREAK OF INFERTILITY

I n looking back on their experiences, the majority of adoptive couples interviewed for this book had one regret in common: not acting sooner to adopt.

Justin, an accountant in Pittsburgh, and his wife Nina, a librarian, were typical. They spent seven years trying to overcome their fertility problems. When they finally accepted the fact that they would probably never have biological children, they began to look into adoption. Only then did Justin and Nina discover that many agencies will not accept applicants over forty. Justin was forty-two.

The agencies that would accept them had waiting times of five years. When those years were added to the number of years they had spent in medical treatment, Justin and Nina found that their wait to become parents threatened to stretch beyond a decade.

Eventually, Justin and Nina were able to adopt an infant more quickly through an independent adoption. Looking back, they still wonder how they let so much time slip by before they took positive action.

Their situation is not unique. Many couples have difficulty in coping with infertility. Taking the next step by deciding to adopt is even more difficult. Yet it makes a great deal of sense to begin looking into adoption while still pursuing medical remedies. No one is advocating that a couple adopt before they are ready, but they should keep their minds open to alternatives and not place all of their hopes on eventually having biological children.

It is not surprising that men and women alike have trouble

accepting infertility. Not being able to have a child always comes as a shock because it runs counter to everything nature had intended.

What could be easier than having a baby? We have all seen the textbook diagrams illustrating the process. It all seems so elemental—thousands of male sperm swim through the female's cervix, then through the uterus to the tubes in time to meet the egg. The female egg, meanwhile, has been released by the ovary and travels through the fallopian tube until it meets the sperm. Fertilization takes place in the tube and the resulting ovum then travels back to the uterus to attach itself to the uterine wall.

The fact is that the human reproductive system is a lot more delicate than we have been led to believe. While the basic process appears simple, there is much that can go wrong along the way. "Human beings are not as fertile as they're given credit for," said Dr. Wayne H. Decker of the Fertility Research Foundation in New York City. "Any time a normal, ovulating woman is exposed to good sperm at the right time, she has a 10 percent chance to get pregnant. This surprises people. But pregnancy only occurs one time in ten."

That rate is present with a "normal, ovulating woman" and a man with "good sperm." With less than optimum conditions, a couple's chances for conception begin to drop lower.

What can go wrong?

Men's infertility—low sperm count, for example—is estimated to be responsible for half the cases of infertility. Hormone therapy can help to raise sperm count. Other men may have a blockage in their testicles that can be corrected through microsurgery. If all else fails and the woman is healthy, artificial insemination can be one solution.

Infertility becomes more complex when the woman experiences trouble. A woman can increase her chances of becoming pregnant by having her children early in life. But, with more women getting married later and delaying childbearing to concentrate on careers, that timing becomes difficult.

Many of the diseases that cause conception failure occur in women over twenty-five. They include the following.

Endometriosis. What happens is that the endometrial tissue that lines the uterine wall actually ends up outside the uterus to form cysts or adhesions. During each menstrual cycle, these cysts grow and soon create scar tissue that can interfere with conception. Treatment for endometriosis includes surgery, during which these implants are excised, or hormonal drug therapy, which may have adverse side effects.

Pelvic Inflammatory Disease. Women who have been sexually active with many partners may contract pelvic inflammatory disease, which includes gonorrhea, chlamydia, and cervical infections. Many physicians believe that pelvic inflammatory disease has been on the increase since many couples have abandoned the use of condoms, which can serve as a protective barrier.

Any woman with an active sex life should take steps to protect herself from these diseases by having her partner use a condom. In addition, an intrauterine device (IUD), which can also cause infections, should never be used by a woman who has not had children.

Hormonal Disorders. A woman who does not ovulate or ovulates infrequently will have difficulty getting pregnant. Many of these women may achieve pregnancy after taking fertility drugs such as Clomid or Pergonal.

Tubal Pregnancies. Scar tissue in the pelvic cavity may cause obstructions in the tube, making it impossible for the fertilized egg to complete its journey. When this occurs the egg may become stuck in the fallopian tube, resulting in an ectopic or tubal pregnancy. This condition can be life-threatening because the tube may rupture. The result may be the destruction of the tube where the ovum was caught, thus further reducing fertility.

In some cases, it is impossible to diagnose the cause of infertility. This situation can be the most frustrating for the couple wishing to become parents.

Physicians differ on the percentages that can be attributed to the different types of infertility in women. Generally, one third will have no detectable problem; one third will have trouble ovulating; and one third will suffer anatomical difficulties attributed to endometriosis, tubal pregnancies, or other factors.

When a couple realize they are having trouble conceiving, they go through several psychological stages. In the beginning there is a feeling of disbelief. "For years we did everything so that I wouldn't become pregnant," said Diane, a teacher living in Texas. "Now it's almost laughable."

When reality begins to sink in, one partner or both may become very angry. The question becomes, "Why us?"

Soon, the anger begins to dissipate and the couple face the question of what to do. If the urge to become parents is very strong and the medical outlook bleak, then the couple may decide on adoption immediately. The more common situation, however, is for the couple to continue medical therapy in the hope that the wife will somehow beat the odds that are stacked against them and become pregnant.

At this point, many couples seek out fertility experts either on their own or through the advice of the woman's gynecologist. Even for those who are helped, however, the medical procedures can be painful and expensive, and may stretch on for years.

If all the false starts and medical tests don't discourage a couple, at some point they may begin to question certain medical solutions. Artificial insemination, for example, can be a convenient solution when the man is infertile and his wife is healthy. It allows the couple to maintain their privacy, since no one has to know that the wife was not impregnated by her husband.

Yet some men are opposed to having their wives fertilized with another man's sperm. Diane said that her husband was one of them. "He said he didn't think he could stand knowing that the child was half mine and half someone else's," Diane said. "He knew he would feel left out and he didn't think he could live with that."

No doubt science has made great strides within the last ten years to aid the infertile couple. But many of these medical techniques have been tried without someone thinking through the eventual consequences and what the effect could be on the child. The techniques include in vitro fertilization and surrogate motherhood.

In vitro fertilization is performed on a woman whose tubes have been damaged. Several eggs are removed surgically from her ovaries and are then fertilized in a laboratory dish with her husband's sperm. The ovum is then implanted in the woman's uterus.

Surrogate motherhood means that the infertile couple pay another woman to be artificially inseminated with the husband's sperm. Or, she could receive the ovum that resulted from in vitro fertilization if the wife for some reason could not carry the embryo to term. In either case, the woman would turn the baby over to the couple after birth.

These procedures seem straightforward enough, but legal experts believe they are creating a potential quagmire that could suck in the infertile couple, the surrogate mother, and the child. Already we have seen some of these dilemmas. In several cases, the surrogate mother has refused to give up the child to the infertile couple. Then what happens? Who are the child's parents? In another instance, a wife separated from her husband sought to prevent her husband from seeing their child by arguing that because the child was conceived through artificial insemination with another man's sperm it was not really his.

The Heartbreak of Infertility   11

Congress has held hearings but has not yet passed legislation on these issues, and few states have laws to deal with some of the complications that could occur. The courts have ruled in individual situations, but it will be quite some time before definitive case law develops.

Another drawback to in vitro fertilization is that it can quickly deplete a couple's enthusiasm and bank account. "In vitro is really the last option," says Johnelle May, a registered nurse who is program coordinator for in vitro fertilization and embryo transplant at the Baylor College of Medicine in Houston. "Patients come to me after they have done everything else. Emotionally, it is very draining to go through in vitro. It's so demanding."

Erica, who underwent in vitro twice in two different medical centers, would agree with Ms. May's assessment of how the process can affect the patient. Besides costing over five thousand dollars, each procedure used up Erica's emotional reserves. When the doctors planted the fertilized eggs in her uterus, the feeling that she might be pregnant was overwhelming. When she eventually found out that the experiment had failed, she was devastated.

Erica's bad experience with in vitro did have one positive side effect, however. "The night we came back, my husband turned to me and said, 'Let's adopt,'" recalled Erica. "I said, 'You're right. We really want a baby and we're not going to get one this way.'" The next day they began to look into adoption.

Some couples discover after they adopt that they have a new perspective on bearing children. Most still want the experience of having a biological child, but, because they are already parents, achieving pregnancy no longer becomes the obsession it once was. Many find that once the pressure is off they have renewed energy and spirit to undergo tests or procedures they had once rejected.

After undergoing five operations and several office procedures, Jennifer, a guidance counselor from New Jersey, said she once felt she couldn't put up with any more tests. But now that she has an adopted son, she is ready to try again. "For a long time, I thought pregnancy was what I wanted," said Jennifer. "But now I have what I want. The only reason I'm continuing with medical tests is because financially it would be easier for us to have a biological child." Jennifer's son came to them through an independent adoption that cost Jennifer and her husband nearly seven thousand dollars. If she has a biological child, her husband's medical insurance will pay most of the hospital costs.

Eleanor, a secretary, and her husband Robert, an accountant, who live in Chicago, adopted a baby boy a year ago when he was only a few days old. "We felt we had gone through heroic efforts for six years," said Eleanor. "But now I'm considering going through more." Eleanor said they have been accepted at an in vitro clinic. "I know three women in my city who have been through it and none has been successful," she said. "I know it's costly and time consuming. But I'm not discouraged. I still want to try it."

Even though Eleanor and her husband will try in vitro, they already are on an adoption agency's list for a second child. "No matter what happens, I know that within a year we will be parents again," she said.

2

DECIDING TO ADOPT

We haven't been able to have children and we really want to be parents. So we're going to adopt."

For the infertile couple, adoption seems like such a logical choice. Yet many couples have incredible difficulty arriving at that decision.

Why? What prevents people from acting soon to adopt?

Some couples may cling to the hope that they will eventually have biological children. But that fact alone should never prevent a couple from considering adoption. The best strategy is to pursue medical remedies and adoption simultaneously.

Dr. Elisabeth Herz, an obstetrician, gynecologist, and psychiatrist at the George Washington University Medical Center in Washington, D.C., said she now advises patients who have a minimal chance of becoming pregnant to look into adoption while they see her. "Then they will have two things running at once," she said.

At the Johns Hopkins Hospital in Baltimore, Dr. Marian D. Damewood said she will mention adoption after medical or surgical therapy, but before in vitro or other last-resort alternatives. "At that point, many couples realize that they have a significant problem and that medical therapy will not work," siad Dr. Damewood, who is an assistant professor of obstetrics and gynecology and director of the in vitro program at Johns Hopkins. "Some say they are glad I brought it up," she added.

One woman whose chances of becoming pregnant were bleak said that her doctor agreed to begin artificial insemination as a course of action only if she and her husband first applied to an adoption agency. "He knew that the artificial insemination might not succeed and he didn't want us pinning all our hopes on it," she said.

Yet many physicians do not believe in advising their patients to consider adoption. "We will continue to treat them as long as we believe there is something we can do," said one infertility specialist. "There are some couples where I say, 'Maybe you should stop trying,'" he said. "But I had a woman who went through one hundred thirty-two artificial inseminations and two operations. And eventually she and her husband had a baby."

He added, "I don't think it's my place to recommend that a couple adopt, or decide on artificial insemination, or in vitro. We lay out the things available to them and then they make up their own minds."

Unfortunately, if the couple experience psychological problems related to their infertility, it may be difficult for them to assess their situation objectively. Few gynecologists, even those that specialize in infertility, have the time or training to help couples deal with the emotional side effects of infertility. "This area needs much more attention than it is getting," said Dr. Marvin S. Kasow, a New York psychologist who counsels infertile couples. "Many doctors are humanistic, but others tend to treat their patients in a mechanistic way. When a couple go to a clinic, they may go for sophisticated medical tests, but the atmosphere may be impersonal."

Some couples seek counseling on their own, but even then it is not aways easy to find the right professional. Marilyn's situation is typical. "I felt like I was living and dying over a thirty-day period," said Marilyn, a textile designer from North Carolina. "I just needed someone to talk to about it. One day I looked in the yellow pages and called a nearby clinic. First of all, I couldn't believe I was calling a clinic. I mean, clinics are places that poor people go to because they have nowhere else to go. But that was me. I had nowhere else to go. When someone answered the phone, I started to cry. I said that I was unable to have a baby and just needed to talk with someone. I began to see a woman there and it has been a great help to me."

Many other infertile couples have found comfort in RESOLVE, a national organization with headquarters in Belmont, Massachusetts, and chapters in forty states, that offers counseling, support groups, medical information, and referral for infertile couples. More than five thousand couples now belong to RESOLVE. The group operates a hotline (617-484-2424) that men and women can call to talk with someone who understands what they are going through.

RESOLVE also publishes a newsletter that is mailed to members. Local chapters sponsor support groups where couples can gather to discuss their feelings about infertility.

Often, couples are too intimidated to talk publicly about their problems. But eventually they begin to open up. Those who are proponents of the RESOLVE approach believe that it not only helped them to deal with their infertility but also served as a mechanism for them to get going on adoption.

A couple may be reluctant to consider adoption seriously because it appears to signal that they are giving up their quest to have a biological child. Jennifer, the guidance counselor from New Jersey, recalled how difficult it was for her to begin the adoption process. "I felt that once I picked up that phone, I was admitting that I had a problem," she said. "It took me a long time before I could do it. Every time I started a new medical procedure that offered us some hope, I would say to my husband, 'Let's wait a little longer.' "

What most couples discover once they adopt is that they have succeeded in their primary goal. They are now parents. They had become so obsessed with achieving pregnancy they may have forgotten that what they really wanted was a child. And adoption can meet that goal quite well.

To understand how a couple can become so obsessed, it is necessary to learn something about the group now having children. Many of these couples are from the baby boom generation—the pig-in-a-python group that continues to change society as it passes through simply because of its sheer size. These people have been America's movers and shakers. They have lobbied for changes in government, business, and society. They are the generation that believes anything can be accomplished with a little energy and inspiration.

Many of these baby boomers are overachievers who have been used to hitting their goals on time. These goals may not be as conscious as those for which you make a list, but if they were, an example might be the following: "College graduation at twenty-one, MBA at twenty-three, marriage at twenty-five, department head at twenty-eight, own home at thirty, vice-president at thirty-two, start own company at thirty-five." By age thirty-five a couple are secure in their marriage, jobs, and home. They are at the perfect point, they reason, to begin a family.

But that schedule cannot be met. Unlike buying a new home or starting a company, having a baby depends on forces unrelated to a couple's education or socioeconomic status. This can be the most frustrating experience of their lives.

How will such a couple deal with this crisis? They are accustomed to being in charge and accomplishing what they set out to do. Suddenly they are confronted with a situation that they cannot control. So they approach having a baby much as they would approach a problem at work.

These women and their husbands will research every new method for treating infertility. Money may be no object: What health insurance doesn't cover, the couple will pay for themselves.

Some couples spend so much time grappling with their infertility that it begins to overshadow everything else in their lives. The strain can sometimes be devastating to the marriage.

In some cases, there are reasons for a couple to be hopeful about their chances for producing a biological child. "Ninety percent of the time we can find something wrong and offer treatment," said Dr. Damewood. Not all cases are easily solved, however, and when a cause cannot be found for the infertility the couple may have difficulty dealing with their frustration.

Relatives and friends may encourage the infertile couple to keep trying for a biological child. Many of these people are well meaning, of course. Chances are, they have never encountered anyone having trouble and so may share the couple's belief that sooner or later the wife will conceive. No one wants to dampen the couple's hopes. Everyone believes a pep talk will help. So rather than help the couple to accept their infertility and look at alternatives like adoption, a parent or good friend is more apt to say, "Sally, don't give up. I just know that if you and Bill keep trying you'll get pregnant."

Such pep talks only increase a couple's anxiety. If this advice comes from a parent, there is the added stress of guilt. An infertile woman looks at the other women in her family and realizes that she is the only one having trouble. How can she let her family down? How can she fail to produce a grandchild?

The infertile couple may also begin to feel that their parents are encouraging them to keep trying because they do not want an adopted grandchild. Usually that is not the case. Most parents probably have not thought the situation through thoroughly, and know only that they have always encouraged their children to do their best. Remember back to that first bike ride? Or learning those multiplication tables in school? Mom and Dad were always there to cheer their children on. How can they now tell them to give up?

The woman's physician, while looking for solutions to a couple's dilemma, may also become part of the problem. Nothing pleases an infertility specialist more than helping a woman achieve pregnancy. The challenge is greater the more difficult her case seems. Of course, it's understandable that the doctor wants to succeed, because that is what medicine is all about—diagnosing the medical problem and then correcting it. But a doctor may become obsessed with a case. "The egos of some of these doctors are amazing," said Erica, a magazine editor, who saw several physicians in Washington, D.C., and New York City over a five-year period.

In some cases, a woman may be worn down physically when she finally decides to throw in the towel. That is because some of the medical procedures are no pleasure to endure: At the least they can be inconvenient; at the worst they can be extremely painful and humiliating. Several years of subjecting oneself to these tests can break even the most stoic individual.

Jessica, a buyer for a department store in Ohio, tells of breaking down after having an endometrial biopsy, a procedure for checking to see if a woman is ovulating. During the test, usually performed in a doctor's office, the cervix is dilated and pieces of endometrial lining are scraped off with a sharp instrument. This tissue is later examined under a microscope for the presence of progesterone effect, an indication that ovulation has occurred.

The test sounds simple, but it can be very painful. Jessica's physician had failed to warn her about that fact. "Midway through the procedure I said, 'This is agony,'" she recalled. "I broke out in a cold sweat. When it was through I went into the waiting room and sobbed uncontrollably. I cried for two solid days. Then the doctor called and said the lab had lost my sample and we would have to do the test again. Even though I said I would never go back there, I did. I took some tranquilizers and the second time it wasn't so bad because I knew what to expect."

Unlike Jessica, some women never go back. They finally reach the point where they are weary of medical procedures that do not improve their chances for pregnancy. Years of hoping and being optimistic come to an end. They then turn their attention to adoption.

There are couples who become discouraged about their chances to adopt even before they start the procedure. Diane, the teacher, and her husband Philip, a banker, live in Texas and are typical. "My husband and I made friends with a couple who were seeing the same infertility specialist that we were," said Diane. "We had dinner at each other's homes and talked often on the phone. At one point, the wife told me they had applied to an agency to adopt a baby. I thought she was wasting her time and told her so. I had heard so many times that there were no infants available for adoption. Philip and I couldn't believe how naïve they were.

"We had been out of touch with them for nearly a year when I called to invite them over for dinner," Diane continued. "Imagine my surprise when the wife told me that she would have to line up a babysitter! Their adopted daughter was already three months old. I hung up the phone and cried for an hour. But that was the shock I needed to take action. I called my friend back, found out more about the agency, and we soon applied there ourselves. Today, the infant we adopted is three years old."

Couples like Diane and Philip believe that adopting an infant is an impossible task. They may have reached that conclusion on their own after reading newspaper or magazine articles, or they may have visited a local adoption agency that confirmed this view.

No one can deny that it has become difficult to adopt an infant, but it is not impossible. Although the waiting times vary, some couples are able to adopt infants within less than a year. Other couples and single adults continue to adopt older children more quickly.

There is the belief that abortion is responsible for the drastic reduction in the number of infants available for adoption. Of course, legalized abortion has had an impact. The number of abortions has increased from 744,610 in 1973 to 1,573,900 in 1982, according to the Alan Guttmacher Institute in New York City, an independent, nonprofit organization that does research and policy analysis in the areas of reproduction, health, and the family.

But the major reason there are fewer adoptable infants has to do with a sociological change that has occurred in our society over the past twenty years.

"In 1949, Ingrid Bergman got pregnant and had a child out of wedlock," said Elaine J. Schwartz, an adoption specialist for the Children's Bureau, a division of the Department of Health and Human Services in Washington, D.C. "She was criticized even in the Congressional Record." That criticism nearly destroyed Ms. Bergman's film career for a time, as she made few Hollywood movies and was shunned at the box office by her former fans.

Times have changed. Unwed mothers no longer are ostracized. As a result, more young women today decide to keep their babies and raise them alone.

The number of babies born to unmarried women is on the increase. According to a 1984 study by the U.S. Census Bureau, the proportion of women who either had a child before they were married or were pregnant when they married went from around 5 percent during and after World War II to 10.7 percent from 1970 to 1974. The study attributed the increase to "a lessening of the social stigma attached to bearing a child outside of marriage."

Because there is a lag between the time the Census Bureau collects its figures and the time it issues a report, its information only covers the period up until 1974. But data from other sources indicate that out-of-wedlock births have continued to increase. According to the Guttmacher Institute, there were 715,227 out-of-wedlock births in 1982. That figure represents 30 births for every thousand unmarried women, compared to 1970 when there were 26.4 births for every thousand unmarried women.

These statistics might surprise some people who have concluded that, since there are so few infants available for adoption, there are fewer infants being born to unmarried women. As these figures show, that is not the case.

What do these numbers mean for the infertile couple who hope to adopt an infant in the near future? How many of these unmarried women will choose adoption? In other words, is the total number of adoptions going up, going down, or remaining the same?

It is nearly impossible to come up with reliable statistics on adoption. That is because there is no one central clearinghouse that must be told every time an adoption is completed. "There is no mechanism to do it," said Dr. Penny Maza, statistician for the Children's Bureau in the U.S. Department of Health and Human Services in Washington, D.C., adding that the cost of maintaining such a system makes it unlikely that the government will create one.

The National Committee for Adoption, Inc., a Washington, D.C., based lobbying group, issued a report in 1985 estimating the number of adoptions in the United States in 1982. According to the NCFA, in 1982 there were 50,720 adoptions by persons other than relatives. Nearly eighteen thousand of these adoptions were of healthy infants, more than fourteen thousand were of special-needs children, and more than five thousand were of children from other countries. The NCFA stressed that the estimate of unrelated infant adoptions may be an undercount and may, in fact, be as high as 30,000. The NCFA also noted that foreign adoptions have risen, with 8,327 in 1984.

The committee's president, Dr. William Pierce, believes that the total number of adoptions is going up rather than going down. He attributes the rise to an increase in the number of adoption agencies (many being started by adoptive-parent groups) and more outreach services by these new agencies.

If the number of adoptions continues to rise, or at the least to remain constant, then the picture might not appear so bleak for many infertile couples. Still, it must be said that the number of infertile couples is continuing to rise also. So, in the years ahead, those who want to adopt will have to work at it.

The first requirement any couple must fulfill before adopting a child is deciding that adoption is right for them. They should handle any anxieties they have early on, before they apply to an agency or investigate independent adoption. All couples arrive at the decision to adopt from different directions, some after long deliberation and soul searching, others more quickly. Take the case of Andrew, a lawyer in Maryland, and his wife Naomi, who had spent eighteen months trying to have a baby and were on the verge of seeking out an infertility specialist.

One day a friend of Naomi's who worked in an abortion clinic called and asked if the couple were interested in adoption. "I couldn't believe it," Naomi said. "A young woman scheduled to have an abortion had decided to have the baby and place it in a home."

Without analyzing the situation, Naomi and Andrew decided they would adopt the baby, which was due in six months. "There was never any of the grief involved with infertility or any questions about whether we really wanted a biological child," said Naomi. "We had wanted a child for a long time and this just seemed the right thing to do."

The baby, a girl, was born in January, and Naomi and Andrew had her in their home for four days when they received a call from their lawyer. The birthmother had decided she wanted the baby back.

"What wasn't a driving force before became a driving force at that stage," said Naomi. "We *had* to have a baby." A year later, they adopted a baby girl from Chile.

Not everyone embraces adoption as readily as Naomi and Andrew did. Even after a couple realize that adoption can be done, they may still have reservations that must be overcome.

The first step is to get each partner's questions out in the open and then deal with them. It is not uncommon for one spouse to be totally committed to adoption while the other has serious questions. In this situation, it is important for the husband and wife to discuss their feelings. Nothing could be worse for the child—and the marriage—than for one spouse to go along with the decision to adopt just to keep peace. Adopting a child is not like buying a new car. There is no trade-in; it is for life. So both parties should be absolutely sure before they proceed.

No one should feel guilty if he or she has questions about adoption. Most people have had little, if any, experience with the subject. "In my family, there are no adopted children," said Diane. "I have five fertile brothers and sisters. I didn't even know anyone who was adopted."

Even though no one in my family was adopted, I had positive feelings about it because of a woman I knew in college who was adopted. I considered her intelligent and well adjusted and knew that she had a very close relationship with her adoptive parents. Ironically, she later encountered fertility problems and adopted two children before having a biological child. I found her willingness to adopt after being adopted herself a further confirmation of the process. After all, if she had had a negative experience as an adopted child, she might have rejected adoption.

My friend and her husband acted quickly to adopt after finding out she would have trouble conceiving. For those who know less about adoption, however, it may take a little longer to warm up to the idea. If the infertile couple have been seeing a psychologist, they could discuss their feelings about adoption with him or her. The psychologist could help answer their questions or help them deal with any fears they may have.

Back in the 1950s and early 1960s, when there were more infants available for adoption, agencies worked hard to recruit qualified couples. It was standard procedure to counsel the couple. These days there are fewer opportunities within the system for a couple to be counseled in this manner. A husband and wife pursuing an independent adoption may never have the chance to discuss their feelings about adoption.

Even at the adoption agencies there is less time and effort spent on helping couples seriously evaluate adoption. The agencies are inundated with applications and so are apt to avoid those couples who appear uncertain. With so many people competing for the few infants available, a couple would be loath to place their application in jeopardy by mentioning any of their reservations. As a result, a couple that need help may not get it just because of the way the system is being run.

Many officials at adoption agencies are aware that the system may be shortchanging the adoptive parents and in turn the adopted child. Several of the agency officials interviewed for this book said that most couples state a preference for infant girls. One agency that specializes in Korean adoptions said that 90 percent of the couples applying to them want girls. While there may be innocuous reasons for this imbalance, several social workers offered explanations that, if true, demonstrate that many couples are still unsure about their decision to adopt.

"Without knowing ahead of time what the child will be like as an adult, many couples, and in particular the husbands, feel less than comfortable with the fact that the child will be carrying on the family name," said one social worker. "The situation is different with a girl. Most likely she will marry and take her husband's surname. There is less concern about whether she will do well in school and go on to a professional career."

Of course, few prospective adoptive couples would actually put their reasons for requesting a girl as bluntly as this. Many may have sublimated their feelings and would be shocked if presented with this analysis. But the fact that there are some couples who feel this way and are being approved for adoption is disquieting to many professionals within the child-welfare community. "This is a very worrisome thing," said Ms. Schwartz.

Because the system has, in effect, abdicated its responsibility to help the prospective adoptive parents, couples must help themselves. Often any problems can be worked out by talking with a psychologist or other trained professional familiar with infertility and adoption. A good first step may be to talk with other adoptive parents by contacting a RESOLVE chapter in the nearest city, or a local adoptive-parents group.

It is not unusual for prospective adoptive parents to be anxious even though they are sincere about adoption. It does not mean that the couple will not make excellent parents. Still, the adoption process itself can be arduous. Only if the couple are committed to adoption will they be able to handle everything that is to follow—the home study, the legal details, and the waiting time.

Some of the most common questions that come up in any discussion on adoption follow. The answers are based on interviews with many adoptive parents who once went through a search for their own answers. In addition, many professionals offered their advice.

What will our adopted child look like? Will it bother me that she doesn't resemble us in appearance?

A decade or two ago, when adoption agencies had many infants to place, great care was taken to guarantee that the adopted child would resemble his or her adoptive parents. One woman whose two adopted children are now in their twenties told me that, with each child, the social worker made a point of saying that the child's biological parents were very similar in appearance to this woman and her husband. "The social worker said with our son, 'If you two had a biological child, he couldn't look much different than this,' " the woman recalled.

Because agencies today have fewer infants, they no longer have the luxury of concerning themselves with physical appearances. Some agencies, however, do try to match the adoptive couple's religion and ethnic background to the child's.

In an independent adoption, it is possible for prospective adoptive parents to search for birthparents who resemble them, hoping that the baby will also resemble the adoptive parents.

In most cases, a couple are so thrilled with the possibility of adopting a healthy infant that they are less concerned with matching up eye and hair color. Many adoptive couples also realize that to start the process with so many requirements might make the going rougher than it might otherwise be.

Others feel very strongly about having children that look like them. There is a natural curiosity on the part of a couple to wonder what their biological child will look like. Not being able to answer that question may come as the biggest disappointment when a couple cannot produce children. "The need to have someone who resembles you, to express yourself genetically, is very real," said Dr. Marvin S. Kasow, a psychologist.

I have a friend who has two biological children. One day when we were having a candid discussion she said to me, "Both of my children resemble me. I can look at Mark and see my nose, or at Katy and see my eyes. I can't deny the fact that it makes me feel good seeing that they look like me."

Still, not all children resemble their biological parents. We all know families where one child stands out because his hair color, eyes, height, or other feature cannot be found among any other family member. Chances are that this child is no less loved than his brothers and sisters. The mother loves him as much as she does her daughter, even though her daughter is the spitting image of the mother when she was a child.

Any couple considering adoption must be honest with each other and themselves about their expectations. If they feel strongly about having a child that resembles them, they should ask themselves why. Do they believe that if the child has their physical characteristics they will be able to pretend the child is biological? That attitude could be very dangerous to both the couple and the child. No amount of pretending will be able to change the fact that the child is adopted. At some time in the future, he will discover he is adopted. If his adoptive parents have hidden that fact from him, he may suffer permanent psychological damage.

Do the couple want a child that looks like them merely to avoid constant inquiries from strangers? Are they worried about having to explain to every passerby how two blond-haired parents had a child with black hair? That is a legitimate concern. But the adoptive parents should know that there is no requirement for them to explain to everyone where the child came from if they don't care to.

One woman I know tells this story. "My husband and I both have dark hair and dark eyes. Our adopted son has blond hair and blue eyes, so naturally we are accustomed to remarks from strangers. One day we were in the park and my husband went to get a soda. A woman had been admiring our son and commented on his very blue eyes. She then said, 'But your eyes are so dark. How did you ever have a son with such blue eyes?' I shrugged and said, 'Gee, I don't know.' She then said, 'Your husband must have very blue eyes.' Imagine her surprise when he returned and she saw his eyes were as dark as mine! She repeated her comments to my husband, who looked very amused. And then, leaving her looking very puzzled, we put our son in his stroller and walked away."

Will we love the child even though he is not our biological child?

Americans have always been interested in tracing their ancestors, often traveling to distant countries to look up relatives. And like people of other cultures, Americans have become intent on carrying on the family line. To most couples that means having biological children.

Obviously, a couple intent on continuing their bloodlines will have tremendous difficulty accepting their infertility. What the couple must come to realize is that while an adoptive child will never be connected to them genetically, he will be connected psychologically. He may not have inherited the family chin, but he will inherit the family's values and traditions. In most cases, the fact that he is not a biological child will be inconsequential.

Some couples have no problem accepting the idea of adoption. What they worry about, however, is how the child will feel about them. An adoptive mother may think about the day when she disciplines her adopted daughter only to have the daughter retort: "I don't have to listen to you because you aren't my real mother."

One the best books ever written to address this question of adopted child and parent relationships was put together by the photographer Jill Krementz. Called *How It Feels To Be Adopted*, the book includes pictures and comments from more than a dozen adopted children, ages eight through sixteen. They talk about themselves and their families. They also talk about searching for their biological parents.

What comes through loud and clear in this book is that these children consider their adoptive parents their parents. Even if they found their biological mother or father, or both—and several of the children in the book did—the majority of these children said it did not change their feelings for or relationship with their adoptive parents.

When we were going through our home study interviews, our social worker made a comment that stuck in our minds. "Biological motherhood is overrated," she told us. Of course, no one would dispute that giving birth to a baby is one of life's great experiences. But what our social worker meant was that the important part of parenting begins after the child is born. And there is no evidence that says a biological parent is an inherently better parent than an adoptive one.

A great deal has been said about the bonding process that occurs between parents and child in those first few weeks and months of an infant's life. With a biological child, that bonding phenomenon begins immediately after birth. That is not possible, of course, with adoption. But many adoptive parents are able to bring their adopted child home after only a few days. Some agencies feel very strongly about placing the baby in the adoptive parents' home as quickly as possible in order to hasten bonding.

The dictionary defines a bond as "a uniting tie or force, a link." That, in effect, is what develops between the child and his parents: They are drawn together. Many adoptive parents begin to feel that attachment to the baby even before they have seen him. We first saw Joseph when he was six days old, but as soon as the social worker called and told us about him, we felt that he was ours. In fact, it was agonizing having to wait even a few days to see him.

Other adoptive parents have expressed similar feelings. I attended an orientation session for couples who were adopting Korean infants. They all had photographs of their children and were waiting for them to be cleared by the authorities in South Korea. These couples had never seen their children, but the manner in which they spoke about them left no doubt that these children were already loved and accepted.

Once the parents and child are brought together, a new element is added when the parents begin to feel needed by the infant. In his eyes, this man and woman who feed him a bottle at all hours of the day, change his diapers, and attend to his every need *are* his parents. When he says his first words, "Ma" and "Da," there is little question of whom he is talking about.

Will our parents love him as if he were their biological grandchild?

Before the adoption actually takes place, a great deal of the couple's anxiety comes from wondering what friends and relatives will think. Uppermost in the couple's minds will be their own parents. How will they feel about this adopted child? Will they love her as much as they love their other grandchildren? Will they treat her differently? If they have trouble accepting the adoption, will their attitude adversely affect the child?

Generalizations cannot be made in this area. How a couple's parents react can depend in large part on the relationship these parents have had with their children all these years. If the wife always has had to struggle for her mother's approval, chances are this situation will not be any different. On the other hand, if the relationship between these generations has been a good one, the adopted child will be welcomed with love and enthusiasm.

How these prospective grandparents react to the adoption may depend on how they are prepared for it. Some couples prefer *not* to tell their parents ahead of time and wait to spring the news on them when the baby has arrived. There are situations where this strategy is very wise.

Remember that once the couple tell their parents that they have been placed on the waiting list at an agency or expect to adopt a child independently very soon, the prospective grandparents will settle in for the wait, too. If the couple already are anxious and nervous, having their parents call every two days to ask them what is happening would be unwanted pressure.

This worrying may take a more serious form if the child expected is from a foreign country. A couple's parents, like other people, may have read about the risks of adopting a child from another country. They may think about diseases or wonder about the child's physical appearance. Many officials who work in foreign adoption advise couples not to say anything to relatives until the baby has arrived.

Still, if a couple feel that withholding the information from their parents would irreparably damage family relationships—possibly making it more difficult for the couple's parents to quickly assume their roles as grandparents—then the couple's parents should be told about the adoption. Sharing the waiting time may help to bring the family closer. Naomi and Andrew did let their parents know they were adopting a baby girl from Chile. "My parents were cautious," said Naomi. "They weren't sure what we were going to bring home. They were concerned that the child wouldn't be healthy. But when we walked off that plane, my mother's eyes lit up and they haven't dimmed since." Naomi said that several of her friends, seeing her mother's enthusiasm, have been encouraged also to pursue foreign adoptions.

The grandparents' attitude also may be affected by their experience with their children's infertility. Often if a mother has seen her daughter go through years of treatments without success she may very well be the one who suggests adoption to her daughter. If the couple's parents were kept in the dark, they might resent that fact and take their anger out on the child. Each situation is different and the husband and wife would do well to consider their parents' feelings before taking action.

Grandparents are important for any young child, but especially so for adopted children. Knowing that they have grandparents, aunts, uncles, and cousins who love and care about them can only increase their feelings of confidence and security.

Yet if a couple's parents are opposed to adoption, particularly in the case of a foreign adoption, what course should the couple decide on?

Ultimately, like everything else in their married life, they must make their own decisions. Once the adoption has happened, their parents will be able to witness its success for themselves. Chances are, they will soon be as delighted as their children.

Will we receive enough information about the birthparents so that we will be comfortable adopting the child?

That depends. If a couple deal with an adoption agency, they will probably receive more than enough information on the birthmother. That information should include any history of physical, medical, or emotional problems in her family. As long as the birthmother identifies the father, there will be sufficient data on him and his family, too. The couple also should learn something about the birthmother's health during her pregnancy, including her diet and whether she smoked, drank, or used drugs.

It may be more difficult for a couple to get background information when arranging an independent or foreign adoption. Unless the lawyer and doctor who are advising the birthmother know her case well, they might not be able to say definitely that her medical or emotional history is acceptable. If the birthmother is eager to place her child, she may not want anyone to know that her family has a history of mental disorders, for example.

With a foreign adoption, many of the children have been abandoned and the parents may not even be known. Remember that in these situations there is always the opportunity for the couple to pass up the adoption if they are unsure about the circumstances.

In the short term, the couple should have the child examined immediately by a competent pediatrician. In the long term, they will just have to assume the risk if they are committed to the adoption. If they have any qualms about accepting such a risk, perhaps they should rethink their adoption plan. Even if the wait is longer, they may feel better applying to an agency.

Will it be difficult handling family and friends who want to know all the details about the child's background and how she came to us?

No doubt once a couple have adopted a baby, numerous friends and relatives will want to be filled in on all the details. Most of these questions stem from normal curiosity. Some neighbor stops over and feels it is a natural reaction to ask where the child came from. Who are the parents? How old were they? Where were they from?

The decision on what and how much information should be given out to relatives, friends, or complete strangers is a personal and private one that will be made by the couple themselves.

I have talked with adoptive parents who were asked by total strangers how much the adoption cost. Some people are honestly interested in knowing what the adoption agency fees were, perhaps because they are pursuing adoption themselves. Other people, however, may suspect that if the child is white, he or she was "bought" illegally. Often this happens because the public has been led to believe that it is impossible to adopt a healthy white infant any other way. "I couldn't believe it!" one woman told me. "The wallpaper hanger, when he found out our daughter was adopted, asked how much we paid for her. I told him it was none of his business and never had him for another job."

That's one way to handle rude people. Remember that most of the questioners do not intend to offend. The sad truth is that many people speak before they think. They may not know anyone who has adopted and so may just want to find out more about it. Another person may know someone who wants to adopt and is gathering information for that friend.

Of course, every now and then the couple will encounter people who are overbearing and rude. They may be so insensitive that they will continue to ask questions or comment on the child long after the couple have indicated that the subject is closed.

With all of these people, it is important for the couple to remain calm. They have nothing to hide. They are not trying to cover up the fact that the child was adopted. Within reason they are more than happy to answer questions. But when those questions become unreasonable, they have every right to deal with the questioner as the woman dealt with her wallpaper hanger.

Each adoptive couple is different. Some may be perfectly comfortable divulging every last fact about the child to strangers, while others prefer to keep everything to themselves.

Most couples fall in between. They don't see any reason to refuse to answer simple questions. But, on the other hand, there are many subjects that are too personal to discuss with close friends, let alone strangers.

There is one thing for the couple to remember: At some time in the future anything said about the child could be repeated back to him. Any disparaging comments made about his birthmother, for instance, could be damaging to his psyche if told to him by a friend years later. Or if he learns that he was abandoned by both his birthparents he may have difficulty living with that fact.

What do a couple say about the child's biological parents? To close relatives, the couple may want to give some of the information they received from the agency or from their lawyer in the case of an independent adoption. When asked about the child's biological parents, most couples are comfortable saying: "We know everything about the birthparents that we needed to know and we are very comfortable with those facts." That response can effectively put aside inquiries regarding the birthmother's age, economic status, or whereabouts.

Occasionally, the couple will be questioned by someone who is interested in adoption, either for himself or for a friend. In these cases, the adoptive couple must decide how they feel about supplying this individual with the details of the adoption. Are this man and his wife people that the adoptive couple would want to recommend to the adoption agency they used? Or, in the case of an independent adoption, would the adoptive couple feel comfortable giving out the name of their lawyer?

Each situation is different and must be handled that way. The adoptive couple should remember that they are never under any pressure to release the details of the adoption to anyone. If they honestly want to help these friends, then they should.

If someone asks about the cost of the adoption, the couple may politely refuse to give out the information. Later on, if the adoptive couple supply another couple with the name of the adoption agency or the lawyer that they used, these sources will be able to explain the costs.

Will it be hard to cope with strangers who make tactless comments either on the dissimilarities in our physical characteristics or on the child's adoptive status?

The temptation when confronted with a rude question is to give a rude response. However, when the child gets older, he may overhear such remarks and misinterpret his parents' anger as being directed against him. That could cause him to become insecure or ashamed of some physical characteristic, believing that that characteristic makes his parents angry.

When a stranger makes a tactless comment, the parents could look upon it as an opportunity to make a positive statement about adoption. For example, a stranger might say, "What dark hair your son has, and you and your husband are both blond!" The parent might respond, "Paul is adopted. And we are very proud to have such a handsome boy for our son."

Remember, however, that there is no reason to explain to everyone that the child is adopted. In fact, if the parents respond to every tactless comment with the explanation that the child is adopted, an older child in particular may begin to feel that his privacy is being invaded. Withholding this information from strangers does not mean that the couple are embarrassed that the child is adopted. They just do not feel compelled to explain his status to everyone they meet.

Will we be disappointed if he isn't as intellectual as we are?

Diane and Philip, who have degrees from prestigious universities and consider themselves intellectuals, wonder what their adoptive son's capabilities will be. "We have talked about that," said Diane. "Both of us having an intellectual bent, what would happen if we have a little plumber on our hands?"

There is no doubt that a child's environment can play a major role in his intellectual development. "My studies show that children's IQs rise if they are placed in homes where there are highly educated parents," said Dr. Gilbert W. Kliman, who founded the Center for Preventive Psychiatry in White Plains, New York. No matter what the child's biological background is, he is bound to be stimulated and challenged by parents who take the time to play with him, read books to him, and help him with his schoolwork.

Even with a biological child there are no guarantees that the child will be as gifted as the parents. And it is possible that the adopted child will turn out to be even smarter than his adoptive parents.

The best attitude for parents to have is to encourage their child to develop his or her talents in whatever area he or she might be interested in. Obviously the parents can help the process along by exposing the child to music, arts, sports, literature, cooking, and whatever else he or she seems to like. But the final decisions—about career and hobbies—must be the child's, and both parents should be able to accept the child's choice.

If we later have a biological child, will we love both equally?

Only the adoptive couple will be able to answer that question when they are actually faced with parenting both an adopted child and a biological child. But interviews with couples who have families made up of adopted and biological children indicate that the adopted children are loved every bit as much as the biological children.

Especially if the adopted child has been with the family since infancy, the attachment is there. This child *is* the couple's son or daughter. Even the addition of biological offspring cannot change that.

Will the adopted child feel like an outsider? How would we handle that situation?

The adopted child will only feel like an outsider if he is treated like one. The adoptive couples I interviewed who have both adopted and biological children report that they make no distinction between them.

William, an advertising executive who lives in Illinois with his wife Anne, a laboratory technician, adopted a baby girl through an agency. Two years later, Anne became pregnant. When William told a friend about Anne's pregnancy, the friend remarked, "Now you will have one of your own." William replied, "We already have one of our own. Now we will have two." Anne gave birth to a baby girl and William reports that they love both girls and never consider their older child to be "the adopted one."

A New Jersey couple, Amy and Michael, adopted a two-year-old boy from Colombia they named Paul and later had a biological child, also a boy. If they have any fears, it is that the biological child, David, will have more of an adjustment problem. "Paul has a wonderful personality," said Amy. "He is really an exceptional child. He touches everyone who meets him. David will have more trouble adjusting, not only because Paul gets so much attention, but also because he has so much to measure up to."

Every couple's experience in raising children—adopted or biological—is different, but many aspects remain the same. An infertile couple may choose to adopt to produce another generation. But their primary reason for adopting is so they can enjoy parenting and seeing a child grow to adulthood. Few experiences in life are as rewarding.

3

DEVISING A PLAN
OF ATTACK

A dopting a child seems like an awesome task. How do a couple begin the process?

If they have decided to adopt, the process has already begun. They should disregard all the discouraging comments from relatives and friends. If the couple want to adopt, even if they want to adopt a healthy white infant, it is crucial that they believe they will accomplish that goal.

To help them toward that goal, they would do well to understand first the different ways of adopting, and what categories of children can be adopted. The chart on the following page lists the main groups of children available.

Already, the couple can see that there is a wide disparity in the waiting times, depending on the race, age, and health of the child and the method used to adopt that child.

The longest waiting times will be experienced by couples who go to an adoption agency hoping for a healthy, white infant. Why? Adoption agencies today have few infants of all races to place. The reasons behind that situation are complex and will be talked about at length in succeeding chapters. At this point, it is enough to say that it is possible to adopt a healthy infant through an agency. It just will take far longer than it did in the past.

Be aware that there are two kinds of adoption agencies, public and private. Public agencies usually are part of a state or city social services unit and have very few infants, either white infants or those of other racial backgrounds, to place. There is still a stigma attached to going to a public welfare agency, so a young unmarried woman probably would not seek out these agencies on her own

Type of Adoption	Children Available	Waiting Times
Agencies (public and private)	All infants	One to eight years
	Older children, some with special emotional and/or physical needs	These children are waiting and usually can be placed as soon as the home study is completed.
Independent	White infants, primarily	Less than one year
Foreign	Infants from Korea and some South American countries	One to two years
	Older children from Korea, some Southeast Asian countries, India, some South American countries	Under one year

and might not even know that a public agency could help her. Because these agencies have limited funds, they cannot afford to spend money on advertising, either to change their image or to describe their services.

I interviewed one couple in New Orleans who waited eight years for an infant girl placed by a city agency. The husband said that so much time had passed that he and his wife had totally forgotten about their application when they received the phone call from the social worker. On the plus side, adoptions through these public agencies typically cost very little. That is because the biological mother's medical and legal costs are taken care of by the city or state.

Because the public agencies have so few infants to place, they have turned their attention instead to finding homes for the many older and special-needs children who find their way into the public foster care system. The agencies are eager to find homes for these children and have special counseling services to help both the child and the parents adjust to the adoption. These public agencies also operate a network that can help pair up an adoptive couple in one state with a waiting child in another.

Private agencies operate differently from public agencies. Rather than being a department run by a city or state, private agencies usually are set up as nonprofit organizations and have a governing board of directors, and many have religious affiliations. Although such agencies often will place children of all religions, a Christian agency will tend to attract Christian birthmothers, a Jewish agency Jewish birthmothers, and so on. Often this occurs because the birthmother is referred to an agency after seeking counseling from her clergy. That is particularly the case if the agency also runs a shelter where the birthmother may live during her pregnancy. Some states require a child to be placed in an adoptive home of the same religion as the birthparents, so it is easy to see how agencies with religious affiliations end up serving only those birthmothers and adoptive couples of that particular religion.

These private agencies have more infants to place than the public agencies, although still far fewer than they did twenty years ago. That is because these agencies do advertise their services to birthmothers and prospective adoptive parents, often using local newspapers or radio. Those agencies affiliated with a certain religion will receive referrals from clergy. The infants placed would include Caucasians and those of other racial backgrounds.

In general, a couple adopting through a private agency would assume responsibility for the biological mother's expenses until the child is placed in the adoptive couple's home. These expenses could include sheltering costs, legal costs, and medical costs. While it is difficult to say how much these expenses can total, they usually range between three thousand and ten thousand dollars. The higher figure would be for a long sheltering period, and for a difficult delivery involving an extended stay in the hospital.

Because private agencies do have some infants to place, nearly all of them have set up a procedure to process the applications they receive from prospective adoptive parents. Depending upon the procedure used, the adoptive couple could wait anywhere from one year to five years. Most private agencies try to keep the waiting times as short as possible. But, in order to do that, these agencies must restrict the number of couples accepted for possible placement. As a result, many couples are turned away.

Many private agencies also have set up systems for placing children from foreign countries. Sometimes these children are infants; other times they are older and special-needs children. A couple hoping to adopt a foreign child would be wise to go through a U.S. agency, as it is very complicated and risky to adopt a child from abroad, even with the help of experienced agency people here in the United States. (More on that subject in Chapter 7, foreign adoption.)

Independent adoptions are used primarily to adopt healthy, white infants. Typically, a pregnant woman looking to place her baby looks for an adoptive couple. She may find the couple through an outside third party (doctors and lawyers are the most common intermediaries) or by reading a newspaper advertisement that has been placed by the couple.

In most cases, the adoptive couple agree to cover the woman's medical and legal expenses, and may also cover some of her housing costs during the pregnancy. The waiting time is under a year simply because the woman already is pregnant when she seeks the couple.

The cost of an independent adoption should be about the same as that of an adoption handled through a private agency, from three thousand to ten thousand dollars. Again, there may be extenuating circumstances that will increase the woman's expenses. But a couple should be wary about agreeing to any expenses that cannot be fully documented. (More on this in Chapter 6, on independent adoption.)

Be advised that as of January 1986, independent adoptions were illegal in at least six states: Connecticut, Delaware, Massachusetts, Michigan, Minnesota, and North Dakota. A number of other states are also considering legislation that would make independent adoptions illegal. A check with a local adoption attorney or the state department of social services is in order before deciding whether to proceed with an independent adoption.

The route that the couple decide to take will depend on several factors, the most important being the type of child they hope to adopt. For a couple looking to adopt an older or special-needs child, the process will be relatively straightforward. The best place to begin is with a local agency, either public or private. Both probably will have programs for placing these children and also will offer follow-up counseling services. Remember, too, that because the public agencies operate as a network a couple may be able to adopt a child from another state. A listing of some of these agencies is included at the end of this book (p. 149).

Information about special-needs children is also available from organizations such as the National Adoption Exchange in Philadelphia, a national network that brings together waiting children with parents who wish to adopt them. More information on these groups is included in the listing at the end of this book (p. 237). Children are registered with the exchange by their agencies; families who have been approved to adopt may be registered by their agencies or may register themselves. Adoption coordinators, using the latest electronic technology, regularly conduct searches for possible matches.

If the couple would like to adopt an older child or an infant from a foreign country, there are many agencies in the United States that have established relationships with adoption agencies in certain foreign countries. That direct contact can eliminate many of the problems and delays that often occur with foreign adoptions.

Agencies also would be the best place to start if the couple want to adopt a non-white infant. These infants might also be adopted independently, of course, but especially in major metropolitan areas, a couple may find that the waiting time at an agency for a non-white infant is not that much longer than if they went the independent route.

It becomes apparent that agencies can be helpful in placing many children within a relatively short period of time. The tricky situation will occur if a couple want to adopt a healthy, white infant for which the waiting time at the agencies can be very long. So such a couple will have to decide whether going to an agency is worth the wait or whether they should try to adopt more quickly by attempting an independent adoption.

Perhaps the wisest strategy is not to discount the agencies without at least investigating them. It is possible that the couple would be ruled out because they fail to fulfill the agency's requirements. If that is the case, then they can proceed with an independent adoption.

What are some of the standards agencies use that could disqualify a couple? These might include the following.

Age. Most agencies have a cutoff age. This cutoff usually ranges from thirty-five to forty years old. There are some agencies that do not have an age requirement per se, preferring to judge each case on its merits. Others have revised their age limit upward in the past decade, mindful of the fact that many people are putting off having children and so may not encounter fertility problems until they are forty.

Still, it is safe to say that if both the husband and wife are over forty, they will probably have a difficult time getting an agency to accept their application.

Marital Status. Most agencies will not accept an application from a couple if the two are living together and not married. In fact, one of the documents the couple may be asked to submit with their application is their marriage certificate. Other aspects of marital status—whether either has been divorced, the length of time they have been married, for example—will also be scrutinized by the agency and could be a factor in whether the couple are accepted.

Financial Stability. The couple would have to prove that their financial circumstances were such that they could adequately provide for the child. If the main wage-earner is out of work, or has a spotty employment record, then the agency will probably reject the couple's application.

A detailed financial statement also will be required with the couple's application. Even if both partners are currently employed and earning good salaries, they must still show financial solvency. Important factors are home ownership, insurance coverage, and savings and other investments. Also considered will be any outstanding debts.

Health. Both partners should be able to prove that they are in good physical health, usually by way of a letter from their physicians. If either person is suffering from a serious disease that could be life-threatening, then the agency could decide not to accept their application.

Most agencies also will want some proof that the couple have not experienced any serious mental conditions that could affect their ability to care for a child. If they have such a history, they would have to demonstrate (either with letters from attending doctors, or through extensive interviews with agency personnel) that they have come to terms with their problems.

There are some agencies that require proof from the wife's doctor, the husband's doctor, or both that either partner or both have fertility problems. Some agencies no longer require this documentation, assuming that any couple willing to wait several years for a baby probably cannot have biological children.

Yet there are agencies that would question a couple's decision to adopt if that couple had only been trying to have children for a short time, say two years. Even if the couple feel they want to start adoption proceedings while pursuing medical remedies, some agency personnel will discourage this strategy. They prefer to concentrate on couples who have exhausted medical remedies and are therefore less likely to conceive and drop adoption proceedings.

Religion. Most agencies with religious affiliations will not turn down applications from couples of another religion, but they probably will be very discouraging to these couples. The agency's reasoning is that the couple would be wasting their time hoping that a baby of their religion would become available for placement.

Every now and then, however, this system works to a couple's advantage. I know of one case where a Christian couple applied to an agency that primarily handled Jewish children. As it happened, the agency found itself with a Christian baby to place, and no one in its files except for this one couple. They got their baby.

Working Wife. Some agencies require a statement from the wife that she plans to quit her job and stay home to care for the child. This may be difficult for a couple to do, since many professional women want to work and there is often no reason they cannot manage both home and job. Other women may have to work to contribute financially to the family. Ironically, many couples may find it impossible to meet an agency's financial requirements test unless the wife does work.

Other Children. Most adoption agencies will reject an application for a healthy, white infant if the couple already have other children, reasoning that childless couples should be given first priority.

Couples applying for an infant may have children by previous marriages. Or perhaps they have one biological child but have been unable to have any others. While most agency officials would not consider these couples for placement of a white infant, there is the chance they may be accepted for placement of an infant or toddler of another race. And, of course, this couple probably would be able to adopt an older child. The couple would then have to decide whether they could adopt one of these other children, or instead pursue an independent adoption.

Aside from these tangible facts, which cannot be changed or altered, the couple may have to deal with the intangible facts: how they personally feel about the method they will use to adopt. Some people are turned off by the bureaucratic red tape they anticipate at the agencies, and many of these people will end up adopting independently.

Other couples may be worried about attempting an adoption on their own without the help of an experienced social worker. These are the people who will prefer to go through an adoption agency, even if that means waiting several years for a baby. Each couple must decide upon the course that is most comfortable for them.

Of course, if the couple live in a state where independent adoption is illegal, then they have no choice but to deal with the agencies. Let's assume that is the case. What should this couple's strategy be?

First, they should make a list of the public and private agencies that they could apply to. Most of these agencies will be those in the couple's state. Years ago, it was not unusual for an agency in one state to place infants and children in many states. Although agencies still do this with older children, the practice is very rare with infants. With so many people applying for infants, agencies have a hard time meeting the demand in their home states, let alone the demand from other states.

Also, some states that prohibit independent adoptions also prohibit agencies outside their jurisdictions from placing babies in adoptive homes. To place babies in homes out of state, agencies would have to establish a liaison with adoption agencies in those states. Again, because agencies see no lack of business in their own backyards, most have been reluctant to make extra work for themselves.

The division may not always be made by state, however. A large metropolitan area may take applicants from several neighboring states simply because many husbands and wives from these states work in that city. New York City agencies, for example, accept applications from couples living in nearby New Jersey.

Couples can begin their own list of agencies by referring to the listing on pages 149–202, which was compiled from information provided by each state in 1985. Keep in mind that this listing serves only as a starting point, as agencies open and close every year.

The first impulse, after assembling a list of agencies, may be to get on the phone and call each one. While that might be a good idea at some future point, it should not be the first course of action. Before they pick up the phone and talk to any adoption agency, lawyer, doctor, or other professional who can assist them in adoption, the couple need to do their homework and gather as much available information on adoption and adoption agencies.

Part of the reason for doing this is defensive. Once a couple begin to call agencies they should be in a position to judge whether they are being dealt with squarely. Unfortunately, information being given out by some individuals is incorrect. For example, a receptionist may tell callers that the cutoff age for adopting infants is thirty-five years old when in fact that agency's policy is to decide each case individually. The couple will be in a better position to challenge a statement if they know that statement to be false.

Where should they go for this information? Local media—newspapers, magazines, radio, and TV—may have done stories on adoption where officials from the state agencies were interviewed and provided useful information. If an agency head tells a reporter the agency will place fifty babies in the current year, then the couple can be prepared to challenge another agency official who turns them away with the explanation that no babies will be placed.

They know there are couples being accepted and their goal will be to find out what they must do to make sure they are one of those couples.

Throughout the entire adoption process, it is essential to keep good records. Before starting out, the couple should set up a system for keeping track of every phone call made, agency contacted, or newspaper story that is clipped. Everything should be dated, especially when dealing with agencies. One agency we dealt with expected every couple to make contact every six months in order to say they were still interested, and any couple who failed to call was automatically removed from the files. Obviously this system places the burden on the couple to keep their application active. Without a good system, it would be easy for the couple to overlook making that contact twice a year.

Records should be kept very organized. One file should be for newspaper, magazine, and other clippings. A second file should be kept to record all telephone calls that were made, the dates, and what information was received.

A third file may be kept to hold other source material that will come in through the mail, such as newsletters, brochures, and application forms. The fourth file, and perhaps one of the most important, should list the names, addresses, and telephone numbers of all people the couple have contacted or plan to contact in their adoption search. If a person was contacted, the file should include a summary of the phone conversation (with the date) or a copy of the letter.

Record-keeping should continue even after the couple have been placed on the list at an agency or are waiting to complete an independent or foreign adoption. There are good reasons to keep up the system. In the event something goes wrong, the couple will have an exact record of what happened. Assuming that the adoption occurs as planned, the couple will then have a complete history of the process that they could use as a guide for a second adoption for themselves or a first adoption for friends.

Once the couple have sufficient knowledge about the agencies in their area, they will begin to understand that all agencies screen applicants. The screening process is a necessary one, as all agencies have too many applicants for too few infants. But that does not mean that the process is always fair, particularly for the couples who are turned away. How do agencies screen applicants?

The three most common methods are as follows.

Opening Intake for a Limited Time Frame. This means that the agency sets up a period when it will accept applications from couples, and accepts applications only at those times. This period may occur every year, every few years, or whenever agencies feel they need more applicants.

Sometimes the agencies advertise the fact that they will open intake—not by taking out a full-page advertisement in the local newspaper, which would obviously bring in more applicants than the agency needs or wants, but by word of mouth. People who call the agency inquiring about adoption will be told that the agency plans to accept applications during the month of May, for example.

Still, the agency could decide to close intake if it receives enough applications the first week, or even the first day. As a result, the couples who get there first stand more chance of being screened through.

Recommendations. There are still agencies that accept applicants solely on the basis of recommendations from officials known to the agency. An agency with a religious affiliation may take a referral from a priest, minister, or rabbi, while the recommendation for a secular agency may come from an outsider who is not necessarily an adoption professional, but someone who knows the head of the agency or one of the social workers.

I know one couple who tried for years to adopt through an agency with no success until a friend of theirs, who served on a committee with the head of an adoption agency, recommended them to that official. Their application was accepted.

Open Meetings. Some agencies periodically sponsor an open meeting on adoption. Couples who call the agency are told when the next meeting will be held and may be asked to reserve a place. At this meeting, a social worker or other official from the agency will discuss the agency's adoption program and the types of children available for placement. Often, the social worker will try to discourage those who want to adopt a healthy, white infant and will stress the agency's program for placing special-needs children.

Couples are then asked to write a letter to the agency stating what type of a child they hope to adopt. Those who decide to adopt special-needs children will be called immediately, while those who state a preference for an infant will wait a longer time. At this point couples will be invited in for an interview with a social worker who will decide whether the couple's application should be accepted.

These three methods are the most common ways agencies screen applicants. It now becomes obvious why calling on the telephone may not be the best idea as a first course of action. If the agency being called is one that relies on recommendations, what will the couple be told over the telephone? Probably that the agency is not accepting applications for white infants. If the agency is one that opens intake during certain periods and the couple happens to call during a time when intake is closed, they will be told, again, that the agency is not accepting applications.

The most positive thing that could occur would be that the couple would be invited to a group meeting to hear about a particular agency's adoption program. Again, merely being invited to this meeting is no assurance that the couple will have their application accepted. Some agencies hold open group meetings, yet those couples who are accepted for placement of white infants are those who also have a good recommendation.

The following chapters will include more information on the actual agency procedure, from the initial interview through the home study and finally the placement. But right now, a couple's concern should be: Is there an agency where they stand a good chance of being accepted? What can they do to maximize that possibility?

Adoptive-parent groups will be one of the greatest resources for couples as they try to formulate their strategy (see the listing at the back of the book, p. 203. Most of these adoptive-parent groups are volunteer organizations, with the phone number given being someone's office or home. It may even take several phone calls before the couple finally get through to someone. But the results may be well worth the trouble.

Adoptive parents have been through the system. They volunteer their time and energies to share the knowledge that they gained during their adoptions and to strive to improve the way the adoption procedure works.

OURS, for example, is a volunteer adoptive-parent group based in Minneapolis, Minnesota, with branches all over the United States. A call to the group's headquarters can help the prospective adoptive couple locate the group nearest them. Another good source of information is RESOLVE in Belmont, Massachusetts. Even though RESOLVE's main purpose is to help couples cope with infertility, many of its members have adopted and can give valuable information.

What type of information should a couple seek from these groups? The most important thing would be the names of couples who have adopted through the same agencies the prospective adoptive parents are considering applying to. Once the couple can contact these adoptive parents, they can begin to learn more about how these agencies accept applicants. The following are some questions to ask.

* Does the agency this adoptive couple used have any requirements that would rule out this prospective adoptive couple?
* If the agency is affiliated with a particular religion, does it only place infants with adoptive parents of that religion?
* How did this adoptive couple first approach the agency? Did they attend a group meeting, were they recommended by a third party, or did they telephone?
* Do the couple know what type of screening mechanism the agency uses? If the agency uses recommendations, who should the hopeful couple enlist to recommend them? (Sometimes an agency will take a recommendation from another couple who adopted there. Perhaps this adoptive couple would agree to so recommend this couple.)
* If the agency is one that opens intake at certain times, does the adoptive couple know (or can they find out) when the next intake period will be?
* If the agency uses group meetings, can the adoptive couple give these hopeful parents any guidance on how to enhance their application? Would a word from this adoptive couple to their social worker help along this couple's application? Would an outside recommendation be of any aid?

If the couple cannot locate other adoptive parents, they will have no alternative but to call the agencies themselves. They should keep in mind that they may not get the whole story over the phone about how these agencies operate. In most cases, they will not be permitted to speak with a social worker or anyone else in authority. If their sole conversation is with the receptionist, the information they obtain may be spotty. But it will be a start. Of course, they should continue to solicit information from outside sources as well.

The following exchange illustrates a typical phone conversation between a prospective adoptive parent and an agency official. It shows how frustrating this telephoning can be.

Agency: Good morning. The Children's Home Association.
Caller: Good morning. I'm calling to inquire about adoption. We would like to adopt a baby and would like to apply to your agency. Can you send me an application, or should I come in to fill one out?

Agency: I'm sorry. If you hope to adopt an infant, we are not accepting applications at this time.

Caller: Can you tell me when you will be accepting applications?

Agency: No, I cannot.

Caller: Do you sponsor any group meetings where prospective adoptive parents may come to hear about your agency's adoptions program?

Agency: Yes, we do. But as I said, we are not placing any infants. Most of the people who come to our group meetings are interested in adopting older children.

Caller: We would still like to come. Can you tell me when the next meeting will be held?

The caller did accomplish something by learning about the group meeting, and making sure to get on the list of those scheduled to attend. While this gathering probably will concentrate on older children, this couple will be able to meet the social worker or agency official conducting the meeting and will thus become two faces to this social worker, not just another couple calling the agency. They may, with persistence and determination, even find out from this social worker what they have to do to have their application for a white infant accepted.

It is easy to see why some couples tire of dealing with agencies and instead decide to adopt independently. Not only do couples often feel they have more control arranging the adoption themselves, but the waiting time is usually far less.

What should a couple do to investigate the possibility of an independent adoption?

The first step should be to see a lawyer who specializes in adoption. He or she can be found by looking in the phone book, calling a local adoption agency (many of these lawyers also do work for the agencies), or contacting a local chapter of the American Bar Association.

The legal profession's role in adoption has become controversial, due to instances where lawyers have profited from handling adoptions. These are the so-called black-market cases, in which an adoptive couple agree to pay an exorbitant fee for an infant. As a result, some states have set up strict guidelines governing a lawyer's conduct in adoption. The lawyer may have to swear that he or she did not receive excessive fees for handling the adoption, for example. In addition, a lawyer is prevented from representing conflicting interests, which might be the case if he attempted to represent both the birthmother and the adoptive couple.

The great majority of lawyers abide by the rules, and those who are well versed in adoption law can give a couple valuable guidance. First and foremost, this attorney can advise the couple on exactly what is permitted in their particular state with regard to arranging these adoptions. Second, he or she may be able to present the various alternatives the couple might want to consider with regard to finding a baby to adopt. Do they want to rely on word of mouth? Should they place ads? Contact doctors? A good lawyer may know which methods will work best for that couple in their area.

Whether a couple hope to adopt through an agency or independently, they should be sure to make their intentions known to certain individuals who can be helpful in locating adoption sources. Oftentimes telling the right person can lead directly to an adoption. Someone who has completed a foreign adoption may be able to take the couple through it step by step and provide them with the name of the agency used, for example. Or a cousin in the Midwest may know a doctor who is looking for an adoptive home for the baby of one of his patients.

How can a couple decide which people they should tell about their plans to adopt? To a great extent, that depends on the couple. Some people are comfortable going public with the news that they want to adopt. Others find they want to keep their plan more confidential.

It should be noted, however, that if the news is made public the couple may have to face talking about adoption wherever they go— work, church, cocktail parties, department stores. Some well-meaning acquaintances, who are unfamiliar with the waiting times in adoption, may put pressure on the couple by constantly asking them what is going on.

If the couple decide to tell only selected individuals, who should those individuals be?

There are some professional people who are obvious choices. Doctors, of course, are a good source, although the doctor of an infertile woman is liable to have many other patients who also are looking to adopt. Unless the doctor would have a reason for considering this couple first, the couple should probably consider notifying other physicians as well.

A good idea would be to contact doctors in both the man's and woman's hometown. If the couple have family still living in these areas, they probably could help in this endeavor. The plus here is that a family doctor will know the man or woman and their family, and would be able to assure the birthmother regarding the character of the family.

Such reassurances may be important to a birthmother who is thinking not only of the parents for the baby, but also of the extended family—grandparents, aunts, uncles, and cousins. In addition, the couple would have peace of mind knowing that the birthmother was in good health and receiving good medical care since they know this doctor and trust his judgment.

The couple also should make contact with local priests, ministers, or rabbis. Because the religious men and women in any community often are active in social services, they may provide a direct link to an agency. It is helpful for the couple not only to belong to a church or synagogue, but to be active and know the clergy well.

If the couple do not belong to a local church or synagogue, they might seek out one on the recommendation of a friend. A good first step would be to set up an appointment with the clergy simply to have a discussion about the couple's inability to have children and the alternatives available to them.

Any friend of the husband or wife who works in a hospital—a nurse, office worker, receptionist—should also be told of the couple's desire to adopt.

After evaluating their chances for being accepted at an adoption agency, and carefully considering their own feelings on whether they could handle an independent adoption, the couple should decide which course to pursue. If they choose to stick with the agency approach, the next few chapters will help them through the process.

4

SEARCHING FOR AN AGENCY

A dopting a baby should be a happy experience. Especially when the couple deal with a reputable adoption agency that employs a sensitive and knowledgeable staff, the entire process can be both enjoyable and educational.

Not all adoptions follow this scenario, however. There are people who dislike dealing with any bureaucratic institution, and they may have a difficult time dealing with an adoption agency. Some may stick it out, knowing that eventually they will be able to adopt an infant. Others drop out, preferring to adopt independently.

Other people may have no problems dealing with bureaucracies in general, but may have specific complaints about agencies. Unfortunately, many of the complaints about how the agencies operate—employing rude, insensitive people, adhering to outdated rules, and being overly secretive—are legitimate ones. The better agencies have begun to address these grievances by actually changing their policies, but others continue to do business as they have done in the past, thus contributing to the increasing number of independent adoptions.

Procedures for good agency adoptions vary, but ideally it should proceed as follows.

The couple call an adoption agency in their area and request an application. The person who answers the phone is helpful and sends the necessary information to the couple, which they complete and return to the agency. Soon, they are called in for an intake interview with a social worker. Several weeks later, their application is accepted and they are scheduled for a home study.

During the home study, the social worker conducts three interviews with the couple—one with the husband, one with the wife, and one with both partners in their home. The couple are then notified that they have been approved for placement of a healthy infant and will be called when a baby has been identified for them.

The couple finally receive the call and go to the agency to pick up their new baby. After the baby is placed, the social worker makes several follow-up visits to make sure the family is adjusting well.

There are agencies where an adoption will proceed exactly in that manner. How about the other ones? What are the complaints that couples have about adoption agencies? These complaints, based on the order in which they may be encountered by the couple, include:

Rude, insensitive staffs. There are agencies that have failed to train their clerical staffs adequately with regard to adoption. Too often these untrained people are the first ones an outsider will encounter. As a result, someone calling to inquire about adoption may very well receive a brusque response from the receptionist or telephone operator.

Elizabeth S. Cole, director of the Permanent Families for Children of the Child Welfare League of New York, said that when she trained social workers for an agency in New Jersey she would send these professionals to pay phones with a list of adoption agencies to call. Inevitably, these social workers would come back furious over the way they were treated.

Unfortunately, at some agencies the switchboard operator and receptionist are not the only ones who may offend those who come to the agency to adopt. Social workers, directors, and even the head of the agency may fail to consider the feelings of the adoptive couple. This insensitivity may take several forms. One couple told me of attending a group meeting where the social worker made those who wanted to adopt healthy, white infants feel guilty for not wanting to adopt one of the special-needs children.

Other couples complain that agency officials often ignore phone calls or letters. The experience of Sally, a medical technician, and her husband George, a salesman, who live in New Jersey, was typical. "I wrote a letter to the executive director of an adoption agency that had placed an infant girl with a couple my husband and I knew," Sally said. "My letter was never answered. Boy, that made me mad. Here I was asking them for help and they completely ignored me." Sally's attempts to follow up with phone calls also failed. She was never able to get through to anyone in authority.

Even if the agency is not accepting applications, anyone who calls or writes to inquire about adoption deserves a response.

Rejecting couples because of age. Some agencies set an age limit for applicants that many couples believe is unfair. Generally, the age cutoff is forty, but there are agencies that refuse to accept applications from a couple where one member is over thirty-five. Adoption officials at such agencies believe it is in the best interest of the baby to have young parents. "With the people who are younger, there is at least a chance that the child may be able to grow to adulthood without losing either parent," said one official. "Those kinds of statements do not endear us to the older adoptive parent. But let's look at it from the child's point of view. Fifty is the age where most people have grand-children."

Many would argue with this official on that point. And some agencies, in fact, have recognized that the population in general is living longer and having children later in life. To bring their policies in line with societal changes, these agencies have revised their age requirements.

Insensitivity toward the birthmother. Years ago, if an unmarried woman got pregnant, going to a public welfare agency for help was a logical step. Today, these women have other choices available to them, including abortion and raising the child on their own, so they may decide against dealing with an insensitive agency.

Yet many women who decide on adoption decide against going to an adoption agency. These women end up pursuing independent adoptions. Why? Some agencies may operate like government bureaucracies requiring the birthmother to fill out form after form, yet allowing her no say in selecting adoptive parents for the child.

There are agencies that have relaxed their policies somewhat and will permit the biological mother to choose a couple by reading autobiographies of those couples on the waiting list. Other agencies permit the exchange of photographs, phone calls, or even videotapes between the birthmother and adoptive couple.

Many birthmothers do not seek out adoption agencies for other reasons. Unless the agency advertises its services, a birthmother may be unaware that it even exists. Some birthmothers worry about privacy. Many agencies still require the birthmothers to come into their offices, and the sight of row upon row of file cabinets, not to mention all the workers present in an agency, may be enough to scare these birthmothers away. Some agencies now arrange to meet birthmothers outside the office in less intimidating settings.

Prejudice against the infertile. Decades ago, before much was known about human infertility, the prevailing notion was that someone who couldn't have children often had mental problems that prevented conception. "When I was doing my training, the model of the home study was built around the question of mental health," said one social worker. "These people were guilty until proven innocent."

It is sad to say that such an attitude still prevails at some agencies. Couples who apply to these agencies will find themselves undergoing questioning during their intake interview and their home study that presumes that they have psychological problems.

Setting unrealistic standards for parenting. Some agency officials have unrealistic images of the ideal parents for the babies they have available. These agencies may expect all couples they select to be attractive, well dressed, socially prominent, and living in a lovely house in the country. Often this attitude develops because the agency has too few babies to place with too many couples. With so many couples to choose from, the agency may get a little carried away with finding the perfect parents for these infants. A couple may rightly feel that one misstep will result in their application being rejected.

Shrouding the entire procedure in secrecy. Too often the agency process is a one-way street. The social worker finds out a great deal about the couple, but their own questions are left unanswered. They may never see their completed home study. They may learn little about how adoptive parents are chosen for the infants and whether the birthmother has any say in the process. Going through an adoption at such an agency can be very frustrating because the couple feel they have placed their fate in someone else's hands.

Rejecting an application without stating a reason. This may be the most frustrating experience: being rejected at an agency without receiving any explanation for that rejection. "There has to be a reason a couple is turned down," said Mrs. Cole. If a couple hope to apply to another agency, knowing what they can improve upon could help them.

Adhering to rigid, bureaucratic rules. While I was working on this book, I interviewed a woman who heads a well-known and highly regarded adoption agency. During the first part of our talk, this official was lamenting the fact that the agencies are finding it harder to compete against independent adoption. Yet minutes later she told me of an incident that showed why agencies like hers are experiencing such problems.

According to this official, a couple who was already on the waiting list at her agency called to say that they had independently found a baby they wanted to adopt. This couple wanted this agency to accept the baby for them and complete the adoption in the same manner they would handle any agency adoption. That would have included counseling the birthmother and submitting the couple's home study along with other adoption papers to the court. This agency is located in a state where independent adoptions are permitted and there was nothing that legally prevented the agency from assisting this couple.

Yet this official refused to handle the adoption because, as she explained to me, she couldn't allow her agency to become involved in what was technically an independent adoption. She told me that she had advised the prospective adoptive father that the agency would be glad to assume custody of the baby, but that it would then go to the first couple on the waiting list. "They were at the end of the list and we don't give preference to anyone," she told me.

As anyone would have guessed, the couple rejected her suggestion. They were fortunate enough to find an agency in another city to help them complete the adoption.

Here is a situation where everyone could have benefited by the intervention of a responsible agency. But this agency refused a call for help and stuck to its old, inflexible way of doing business.

The one positive note is that this couple eventually found an agency that would assist. That fact should be encouraging to a couple who would prefer to adopt through an agency. There are good agencies out there. No one should be put off by all the negative publicity or by agencies that are bureaucratic and rigid. It is the couple's goal to find a responsive agency that they can work with.

Even at the best agencies, couples may find there are rules and regulations that they object to. In defense of the agencies, there are reasons for many of the policies they must follow. For a moment, consider the situation from the agency's point of view. A birthmother has come to the agency asking its officials to find a good home for her child. This is a heavy responsibility and one that most agencies take very seriously. Yes, agencies make mistakes—they are, after all, made up of human beings who are required to make difficult decisions. But most agencies do a competent job of interviewing applicants and selecting the best families to care for these babies.

There are many advantages in dealing with a reputable, efficient, and sensitive agency when going through the adoption process. Adoption agencies are concerned with all the parties involved in an adoption—the birthmother, the adoptive couple, and the child, a group referred to as the triad. A good agency will strive to meet the emotional needs of each member of the triad throughout the entire adoption process.

This will mean counseling the birthmother before the birth of the child so that she is fully aware of what is happening to her and of the alternatives available to her. A good agency also offers counseling services to birthmothers after the birth of the child. "Just as with a woman who has had a miscarriage, there's a tremendous sense of loss for women who surrender their babies," said Dr. William Pierce of the National Committee For Adoption. "Counseling is required to help these women get through it."

Counseling should also be available to the adoptive couple as they proceed. There should be an opportunity for them to talk out any concerns they have about infertility or adoption with a qualified social worker. Follow-up services also should be available for the couple.

In working with the birthmother and the adoptive parents, the adoption agency is directly looking out for the most important member of the triad, the baby. Everything should be done to ensure that this baby will have a good, stable home filled with love and understanding.

There are a number of safeguards for everyone involved when working through an adoption agency. The birthmother will have peace of mind knowing that the baby has been placed in a good home. The couple will be reassured knowing that the birthmother was confident in her decision to choose adoption. The possibility that the woman will show up in two years and try to convince a judge that she was paid or coerced into giving up the child is remote. Also, the couple will have some knowledge about the woman's health during her pregnancy, particularly if she was living at the agency's shelter. They will know that she wasn't drinking or taking drugs, for example.

In future years, all three members of the triad will have an agency that they can come back to for help and information. This fact could be important to both the birthmother and the child if they decide to search for each other later on. It also will be comforting to the adoptive parents in the event a medical emergency makes it necessary to obtain detailed health records on the child's birthparents.

When the agency process works as it should, it is a hard system to beat. Once a couple have found an agency they would like to work with, what should they expect during their intake interview?

The format will be simple enough. The couple will meet with a social worker or other agency official who will talk with them about their interest in adoption. The couple's purpose is to impress the individual conducting the interview with their qualifications for being parents. The best advice would be for the couple to relax and be themselves.

Any display of emotion should be avoided (more on this topic in Chapter 10, coping emotionally). This is not the time or place for a couple to talk about all they have been through in their efforts to have a child. Everyone coming into the agency has a story to tell, and this recital inevitably leads to tears.

Not every couple develop a warm relationship with their social worker. In fact, there are cases where the personal chemistry is wrong, setting the stage for a possible disaster. The couple need to be prepared for such a situation and should avoid any display of hostility, even if goaded by the person doing the interview. One couple I know was confronted with a combative individual during their intake interview. The woman conducting the interview discovered the husband was a lawyer, and she went into a tirade against the legal profession. The husband managed to keep his cool, listened to her complaints, and soon managed to get the discussion back on track. Even this disagreeable woman was forced to pass them after such an exemplary performance.

The couple should discuss beforehand their responses to a number of questions they know will be asked. Following are some of the most commonly asked questions with appropriate responses.

Why Do You Want To Adopt?

"We are eager to have a family, and because we cannot have biological children, we would like to adopt."

Another response may be: "We have a very good marriage based on love and understanding. We feel we would grow by opening our home to children. And we also feel that the child would benefit by being able to share our love."

Are there any reasons for adopting that would disqualify a couple in the mind of the social worker? Yes, according to Margarett Helms, executive director of the Children's Home Society of Missouri in St. Louis. These reasons include: "So my wife will have someone to keep her company while I travel." Or, "So I will have someone to take over the family business." Mrs. Helms tells about one couple with three biological daughters who came to her agency hoping to adopt a son. The husband was the fourth generation of men who had gone to a particular southern school. He wanted a son to keep that tradition alive. "That's not a good reason to adopt," said Mrs. Helms.

How Does Your Family Feel About Your Decision To Adopt?

"Our families are very enthusiastic about our decision. They know how much we have wanted a family, and they feel that adoption is a very good way to achieve that goal."

What happens if the couple's families are opposed or do not know about the couple's decision to adopt? There is no need to go into specific details if the couple's desire to adopt has touched off a major family battle. It would be sufficient to say, "Our families know how much we want children, and we're sure when they see how happy we are with the child we adopt, they will be very excited."

Would You Accept an Older Child or One with Special Needs?

Chances are good that this question will be put to the couple during their intake interview; if not then, definitely during their home study. It is best that the husband and wife discuss this issue fully before facing agency officials.

Some couples who have their hearts set on adopting an infant believe that they will eventually accomplish that goal if only they can get their foot in the door at a reputable agency. Therefore, they tell the agency they would accept an older or special-needs child, hoping this will get them on an agency list sooner. Later, they reason, they can switch their request to an infant without harming their position.

I have never heard of an instance where this ploy has been successful. Usually, it merely serves to antagonize agency officials. Most agencies have different procedures for handling the applications of those who request older or special-needs children. Typically these applications are processed more rapidly because these children already are waiting and so can be placed immediately.

If an agency jumps a couple's application ahead because it believes they are sincerely interested in a hard-to-place child, it does not mean they will automatically jump that couple ahead when they later request an infant. In fact, it may end up delaying the entire process and alienating the social worker who has already invested some of his or her time and the agency's resources in the couple's case.

Because the agencies have more older and special-needs children to place than infants, they obviously are eager to find good homes for these children. To that end, many social workers resort to the hard sell when talking about these children. This tactic usually is first displayed at the group meetings. This theme is, there are so many children who need homes, why not take one of them instead of an infant?

It is possible that after some soul searching the couple may indeed reach that conclusion. Yet the infertile couple may opt for an older child for the worst possible reason—guilt. They begin to think, "If I really want to be a parent, then I should be willing to accept any child, not just an infant." They end up talking themselves into doing something that may not be right for them. They may have the best motives, but if, deep down, they are not totally sure about whether they could parent an older or special-needs child they shouldn't do it.

In fact, no couple should feel guilty about wanting an infant. "It is wrong to discourage the elemental desire on the part of new parents to want an infant," said Mrs. Cole. "It has less to do with the fear that an older child will already be molded. It's just the joy of wanting to see an infant grow and develop."

If a couple honestly want an infant, they should not let anyone discourage them. Beginning at their intake interview, they should state their preference. If asked to elaborate, they could say that they are eager for the experience of parenting an infant. They could add, however, that they would like to adopt more than one child (if that is the case) and would certainly consider a hard-to-place child in the future.

Some couples may go into their intake interviews preferring an infant but ambivalent about an older child. At this point, it certainly would help their case to keep an open mind. When asked what type of child they would like to adopt, they may say, "We would prefer adopting an infant, but we have not ruled out an older child."

If this is an accurate statement of their feelings at that point in the adoption process, it will not hurt them during their intake interview. Later on, the social worker may want to discuss with them the challenge of adopting an older child and would probably be interested in hearing about their life-style and how they would cope with opening their home to an older child.

Is This the First Agency You Have Contacted About Adoption?

There are agencies that require that a couple work only with it. The agency's rationale is that, once it decides to consider seriously a couple for adoption, it is dedicating its scarce resources for the counseling and home study. The agency wants to make sure that those efforts are not wasted.

From the couple's point of view, this could be a drawback. They may be reluctant to remove their names from consideration at another agency. I interviewed one couple who ended up on the waiting lists of two agencies, even though each agency had asked for exclusivity. "I wasn't going to remove our name from anywhere until we were sure we were going to get a baby," the husband told me. He said he did not feel guilty about this small deception since each agency was quoting long waiting times and refused to be specific about when this husband and his wife would have a baby. The agencies never compared their lists and the couple soon adopted a baby from one of them without jeopardizing their position.

What questions should a couple ask the social worker during this intake interview? Some couples are so worried about alienating the interviewer that they decide not to ask any questions for fear of making a bad impression. As a result, these people leave the interview knowing little more about the agency than when they arrived.

Of course, it is not a good idea to put the interviewer through the third degree. But the social worker no doubt will be prepared to answer some queries, and would probably be surprised not to be questioned about the agency. The couple should regard this session as an opportunity to assess their situation and to find out some important facts in evaluating the agency. Some things to find out:

- Does the agency have any requirements—age, income, family size—that would eliminate this couple?
- What is the waiting time for a healthy infant? For an older or special-needs child?
- How long will the home study take?

- What are the financial obligations for the adopting couple? (If the interviewer says the couple would cover the cost of the birthmother's medical and legal expenses, then the couple should try to get an estimate as to what that amount would be.)
- How is it decided which baby is placed with each couple?
- Does the birthmother have any say with regard to where the baby is placed?
- Does the agency have any adoptive-parents groups that work with it? (This could be important to the couple later on if they need the emotional support provided by other parents who have adopted.)
- What follow-up counseling does the agency provide?

What happens after the intake interview? The social worker will submit a written report with the recommendation that the couple be accepted or rejected. If they are rejected, they will receive a form letter that will be of little comfort.

Any attempt on the couple's part to find out why their application was rejected will probably meet with little success. But the couple should try to find out the reason anyway. Very often the social worker or the director of the adoption program will be sympathetic and understanding and will explain why the couple was not accepted and may be able to offer alternative suggestions, such as foreign adoption.

What happens to the couples that are rejected by all the adoption agencies they approach? Some may decide on adopting a foreign child, while others may go back to one of the agencies that rejected them and apply instead for an older or special-needs child. There are those who will give up totally and adjust to a life without children. Many will refuse to take no for an answer and will pursue an independent adoption.

Whether a couple adopt through an agency or independently, most states require that they undergo a home study. But there is an important difference. With an independent adoption, the couple have identified a baby they want to adopt. In most states, the baby has already been placed in the couple's home before the licensed social worker comes to complete the home study. The social worker has no role in selecting a baby for this couple and, in fact, it is extremely rare that a couple would "fail" the home study for an independent adoption.

When dealing with an agency, the process is different. The couple must pass the home study in order to be placed on an agency waiting list. The following chapter will help them through the process.

5

GETTING THROUGH THE AGENCY INTERVIEWS AND HOME STUDY

Whether the couple hope to adopt through a U.S. agency, through a foreign agency, or independently, they probably will be required to go through a home study after the acceptance of their application.

Who requires a home study? For a foreign adoption, the U.S. Immigration and Naturalization Service does. For a domestic adoption, most states require that the couple and their adopted child have a court hearing before the adoption becomes final, and most courts stipulate that a home study be submitted with the adoption petition. (This stipulation may be waived by the judge in some states, however.)

What is a home study? A home study is a report written up by a licensed social worker who either is affiliated with an adoption agency or operates independently. This report includes factual information on the adoptive couple (their ages, occupations, income, for example) as well as subjective information provided by the social worker that will help illustrate the couple's suitability for parenthood. The social worker puts together the information after conducting an interview or series of interviews with the couple. In the case of an agency adoption, additional information may be supplied by the couple's application form.

As noted earlier, the way the home study is conducted and the way it is to be used differ depending on the type of adoption the couple hope to complete. These differences can be summed up as follows.

Agency Adoption. For those adopting through an agency (this includes those adopting infants, older and special-needs children, and foreign infants and children), the home study begins once the couple's formal application to adopt has been accepted.

Being accepted for a home study represents a certain commitment by the agency to that couple, as an agency only decides to dedicate its resources and efforts to those couples it deems suitable for adoption. However, the couple should know that, until their completed home study has been accepted by the agency, they are not assured of being placed on the agency's list to adopt. Therefore, they should be careful not to do anything during the home study that would disqualify them.

Most adoption agencies do not allow prospective adoptive couples to see their completed home studies, although some will upon request. Others have become more liberal and now have the adoptive couple cosign the home study with the social worker. If a couple feel strongly about seeing their home study, then they should make that fact known to their social worker. Often, if the agency is pressed hard enough, it will fulfill the couple's request.

Independent Adoption. With an independent adoption the couple have identified a baby or child they wish to adopt and, in most cases, the baby already has been in the couple's home for several months by the time the home study is done. The home study is conducted by a social worker, usually from the state adoption agency, who is called in to complete what is sometimes called an investigator's report, which will be submitted with the couple's adoption petition to the court. Most couples are able to see their completed home study and may have the opportunity to correct or question the social worker's conclusions.

The social worker has no role in selecting a baby or child to place with the couple in independent adoptions. In fact, critics of independent adoptions believe that the home study becomes little more than a rubber stamp to approve a placement that has already occurred.

There are some agencies, particularly those that hold group sessions for the home study, that now encourage those adopting independently to go through their program. The agency plays no role in selecting or placing a child, but it can play an important role in helping prepare the couple for the child.

"Couples adopting independently are not getting the benefits of what we know about adoption," says Reuben Pannor of Vista Del Mar Child Care in Los Angeles. Mr. Pannor's agency is one that encourages those adopting independently to come in for a home study or to attend orientation sessions.

Foreign Adoption. In a foreign adoption, a home study may be done either before or after a child has been identified for the couple. If it is done beforehand, a well-written home study that presents the couple in the best possible light can be a persuasive tool in their attempts to sell themselves as parents to a foreign adoption agency.

In these cases, couples should be sure to read their completed home study and correct any mistakes. Also, the couple should keep in mind the countries to which this home study will be sent. If there is something in the home study that might be offensive to people of another culture (the fact that one of the partners has been married before, for example), they may wish to ask to have that section deleted.

Most couples will be apprehensive about the home study, and the most anxious are likely to be those going through an agency adoption, since there is still a chance their application could be rejected. Often the excitement of finally being accepted by an adoption agency evaporates when the couple are faced with the detailed application forms and the prospect of a home study—steps that may be viewed as an unwarranted intrusion into their personal lives.

The couple's anxiety may be heightened by the secrecy surrounding the entire procedure. An agency may ask on the application form for very personal information—childhood experiences, relationship with parents, for example—and then give the couple no idea how this information is to be used. Are these forms passed around the agency and read by everyone in the office? Are they shown to the birthmothers to help them select homes for their babies? What happens to these forms once the adoption is completed? Are they kept on file or destroyed?

Under typical agency procedures, the couple probably will never find out. If they are assigned a caseworker (most couples are), they may find out during later interviews how their application forms will be used. However, most couples will be too intimidated to press for answers, believing that to do so might antagonize agency officials and place their application in jeopardy.

How the applications are used varies from agency to agency. In general, it is safe to say that applications will be read by most people on the adoption staff at the agency. Often it is not the sole decision of the couple's social worker as to which baby will be placed with them but a joint decision with other social workers, including those who work with the birthmothers. At some agencies, the birthmothers may read profiles of those couples who have been approved for adoption and may even be given the power to select the parents they prefer for their babies.

Why do some agencies insist on being so secretive?

Traditionally, agencies have viewed themselves as protecting the privacy of the birthmother and the adoptive couple. And in most cases, that is the way it should be. Usually the adoptive couple want to raise the child without the thought that the birthmother knows where the child has been placed and is watching. Similarly, many birthmothers want to get on with their lives after they decide on adoption.

Unfortunately, this penchant for secrecy has spilled over into other areas of agency operations. Elizabeth Cole of the Child Welfare League is one professional who believes that home studies should be cosigned. "If I have been honest with you all along, then I shouldn't care if you see what I have said about you," she said. "If I'm a confident professional, why should I be afraid to show you what I've written?"

Instead, most couples come out of their interviews never knowing how they did. "It causes needless anxiety in most, but it doesn't raise enough anxiety in others," said Mrs. Cole.

Generally, once the home study is completed, a couple will be told that they have been approved for a placement and have been placed on the waiting list. Although there are cases where a couple have been rejected by an agency after their home study was completed, that situation would be unusual. A more likely scenario is that the home study would be suspended while still in progress if the social worker felt one or both partners had a serious problem that needed to be resolved before they could be approved for an adoption.

Many agencies are attempting to make their home study process more responsive to the needs of the adoptive parents. One of the ways the agencies receive suggestions is through adoptive-parent groups that have been formed in all parts of the United States. The Children's Home Society of Minnesota, for example, works with OURS, an adoptive-parent group that was founded in that state and now has branches nationwide.

"There's no question that if you're going to have a quality program there have to be certain procedures people have to go through," said Roger Toogood, executive director of the Children's Home Society of Minnesota. "But it can be done in a sensitive and loving way.

"Our experience has been that if you are open with people and make it clear to them what is involved and never overpromise, it helps," Mr. Toogood continued. "Most people in our society are accustomed to the fact that good-quality results require a commitment whether it be in purchasing a home, doing adequate preparation in getting married, or in preparing a child for college."

Or in adopting a child. A good agency program can help the new adoptive couple to adjust to their new status in many ways. "We approach the home study as an educational process," said Mr. Pannor of Vista Del Mar Child Care in Los Angeles. "We say we're not going to play God and decide whether they are good parents or bad parents. We are going to try to help them understand adoption. We help them see it as a lifelong process. And we encourage them to ask questions."

If the couple are assigned an experienced caseworker, this person can be an invaluable source of information even for years after the adoption. To some, the caseworker became a friend and ally, someone the couple could turn to whenever they had a problem or question, or whenever they just wanted to talk about the joys of being an adoptive parent.

Unless the couple have reason to suspect otherwise, they should enter the application, interview, and home study phase of the adoption expecting nothing short of an exemplary performance by the agency. It is hoped that they won't be disappointed.

Once a couple have been given an application (and by that I mean the long-form application and not the short one that is handed out to everyone who inquires about adoption) and scheduled for a home study, it is pretty much expected that sooner or later they will be on the agency's list to adopt a baby. Rarely would a couple be rejected for an adoption after being accepted for a home study, but it does happen.

There also have been cases where a couple's home study was interrupted because the initial interview with either the husband or the wife raised questions in the social worker's mind. Such interruptions could delay a couple's application indefinitely.

One thing that could hurt the couple is displaying the wrong attitude at the beginning of the interview and home study process. These feelings may stem from the couple's resentment at being evaluated by someone else as to whether they are fit to be parents. No doubt the couple know their fair share of bad parents and are angry that they are being forced into a position where they must defend themselves.

The couple should realize that these feelings are common. Everyone knows that there are many children being abused and neglected by their biological parents. Who is out there evaluating the job that these parents are doing? It is quite possible that if all parents were required to go through some sort of parenting course before having children those incidents of child abuse and neglect would decrease dramatically.

Rather than resent this part of the agency process, the adoptive couple should regard it as a unique opportunity to sharpen their parenting skills. Any information about parenting that the couple can get from the social worker in the days ahead can only add to their storehouse of knowledge on children.

It should be noted that much of the discussion about parenting also will include advice for raising an adopted child. While the adoptive parents would like to feel that they will take their baby home and it will be no different than raising a biological child, it *is* different and no amount of denial will change that. At some time in the future, the adoptive couple will face the challenge of telling the child he is adopted. They must be prepared to deal with his questions regarding his birthparents. These sessions with the social worker will help prepare them.

Throughout the entire agency process, it will help the couple to keep focused on the end result—the baby. Whenever they are depressed, upset, or angry about what they are going through, they should remind themselves *why* they are going through all of this. They want to adopt a baby. Like many other things in life, it sometimes is necessary to put up with a difficult interlude in order to obtain something that is valued highly. Learning how to be a parent might not be much fun, but the actual activity of parenting will be.

The first requirement an agency makes of a couple after accepting them is to fill out a long and detailed questionnaire. Questionnaires vary from agency to agency, but their purpose is the same: to educate the agency—specifically the social worker who will handle the case—on the couple's background. This application will serve as a basis for all future discussions during the home study.

What types of questions are included on the application?

These questions will range from the factual—name, address, religion, occupation—to the subjective. Not surprisingly, most people find the subjective questions—those that probe their feelings on parenting, families, marriages, and careers—the most difficult to answer.

On most applications, the answers to these questions should be brief—usually a sentence or two will suffice. The responses will give the social worker some background information to work with, which can be discussed more fully during the interviews.

Questions likely to appear on the application include the following.

- How would you describe your spouse?
- What goals do you work toward in your marriage?
- How do you resolve disputes in your marriage?
- If you have been married before, what were the reasons your other marriage(s) ended?
- What role does your extended family play in your marriage?
- Do you anticipate that having a child will change your relationship with your spouse? In what way?
- How will a child affect your life-style? Are these changes that you are prepared to make?
- What are your own personal goals? How did you decide on these goals?
- Who is the person who has had the most influence on your life? In what way?
- How will your work life accommodate the addition of a child? Do both parties intend to keep working full time? If so, what provisions will be made for child care? What provisions will be made for creating family time?
- What are your feelings on how a child should be disciplined?
- Why do you want to adopt?
- What type of child do you want to adopt?
- What qualities do you possess that you feel will enable you to become a good parent?
- What are the most important things you feel you can teach a child?
- Do you spend any time with children now? How has this influenced your views on parenting?
- Are there goals that you would want your child to achieve? What would they be?
- Are there things that you could not accept in a child? What would they be and why?

The responses to these questions will help the social worker understand the couple, giving him or her an idea of how each spouse regards the marriage and their future roles as parents.

Along with answering this questionnaire, each partner may be asked to write an autobiography. In putting together this life story, each person will be asked to talk about his or her family, marriage, infertility, and their decision to adopt. Here are some areas a couple may be asked to talk about in an autobiography:

- Early Childhood. Describe your childhood years and your relationship with your parents and family members during this time. Include any recollections of family events, celebrations, or tragedies that may have had a lasting effect on you.
- Adolescent Years. Talk about your school years, what you found enjoyable, your dating experiences. What experiences helped you in terms of establishing personal and career goals for later in life? Describe your relationship with your family during these years.
- College Years. Discuss what you found enjoyable about your college years. Were there professors or other individuals that you met during college who profoundly influenced you? How did college prepare you for what would occur after graduation? Talk about your dating experiences.
- Time After College. Talk about your work experiences after college. Under what circumstances did you meet your spouse? What first attracted you to him/her? What activities, hobbies, and other interests do you share? What roles do your family and your spouse's family play in your marriage?
- Adoption. How did you reach the decision to adopt? How do you expect a child will change your lives?

Initially, each partner may balk at the idea of answering all these questions and writing an autobiography. While the questions appear simple and straightforward enough, they can actually be very difficult to answer. Then again, each person is wondering whether his or her answer is the wrong one. ("If I say that I believe a child should be spanked, will that be held against me?")

The apprehension may be even greater when putting together the autobiography. What happens if one of the partners had parents who were divorced and, as a result, had a very unhappy childhood? Would admitting that hurt their chances for a baby? What if the husband has never been accepted by his wife's family? How does one deal with that when talking about the extended family?

The best advice that can be given is that the couple should never lie when filling out any of these forms. Chances are, once the couple begin a more in-depth discussion with the social worker, the truth will come out anyway. It will only make the couple more tense if they feel they have to cover up something in their past.

Instead, they should view any negatives in a positive manner.

For instance, if the husband did have an unhappy childhood, it may have made him all the more determined not to repeat the mistakes made by his parents. If he were all that negative on being a parent, he wouldn't be trying so hard to adopt. The fact that he is going through the process says that he is sincere about being a good father.

If there are strained relations with one set of parents, there is no need to stress that fact. A simple answer to the question about the extended family would be: "We see our parents whenever we have the chance and hope that they will play an active role as grandparents." Who could say that was a false statement?

Some agencies show some form of the application and autobiographies to birthmothers so they can choose the adoptive couples they want for their children. "The agencies may give sketches of the adoptive couples to the birthmother to allay fears on her part," said Frederick J. Magovern, a New York attorney who specializes in adoption. "Most birthmothers want the security of knowing that the child has gone to a better home. In most situations, she may be estranged from her family and have little money. Knowing that the child will have a good future will help her."

Before the home study actually is begun, the couple may have to add to their application certain other documents, usually a certificate of marriage, birth certificates, divorce decrees, financial statement (this could include the couple's income tax form for the previous year and a bank statement detailing their savings and other assets), insurance policies, medical reports from each partner's physician, and several recommendations.

The couple will be asked to submit some names for recommendations. These people will be asked to write letters vouching for the couple's character. When choosing these people, the couple should select at least one person who has known them for a long time, over ten years. The second person could be a priest, minister, or rabbi who could attest to the couple's spiritual qualities. A third might be a couple with children who could say something about how well their friends interact with children.

Once these papers are all together, the couple will be scheduled for a home study.

Too often just the words *home study* strike terror into the hearts of the couple. Some people take the words quite literally and believe that someone will be dispatched from the agency to study their home. In the past, terrible stories were circulated about agency officials making surprise visits and then rejecting a couple because their home was in disarray.

Be reassured that agencies no longer—if they ever did—make surprise visits. Resources are too scarce to send caseworkers out to interview a couple when they might not be at home. Especially now with so many women working outside the home, the social worker would probably waste time and effort trying to catch the couple off guard.

Usually, the home study process begins with interviews at the agency. Most often three interviews are scheduled, one with the wife, one with the husband, and then one with both partners together. The latter interview is the one likely to be scheduled for the home. (Some agencies do the first two interviews in a group meeting held at the agency. The third interview is then held with each couple in their home.)

During the separate interviews with the husband and the wife, the social worker may do as much talking as questioning. A good agency wants these sessions to be informative on both sides, and ideally they will cover many aspects of the adoption process.

Each partner can expect some discussion on their marriage. Most agencies know that trying so hard to have a child may place strains on a relationship, and the social worker will want to make sure that the marriage has come through this difficult time strengthened. No agency wants to place a child in a home that is about to fall apart.

Naturally, there will be some talk about infertility. Some people are so excited that they are finally on the sure road to adoption that even a discussion about their infertility won't dampen their spirits. For others, however, just the mention of the reproductive system is enough to start the tears flowing.

If either partner is worried about discussing infertility, he or she should try to keep answers short. (More on coping with the emotional aspects of infertility and adoption will be covered in Chapter 10.)

There will probably be some discussion about the birthmother. This will be a general discussion since, at this point, the agency couldn't possibly know which baby was going to be placed with the couple. What the agency official will want to know is how the couple feel about her. Do they view her in a negative way—either because she ended up with an unwanted pregnancy or because she chose not to raise the baby herself? Or, do they see her as a caring human being who is trying to ensure her child a warm, loving home and a good start in life?

How the couple regard the birthmother is important because years from now they will be faced with the challenge of telling the child about her. If they harbor a negative attitude about her as the child grows up, it will be difficult for them to paint a positive picture for him. It is critical that the child understand that he was given up by his mother not out of neglect or selfishness, but because she cared about him. For the adoptive parents to make that a convincing argument to the child, they must believe it themselves.

A good social worker will be able to tell a couple during home study interviews something about the young women who come to the agency for help. Often the birthmother will write a letter to the adoptive parents after her child has been placed with them. Some agencies will show these letters to couples going through the home study in order to help them understand that these young women care about their children. In most cases, the decision to have the child and offer it for adoption was arrived at after much thought and pain.

Of course, some adoptive parents want to forget the existence of a birthmother or birthparents. Most adoption agencies today discourage that type of attitude. Even if the child does not want to search for his birthparents when he becomes an adult, chances are he will still ask questions about them. It is only natural, and the adoptive parents should not feel threatened by his curiosity.

Some birthmothers who go to agencies express a desire for some sort of contact with the child's adoptive parents. The social worker will ask the prospective adoptive couple how they feel about having contact with the birthmother.

This contact can take several forms. The birthmother may merely want to receive a letter from the parents after they receive the child, so she can be reassured that she made the right decision and that the child has been placed with a good family.

Most adoptive parents would not object to writing such a letter. However, if the birthmother is looking for more than a letter, the couple may have reservations.

What if the birthmother wants to talk with the couple over the phone? She may go a step further and actually want to meet the couple in person.

It is possible that she may be looking to maintain contact after the child is placed. This could take the form of receiving a letter from the adoptive parents each year, telling her how the child is doing.

If a couple agree to any of these situations, that fact will be noted on their home study. If a birthmother makes a request for contact, it is likely that one of these couples would be chosen.

A couple's initial reaction might be to agree to anything, thinking that they might get a baby that much sooner. They should realize, however, that agreeing to such conditions does not necessarily mean they will be moved up the agency's list. And it also might mean that they could be stuck with their decision for years to come.

They need to be totally honest with themselves. How do they *really* feel about meeting the birthmother? Would it make them uncomfortable? Would they be worried about running into her years later on the street? "It takes a special, secure adoptive couple to agree to meet the birthmother," said Mr. Magovern, who often represents adoptive couples.

What about the adoptive couple maintaining an annual correspondence with the birthmother? Would they resent having to tell her about the child? Would they see this as an invasion into their lives?

Traditionally, adoption agencies have sought to protect the identities of the birthmother and the adopting couple. Many agency officials are opposed to so-called open adoptions, arguing that it may be confusing to the child having both adoptive parents and biological parents in his life.

Mr. Toogood, of the Children's Home Society in Minneapolis, said that his agency will try to accommodate a birthmother who requests meeting the adoptive parents. In his experience so far, three birthmothers made that request at the outset, but all three ended up changing their minds after the births of their babies.

It would be rare for a social worker to hold it against a couple if they decided they wanted no contact with the birthmother. That does not necessarily mean that they feel negatively about her, or are trying to deny her existence.

There are still a few agencies that insist on pairing up adoptive parents and adopted children based on physical characteristics. While that might seem to be an admirable goal, most couples who go to these agencies find it a frustrating system because they often end up waiting longer for a child that the agency feels is suitable for them.

Other agencies cannot afford the flexibility of waiting for a blond-haired baby to place with a blond-haired couple, although some insist on finding an adoptive couple that matches at least some of the characteristics of the child's background. "We look very carefully at the background of the birthparents and adoptive parents to try to find a home that will be compatible with the child's heritage," said Mr. Toogood. "From the religious perspective, we respect the wishes of the birthparents. But many of them do not specify."

Some state laws require that a child be placed in a home where one or both of the parents are of the same religious background as his birthparents. Beyond that, agencies might consider matching nationalities when placing a child, reasoning that having this common bond could only help the relationship between the adoptive parents and the adopted child.

However, it would be nearly impossible for an agency always to be able to match perfectly the ethnic backgrounds of the adoptive parents and adopted child. So, sometime during the home study the couple probably will be asked what type of ethnic background they feel they can accept in a child.

The husband and wife should discuss their feelings on this point ahead of time, and they should be perfectly honest with themselves. Again, they should not feel compelled to accept a child they do not want. That would not be a positive situation for either the couple or the child. Also, they should not say they will accept any child, feeling that to do so will get them a child quicker.

These discussions on all of these points will take place between the social worker and one partner. After these two interviews, the social worker will make an appointment to visit the couple in their home.

What does the social worker look for during these visits? Obviously the social worker will look to see that this is the type of home where a child will be nurtured, both physically and spiritually. Rarely would a couple be turned down because of the physical appearance of their home. "It would have to be pretty bad for them to be turned down on the basis of their house," said Irene Moses, of the Catholic Community Services in Miami. "It's an opportunity to see them in their own setting, to observe what kind of people they are, to see them one on one."

Ms. Moses's agency is one that conducts its first two home study interviews in group meetings, usually with twenty couples in a class. So the home visit takes on added importance. "Some people don't shine in a group," she said. "Others do, but that doesn't mean they will be better parents."

Most agencies do not require that the couple have a separate room for the child, although if they do have a separate room in mind it wouldn't hurt for them to point out that fact to the social worker. More often, however, the social worker will want to know that there will be room enough for the child to sleep and play.

Will the social worker actually go poking into closets or looking in the refrigerator? There have been cases where this has happened, but those situations are rare. The couple, after two individual interviews (or two group discussions), will probably know this person and what he or she is like. If the social worker all along has presented the unlikely image of one who would look under rugs, then they should be ready for that.

In fact, many social workers actually dislike this part of the home study and are eager to get a quick tour of the home and then settle into a comfortable area to conduct the third and final interview.

The best preparation for the home visit is to tidy up the home and prepare some simple refreshments—cookies and a beverage are a good choice. Have a cozy part of the home or apartment chosen that everyone can retire to after the social worker has been shown around.

Until now, the discussion on the interviews and home study has assumed that the agency the couple is working with is a good one and that the social worker is competent, sensitive, and responsive to the couple. But what if the worst happens? What if the agency and its personnel turn out to be rude, critical, and difficult to work with? What should a couple do?

First, the couple should understand that they may not have done anything to cause agency personnel to act negatively toward them. Perhaps they have a personality conflict with their social worker. Or, it is possible that agency personnel still cling to outdated agency procedures, adopting a bureaucratic demeanor and judging the couple every step along the way.

The couple's most immediate reaction may be to walk out and hope that they will find another agency. However, they may have no other choice. It may be this rude agency or an independent adoption. If their state doesn't allow independent adoptions, or if they are committed to dealing with an agency, then they have no alternative but to stick it out.

It would be unfortunate if the home study turns out to be an ordeal. The couple no doubt will be disappointed that they are being denied a valuable learning experience. If they opt to stay with the agency, then they should try to get through the interviews as best they can. After they have adopted the child, they could ask a local adoptive-parents association for the name of a good professional who might provide them with some of the information they did not receive during their home study.

Since a couple cannot hope to revise agency policy overnight, they should be concerned with handling a bad situation without jeopardizing their application. Here is one sample crisis and advice on how to get out of it:

The wife enters her first interview with the social worker, feeling calm and composed. However, after about a half hour of questions about her infertility, the wife begins to suspect that the social worker is trying to turn the wife's inability to have children into a mental problem. The wife does not want to become angry (thus perhaps confirming the social worker's opinion), yet she does not want to give the impression that she has psychiatric problems.

Anyone who is confronted with a situation where their infertility is being made into a much broader problem should not take the bait. Getting angry will defeat the purpose. The couple should continue to answer the social worker's questions honestly and calmly. Chances are, the social worker will realize this line of questioning is wrong and will drop it.

The other problem a couple may run into may not be as easy to spot during one set of questions, but it also stems from longtime agency attitudes. That attitude is that adoptive parents should be required to meet standards so high that most biological parents would fall short.

A couple will sense this attitude on the part of their social worker if everything they say seems to be wrong. There is little a couple can do when placed in this situation except try to remain calm and to give honest answers. Unless the couple spark a real confrontation with the social worker, it is unlikely that their application will be in danger of being rejected.

Sometimes the chemistry between the social worker and the couple is wrong. Every question the social worker asks seems an invasion of privacy, while to the social worker the couple appear hostile and uncooperative. In this case, the couple should ask to meet with the head of the agency and ask to be assigned another social worker.

If the agency turns down the request, then, through an adoptive-parent group, the couple might seek out other couples who have worked with this social worker who may have advice on how to get through the process. As a last resort, the couple may have to consider going to another agency or adopting independently.

When the home study is complete, the couple will receive a letter from the agency telling them that they have been accepted for placement of an infant and will be notified when one has been identified for them. Now begins the most difficult time—the waiting period.

This time period will be different for each couple: Some couples will wait years, whereas another couple could get a baby in a matter of days if one comes into the agency that is perfect for them and no other couple.

The couple should ask their social worker how long they will have to wait. While each situation is unique, the social worker should be able to offer some guidance. When did a couple that received a placement in the last month first go on the agency's waiting list? Knowing the answer to that question may help a couple figure out their own situation.

Many factors will influence the waiting period. The number of other couples on the waiting list is always a factor, yet some couples wait longer than others. Why? If the agency is one that matches ethnic backgrounds, it may help the couple to be of a certain nationality. Aside from that, there are subjective decisions to be made on the part of agency officials and on the part of the birthmother, if she plays a role in the selection process.

The couple should keep in touch with their social worker during the waiting time. Remember that the social worker has many other couples whose home studies he or she completed, so it will not hurt the couple's case to be diligent in reminding the social worker that they are still eager to become parents. And talking with the social worker can help a couple cope during the wait. Many agencies also can refer a couple to an adoptive-parent group. (See the listing in the back of the book, p. 203.) These are the people who also had to wait for their babies. They know what it is like and can help.

How much advance notice will a couple have before their baby arrives? This time could vary. If an agency places a child into a home as soon as it has been discharged from the hospital, then the couple may have only a few days to prepare. Other agencies may place the baby in foster care until the biological mother's surrender becomes final. In most states that period is for thirty days after the birthmother has signed the surrender papers. At that time, her decision is binding; she cannot change her mind and ask to have the baby returned to her.

Does a birthmother ever change her mind and ask for her baby back? Yes, it does happen, although most agencies report that these cases are few. The effect on the adoptive parents cannot be minimized. It is like experiencing a death in the family. The baby is taken away, never to be seen again by that couple.

Dealing with an agency, however, the couple have several safeguards. First, the birthmothers receive extensive counseling during their pregnancies. A good caseworker can tell when a birthmother is unsure about her decision to place the baby in an adoptive home. The caseworker will advise his or her superiors of that fact and the baby will be categorized as a legal-risk baby.

If permitted, an agency might choose to place the baby in a foster home until the surrender is final. If state law requires that the baby be placed in an adoptive home before the thirty-day period can begin to run, then the agency would tell the couple that the baby was a legal-risk case.

It would remain up to the couple to decide whether they are up to the challenge. However, they should know that if the birth-mother does change her mind many agencies would act soon to place another baby with them. That, of course, would not make up for the baby they lost. But it would mean they wouldn't have to wait years for another shot at becoming parents.

After the baby is placed in the couple's home, the first thing that they should do to help avoid future problems is to engage a qual-ified adoption attorney to handle the legal aspects of the adoption. Probably the most important matter from the couple's point of view is making sure the biological mother's surrender statement is properly completed. Unless the paper is properly signed by the birthmother and notarized, someone could challenge the adoption later on. A couple's attorney can check to make sure that this paper has been executed properly.

There is another important reason to hire an attorney. In some states, the couple have a choice of where to file their petition for adoption. In Louisiana, for example, the couple may choose be-tween family or juvenile court. Plainly stated, some courts are more expeditious than others. The couple will want to have the adoption finalized as soon as possible and will therefore want to choose the fastest court.

In addition, adoption hearings run smoothest before judges who are familiar with these cases. A judge who does not routinely han-dle adoptions may question certain facts that another judge would not. Such questions could threaten to drag the adoption hearing on indefinitely or to revoke the adoption.

One attorney tells of a case where his clients were adopting a baby whose birthmother was only thirteen. The judge, who was unfamiliar with adoptions, felt that the birthmother was too young to make such a decision and insisted on issuing a subpoena for her to appear in court. Therein followed a hearing that was pain-ful for the birthmother (who reaffirmed her decision to place the child in an adoptive home) and the couple (who feared losing their baby).

The actual steps from placement to the time the adoption is finalized vary from state to state, but the following is fairly rep-resentative.

1. *Placement.* The baby is placed in the adoptive couple's home. They are required to sign certain documents, including a peti-tion, which states their intention to adopt the child.

2. *Surrender.* The birthmother signs the surrender papers and the thirty-day period begins.
3. *Termination of Birthmother's Rights.* The thirty-day period ends and the biological mother's release is irrevocable.
4. *Waiting Time.* The adoptive couple must wait a certain time period (in most states six months) before they can move to make the adoption final. During this time, the couple will continue to be visited by the agency's social worker, who will file reports on the family's progress.
5. *Preparation for Court Hearing.* The agency and/or the couple will be required to submit several documents to the court in preparation for an adoption hearing. These documents may include:

   • A petition of adoption, which gives biographical information on the adoptive couple, including their earnings, religious background, the agency handling the adoption, and how and when the child came into the couple's care.
   • An agreement of adoption, which is a contract between the adoptive couple and the adoption agency. The couple state that they agree to assume all rights for the child. Both parties also agree to a name change for the child.
   • An affidavit pursuant to the social services law that details the financial aspects of the adoption. (In an independent adoption this document would also have to be submitted by the biological parents, who would attest to the monies they received from the adoptive couple and for what purposes.)
   • An affidavit of marriage.
   • An affidavit of medical history of the child.
   • Notification of the order of adoption, which is sent to the state so that a new birth certificate can be issued.

6. *Court Hearing.* The couple and their child appear in court where the judge rules on the adoption. The hearing is private, often in the judge's chambers. After the hearing, the adoption records are sealed. These records, in most states, can only be opened upon "good cause."
7. *Adoption Final.* The adoption is now final and within a few weeks' time the couple will receive a new birth certificate for the child. The old birth records are removed and sealed along with the other adoption records.

In most states it will take about a year from the time the child is placed in a couple's home until the time his adoption is legal.

6

INDEPENDENT ADOPTION

A dopting through a reputable agency offers certain safeguards to both the birthmother and the adoptive couple. Yet each year there are many birthmothers and couples who shun the agencies in favor of arranging the adoption themselves.

The great majority of independent adoptions are white infants, because it is easier for someone to adopt an older, handicapped, or minority child through an adoption agency. These children already are waiting for homes and agencies actively seek parents for them.

Agencies do place healthy, white infants, of course. But some couples may have been turned down by all the agencies in their state or community. Perhaps they were rejected because of their age. Possibly they received no explanation about why their application was not accepted, adding to their frustrations.

But it is wrong to assume that everyone who pursues adoption independently does so because they would not be accepted by an agency. Many people—and that includes both the birthmothers and the adoptive parents—decide on this route because they believe it offers them the flexibility and independence they feel would be missing in an agency adoption.

First, let's talk about the birthmother. Why would she choose to place the child herself, instead of depending on professionals at an adoption agency who are trained specifically for that task?

She may feel very strongly about being the one who selects a home for her child. She may decide to interview several couples, either over the phone or in person. While some adoption agencies now permit an active role by the birthmother, she might feel that if she goes to an agency she will be losing control.

Desire for privacy is another reason birthmothers may avoid agencies. "If the girl is middle class, it's embarrassing," said Elizabeth Cole of the Child Welfare League. "She may always have connected agencies with poverty."

The birthmother also may want to avoid an agency's counseling services, believing that agency officials will attempt to talk her out of her decision to place the child in an adoptive home. In most cases, that is not true. A good agency merely wants to make certain that the young woman has considered all the alternatives and is certain about choosing adoption.

Assuming that a couple could find an agency to accept their application, why would they decide to go the independent route instead? Many couples are turned off by the agency system—they are annoyed by the applications and they resent placing their fate as parents in someone else's hands. No doubt other couples are discouraged by the long waiting times quoted by some agencies. They think, "Why should we wait for three years when we could have a baby in nine months through an independent adoption?"

An adoptive couple may like the idea of being selected by the birthmother. "If agencies could place babies perfectly, then fine," said Susan, a financial analyst from Florida who adopted her son through an independent adoption. "But agencies make mistakes, too."

Independent adoption often is categorized as the "gray market." Although these adoptions are perfectly legal in most states, many agency professionals still object to the procedure, citing the fact that there is no screening mechanism for deciding whether an adoptive couple are ready for a placement, and no counseling for determining whether the birthmother is aware of the alternatives available to her.

How does an independent adoption work? The adoptive couple would find the birthmother on their own, either through a third-party referral or by placing an advertisement in a newspaper. Both the adoptive couple and the birthmother should be represented by lawyers throughout the procedure, who can help work out arrangements such as expenses.

The National Committee For Adoption in Washington, D.C., estimates that perhaps as many as thirty thousand healthy infants were adopted in 1982. Half of those adoptions, the group believes, were done independently. There are other officials, however, who believe that the proportion of independent adoptions is larger than half and continuing to rise.

A couple opting for independent adoption should be cautious.

Even though they have good intentions, they may encounter nefarious individuals who hope to make a handsome profit. This request for a large sum of money may come from a lawyer, doctor, other middleman, or the birthmother herself. This quickly moves the adoption from the gray area into the black market.

No matter how desperate a couple may be, they should never resort to dealing in the black market. This admonition may fall on deaf ears if the couple are determined and wealthy enough to pay any sum without hardship. While most authorities view the couples who get tangled up in the black market as victims, these people cannot be totally exonerated, since their very participation in the black market ensures its continuance. They are taking part in the worst possible transaction, one that places a price on the head of a helpless infant. How would these parents explain their behavior to that child years from now?

An independent adoption does not have to wander into the black zone. Many are completely legal and benefit all the participants—the birthmother, the adoptive parents, and, of course, the child.

Because couples adopting independently won't have an agency looking out for their interests, they will need to do their homework and be prepared to handle any crisis that comes their way. The first step will be for a couple to find a reputable attorney who can advise them on the many legal questions they will encounter. The best choice would be to locate a lawyer who is completely up-to-date on adoption law on the state and national level. With independent adoption, it is possible the couple will be dealing across state lines. These interstate adoptions are governed by the Interstate Compact on the Placement of Children, an agreement that has been signed by all but three states (as of June 1985 the matter was before the legislatures in Nevada and Hawaii and had not yet been considered in New Jersey). Under the terms of the compact, an adoption that crosses state lines cannot violate the adoption laws in either state. "If independent placements are illegal in Minnesota, then the receiving state cannot say the placement can be made," said Betsy Rosenbaum, project manager for the American Public Welfare Association in Washington, D.C.

Therefore, having an attorney who is completely knowledgeable on different state laws and the interstate compact is essential. A knowledgeable attorney not only will help the couple not do anything illegal, but he or she also can prove to be a great support system when the going gets rough.

Susan and her husband Drew found their attorney through a referral and were impressed on their first meeting. "The lawyer told us, 'I don't do anything illegal, and will no longer handle your case if you consider doing anything illegal,' " recalled Susan. "We said that was the way we felt, too."

How much help a couple can expect from their attorney will vary. The couple should remember that attorneys are prevented from representing both the birthmother and the couple. Some states also have laws preventing anyone—a lawyer or other individual—from pairing up birthmothers and adoptive couples. Under some state laws, only licensed agencies may perform that matching function. So it will be up to the adoptive couple to locate a birthmother on their own.

The lawyer can, however, advise on the best methods for finding a birthmother. The most common is to place an advertisement in a newspaper. Often the lawyer can provide the couple with a list of newspapers that accept such ads—not all newspapers do. Some papers, simply because of where they are located, produce a greater response. Many of these publications have become known for carrying these ads and a birthmother who is looking for a home for the baby will know enough to look in one of them. Most of the newspapers used tend to be in smaller cities and towns. Some have religious affiliations, while others are located on college campuses.

Some couples go overboard and place ads in dozens of newspapers around the country. A better method is to limit the advertisements in the beginning to a handful of newspapers, and to limit the time these ads run. Some couples report that after being fairly conservative with running these ads they were able to find a birthmother they felt comfortable working with. Others found they needed to advertise more than once.

"A lot of lawyers will tell you to flood the newspapers," said Beverly, a secretary from Cleveland who, along with her husband Frank, a teacher, did an independent adoption. "We stuck to three newspapers and did them for two weeks at a time."

Before placing any of the advertisements, a couple will need to consider how they will handle the responses. The most frequently used method is for the couple to have a separate phone line with an unlisted number installed in their home. Whenever that phone rings, the couple will know that it is someone answering their ad.

What should the newspaper advertisement say? Certain things should be included. The couple might want to state their religion. They should emphasize their happy marriage, warm home, financial security, and ability to provide for the child's spiritual and physical needs. They might want to state their occupations.

The phone number should be given. With out-of-state ads, the couple may want to say that they will accept collect calls. They may want to give the best hours to call. If both the husband and wife work, they may want to hook up an answering machine to the telephone. Most of the young women who call probably will not leave messages, but the recording could remind them of the best times to call.

Here are some sample advertisements:

> ADOPTION NOT ABORTION. We are a happily married, Catholic couple eager to adopt a white infant. We offer love, warmth, and financial security. All medical, legal, and other expenses will be paid. Confidential. Please call us collect 212-555-5555, evenings after 7 p.m. and weekends.
>
> ADOPTION. We are a professional couple looking for a newborn or toddler to adopt. We are happily married, financially comfortable, and wish to share our love with a child. Answer our ad and answer our prayers. We will pay all expenses. Telephone collect 312-555-1212, anytime.
>
> ADOPTION. Pregnant? Need help? Please let us adopt your child. We will pay all expenses. We are a mature couple who want to adopt a white newborn. We can provide love and affection. Call collect 804-555-1212.

Once the phone has been put in and the advertisements placed, then the couple sit and wait for the phone to ring. Be prepared for some crank calls. Some individuals see the ads and can't resist making a nuisance of themselves. Also be prepared to receive calls from other prospective adoptive parents who are interested in finding out what success the couple are having with the ads. Perhaps these people have ads running in some of the same publications, or are thinking about trying this method to adopt and merely want to find out how the procedure works. In any event, these people could provide valuable information if they have been talking with other couples who have placed ads.

But the calls the couple will really be interested in receiving will be from birthmothers who are looking for homes for their children. The number of calls a couple can expect to receive will vary. The couple from Cleveland, Beverly and Frank, said that their ads produced thirty phone calls. One couple interviewed for this book reported receiving dozens of calls from just one ad, while another couple received far fewer. The latter couple placed ads on five different occasions in thirteen newspapers before finally locating a birthmother they felt comfortable with.

Susan recalled that the very first call she received was from a birthmother's mother who was looking for a Catholic home for her daughter's twin girls. Susan and her husband Drew are not Catholic and, to their disappointment, did not qualify.

Susan soon discovered that disappointment became part of the process. It was not unusual for a birthmother to have very specific requirements in mind for the child's future parents and often Susan found that she and Drew did not measure up. A number of the birthmothers wanted Catholic homes, while one asked for an Episcopal couple. Susan encountered one woman who was determined to find a home in the country for her child and rejected Susan and her husband because they lived in the city.

Susan soon learned after those first few calls not to volunteer any information. She waited for the birthmother to ask her questions instead.

Beverly and Frank first placed their advertisements in July. They had one adoption fall through in December when the birthmother changed her mind. They finally adopted a baby boy in January after locating another birthmother.

Beverly recalled that some women who called were not serious about adoption. "One woman told me she was pregnant and wanted to give the baby away but her husband wanted to keep it; they decided to keep it," she said. "Another woman told me that she was going to have a test done and if the baby belonged to her boyfriend, she would keep it. If not, she would give it away.

"At one point every girl we talked with wanted money. You fight the urge to say something nasty. I was working full time just to save up the money for an adoption. In addition, we were paying out a lot of money every month for my own medical bills. There are a lot of things in fertility workups that the medical insurance doesn't pay for.

"I also felt that if we paid a birthmother anything, she could blackmail us for the rest of our lives," Beverly continued. "Our lawyer firmly discouraged us from paying any woman money. He kept saying, 'You can do it without paying the money.'"

It is not unusual for the birthmother to request a face-to-face meeting with the adoptive couple. She might even make that a condition for accepting the couple. Many couples actually choose independent adoption in order to be able to meet the birthmother, reasoning that some agencies would not permit such meetings. But other couples hope for the same confidentiality that they would be guaranteed in an agency adoption.

A couple should be honest with themselves and their attorney about how they feel regarding this issue. If they would feel threatened or insecure actually seeing the birthmother, then they should admit that fact and stick to their plan. However, if they would have no objection to one meeting, either during the birthmother's pregnancy or when she places the baby in their care, then perhaps they should consider it.

A couple may not object to one meeting, but might decide against it if the circumstances are not ideal. Beth, a lawyer living in Illinois, for example, said that the first birthmother she and her husband talked with lived in the same city. "I had no problem with meeting her once," said Beth, "but the idea that I could run into her at some time in the future in the local department store led me to reject that suggestion."

The second birthmother, and the one whose child Beth and her husband adopted, did not want such a meeting. "I would have done that one," said Beth. "The woman lived far away, and there was little chance I would ever see her again."

It might help a couple to decide this issue by hearing about the experiences of three other couples. Each couple handled the question of meeting the birthmother differently; all were pleased with the outcome.

Susan and Drew decided ahead of time that, although they had to talk with the birthmother over the phone, they had no desire to meet her. They advised their lawyer that they wanted the adoption handled in the strictest confidence. They had regular reports on the birthmother, but they did not speak with her again after turning the adoption over to their attorney. Both Susan and Drew were pleased with the manner in which the adoption was completed.

Beverly and Frank felt similarly about protecting their privacy. "I didn't want to get involved with the birthmother knowing us," said Beverly. However, when the birthmother asked to actually hand the baby over to Beverly and Frank at the hospital, the couple agreed to the meeting.

As Beverly and Frank expected, the entire experience was very emotional. As Beverly recalled, she and Frank had gone to the hospital to receive the baby. Their lawyer called to say that there would be a delay, as the birthmother was very upset about transferring the baby. She was afraid to look at him or touch him. The lawyer asked Beverly to talk with the birthmother on the phone.

"For the first time, I felt sorry for her," said Beverly. "All this time I didn't, because I thought she was being very calculated about the adoption. But when I spoke to her on the phone she was crying. I suddenly realized, 'Hey, I'm not the only one going through this. She's giving up her baby.'"

Beverly said she was grateful for that phone conversation, because she had the opportunity to express her feelings to the birthmother. "I wanted her to know that her son was going to be loved and taken care of and would have a good life," Beverly said. "I felt glad that I could tell her that. To reassure her one last time."

The encounter finally did take place at the hospital, with the birthmother seeing her baby placed in Beverly's arms. Neither the birthmother nor Beverly and her husband said anything during this meeting. "When I saw her, my first thought was that she looked a lot like me," said Beverly. "She was the same height and weight. She even wore her mascara like I did."

Beverly feels that seeing her son's birthmother had a positive affect on her attitude. Rather than feeling threatened, she feels more secure. "I know this woman has a nine-year-old son," Beverly said. "I told our lawyer that when our son gets older and wants to meet his brother, we can arrange it. I'm not nervous about it anymore."

Until that time, however, Beverly and Frank took steps to protect their identities. "Our lawyer was great," said Beverly. "Any money that was paid went through our lawyer. We gave him a check and he wrote the check to her so that it couldn't be traced to us. For that reason alone, it's important to get a lawyer who wants to do more than just the paperwork."

Gloria and Anthony, two teachers who live in upstate New York, went farther than perhaps any other adoptive couple have ever gone in their relationship with their son's birthmother. The couple felt very strongly about not only meeting the birthmother, but getting to know her.

This birthmother, Terry, was from a midwestern state and had found a couple in the East that was going to adopt her child. Unfortunately, two months before the baby was due, her adoptive couple changed their minds. About the only thing Terry had was the name of the lawyer who had been representing her adoptive couple. That lawyer then agreed to represent Terry. He contacted a colleague who found another adoptive couple—Gloria and Anthony—eager to adopt the baby.

Because Gloria and Anthony couldn't afford to pay for a hotel for Terry, they offered her accommodations in their home. No doubt most couples would have found such an arrangement uncomfortable, but Gloria and Anthony were thrilled with the opportunity.

"We thought it was great," said Gloria. "We wanted to meet her and be able to tell our son all about her.

"I felt so strongly that Terry and I were going to have a good relationship that I never felt threatened by her," said Gloria. During their time together, Gloria and Terry had long conversations about the baby. "She had another child and she was only seventeen," said Gloria. "She made the wisest decision and I told her I thought it was the right thing to do."

Not only did Terry live with Gloria and Anthony for two months, but she gave birth in their home after a long and difficult labor. Sharing the experience is one memory that Gloria will treasure.

Terry went back to the Midwest shortly after the baby was born. In the first few weeks, she wrote to Gloria regularly. She writes less frequently now, but Gloria is eager to maintain this correspondence.

"I feel so proud of myself for the way I handled the adoption," said Gloria. "I feel I've really made a difference in Terry's life. I want her to feel free to have contact with our son."

There are ways to find a birthmother other than placing advertisements in newspapers. If a couple has told enough of the right people that they are interested in adoption, then it is possible one of these people will prove to be the key.

Blanche Gelber, a New York attorney, advises her clients to "spread the net as wide as possible." In response, some of her clients tell their friends and relatives. Others write letters to obstetricians all over the country. Which tactic is chosen often depends upon the individual couple, and there is no one set plan for success.

What would a couple say in a mailing to doctors they have never met? Some couples actually type up a résumé listing their ages, occupations, etc. A better approach is to type a letter with a more personal tone. They should talk about themselves, their jobs, their hobbies, their families, their home life, and why they are so eager to adopt. They should enclose a photograph.

The couple should not let down their guard just because a certain birthmother was referred by a reputable physician, a trusted friend, or a close relative. The person who makes the referral may not have talked with the young woman very much and will not know what she expects from the couple. Couples should always beware of demands for money or any actions that may carry the adoption into the black market.

No matter how the couple locate the birthmother—through an ad, by a referral, or with sheer luck—they should put this woman in touch with their lawyer immediately. Their attorney will arrange for another lawyer to represent the woman.

It is important that the birthmother have her own legal representation. Her lawyer will look out for her interests throughout the entire process. From the couple's point of view, it would be difficult for the woman to claim years later that she had been coerced into the adoption if she had proper legal help.

Even with certain safeguards things can go wrong. Perhaps the worst thing that could happen is for the birthmother to change her mind. Of course, this situation can also occur when dealing with an adoption agency, but in such a case an adoptive couple that were forced to surrender the baby would be placed back on the agency's list. In all likelihood they would not wait long before receiving another placement.

With an independent adoption, there is no such guarantee. If a couple lose the baby, they must start all over again. They must locate another birthmother and go through the entire procedure.

For that reason, when a couple see an independently arranged adoption fall through, the effect can be devastating. Beverly and Frank had that experience. "We had worked out everything with a young woman in Pennsylvania," said Beverly. "The baby was going to be born around Christmastime. My husband kept saying, 'Let's not count on it,' but you start to dream anyway."

Shortly before Christmas, Beverly and Frank's lawyer received a letter from the woman saying that she had changed her mind and wanted to keep the baby. "That was it for me," said Beverly. "I said to my husband, 'I can't do this anymore,' but my husband and our lawyer kept me going. My husband kept saying, 'We'll just keep putting the work in and it will happen.' "

Naomi and her husband Andrew, a lawyer in Maryland, had a worse time. They had the baby in their home for four days when the birthmother decided she wanted her infant daughter back. "Losing the baby was a moment of high drama," said Naomi. "The lawyer came, took the baby, and drove away leaving me weeping on the porch."

Naomi and Andrew—like Beverly and Frank—redoubled their efforts and soon adopted a baby girl from Chile.

Another negative factor in independent adoption may be the cost, which is difficult to predict, although estimates are possible. The lawyers' fees, for both the couple and the birthmother, should be known beforehand. The couples interviewed for this book reported fees that ranged from $1,500 to $3,500—the latter fee is on the high side.

Medical bills for the birthmother can range widely. If it is a normal, spontaneous delivery, and the mother is in the hospital only a few days, the bill should be around $3,000. Bills can soar, however, if the birthmother encounters difficulties. One attorney reported a case where the birthmother had hospital bills totaling over $20,000. It turned out that the mother had been on drugs and the baby was born with serious problems.

That is an extreme case. But there are occasions when the birthmother delivers by cesarean, which carries higher doctor fees and calls for a longer stay in the hospital.

What also must be figured into the total are any necessary expenses that the birthmother incurs. However, the adoptive couple need to be wary here. "When you start to hear about expenses, the danger flags should go up," said Frederick Magovern, a New York attorney.

Sometimes a birthmother decides to go the independent route because she doesn't have a job or any savings and she needs someone to help her pay the rent. If she went to an agency, she would be able to stay in a shelter. But many young women reject that alternative.

Any expenses paid to the birthmother by the adoptive couple are closely scrutinized by the courts, which must approve the adoption petition. Some jurisdictions are more lenient than others, but in general a judge is not going to sanction a large, lump-sum payment to a birthmother, even if she claims loss of earnings.

It goes without saying that all payments to the birthmother should be verified. The couple should receive a full accounting with an itemized list from their attorney. Anything they are unsure about should be questioned.

All things considered, and under normal circumstances, an independent adoption should cost around $10,000. If a couple find that they are paying substantially more than that, then they should ask why. Are there legitimate reasons the bills got so high? Or are they being taken for a ride?

Independent adoption can cut down on the waiting time a couple will face, but it carries added risks. "You run the gamut of extremely fortunate coincidences to disasters," said Mrs. Gelber, the New York attorney. Yet despite those occasional disasters, she remains a supporter of the system. "People think that independent adoption is evil," she said. "It's not. It's beautiful."

There are many officials who disagree, however. "We all know that there are some payments, gifts, given to people in these adoptions that are unethical and, in fact, illegal," said Dr. William Pierce of the National Committee For Adoption.

Independent adoptions are illegal in Connecticut, Delaware, Massachusetts, Michigan, Minnesota, and North Dakota. Massachusetts and Connecticut do permit what is called identified adoption—the couple identifies a baby they want to adopt, then the agency comes in to counsel the birthmother and complete the couple's home study.

Social-work professionals, like Elizabeth Cole, endorse this approach. "Independent adoptions are risky, but they shouldn't be outlawed," she said. Mrs. Cole worries that all three parties in these adoptions—the birthmother, the adoptive parents, and the baby—are at risk.

The child may be at risk because the adoptive parents chosen may not be suitable. The birthmother might be harmed because she would not receive counseling and may be at the mercy of unscrupulous attorneys. And the adoptive couple may suffer because they may not receive enough information in order to make an informed decision. Mrs. Cole believes that all those risks could be minimized if a reputable agency were required to see the birthmother and the adoptive parents before the adoption was completed.

Perhaps someday there will be safeguards for those who want to adopt independently. But until there are, anyone deciding upon this course should go in forewarned and tread carefully indeed.

7

FOREIGN ADOPTION

On a hot and steamy summer afternoon, four couples gathered in a conference room at the Spence-Chapin adoption agency in New York City to watch a slide show on Korea. Many of the slides showed the modern Korea—Kimpo Airport, high-rise office buildings, gambling casinos, elegant restaurants, and fancy night-clubs. Other slides—including one of a gilded statue of Buddha—displayed a country whose cultural heritage goes back thousands of years.

The slides for this show were provided by the Korean Travel Bureau, but the couples who attended had more than a typical tourist's interest in this Far Eastern country. Each of these couples had been approved by the adoption agency for placement of a Korean infant. Not only had these couples been approved, but they each had been matched with a Korean child.

During the coffee hour that preceded the slide show, photographs were passed around. From the comments that were made one thing was apparent: Even though these couples had yet to see these children in person, they had already accepted these Korean babies as their own. "This is my daughter," one woman said to another, proudly offering the picture of a three-month-old girl. "Isn't she beautiful?" The other woman agreed, then added: "I haven't seen one who isn't absolutely adorable."

This scene at Spence-Chapin is becoming a common one at adoption agencies across the United States as more Americans—eight thousand in 1984—decide to adopt children from foreign countries. To ensure a smooth transition for both the child and the parents, adoption agencies hold orientation sessions whose formats vary, but which often include a slide show of the children's country, a lecture by an agency official, and a question-and-answer period.

There are a variety of reasons Americans are adopting foreign children. Perhaps the major reason is a lack of healthy white infants in the United States. Many couples who are turned down for these babies decide to adopt a foreign infant.

Rosemary Stowe, director of adoption services at Spence-Chapin, said that at her agency many couples who are not accepted for placement of a white infant later are accepted to adopt a Korean infant. At Spence-Chapin, as at most agencies, a couple would stand a better chance of being accepted for the placement of a foreign infant simply because there are more of these infants to place. Spence-Chapin places about 170 Korean infants a year, compared with about 25 white infants.

But it is wrong to think that everyone who adopts a foreign child is doing so just because they can't adopt a white infant. Many couples and single people are eager to adopt foreign children. Some couples, when they discover they cannot have biological children, quickly choose to adopt from abroad. Other couples already have biological children, adopted children, or a combination of the two, and then decide to adopt a child from another country.

Where do these children come from? In 1957, more than 70 percent of all children adopted from abroad were from European countries; today, few are. More than 50 percent now are from Korea and a large percentage are from Latin America. Other agencies report placing children from the Philippines, India, Hong Kong, and Greece. All together, foreign adoptions make up between 10 and 15 percent of all adoptions by non-relatives completed in the United States each year.

Adopting a foreign child can be a thrilling experience, yet it can also be a greater challenge than parenting an American child. Before anyone makes this decision, some serious thinking must be done about what is involved in taking on this lifetime responsibility.

Perhaps the first issue the couple or single parent will have to face is the child's physical appearance. A couple may already have accepted the fact that they will not have a biological child and will adopt a child that may or may not look like them. But it is a big jump from adopting an American child who may have some features similar to those of his adoptive parents to adopting a foreign child who very likely will not have any similar features.

In fact, if the adoptive parents are white or black and the child they are adopting is from Korea, India, or one of the Latin American countries, there is a good chance that his appearance will make it obvious that he is adopted. Anyone considering a foreign adoption needs to be honest with himself about this issue. Will the adoptive parent feel uneasy if the child attracts stares in the supermarket?

How will relatives and friends adjust to a foreign adoption? Resistance on their part could make the transition more difficult. What happens when the child grows up? If he is being raised in a mostly white suburban area, how will he fare socially? Will he be able to date? How do the couple—and how do their friends—feel about interracial marriage?

Discrimination still exists in the United States, and anyone adopting a foreign child will face that discrimination on a regular basis. If that strain will be too much to bear, a couple or single parent should admit that fact now and pursue another avenue.

Those who are unsure about adopting a child from another country would do well to talk with someone at an agency that handles foreign adoption. Social workers are accustomed to answering questions facing a couple who are thinking of adopting a foreign child. In addition, there are many adoptive-parent groups—national and local—whose members have adopted foreign children and who can offer advice and guidance.

Once a couple are sure about a foreign adoption, they face the question of how they should accomplish that task. There are several different ways of arranging an international adoption. These include:

Working Through a U.S Agency. This is perhaps the safest method for adopting from abroad. Many U.S. agencies have become very skillful at handling foreign adoptions and in most cases have established good working relationships with adoption agencies in foreign countries. Often social workers from the U.S. agencies will make regular trips to the foreign countries to meet with officials there.

How does it work from the couple's point of view? The couple probably would have to go through the same application, interview, and home study procedure set up for those couples who want to adopt white infants. Unfortunately, some agencies accept only a certain number of applicants each year. If the couple fail to get accepted by an agency in their area, then they could try contacting other agencies around the United States that place foreign children (see listing at the back of the book, p. 234).

Working Through a Facilitator. A facilitator serves as an intermediary between couples in the United States and foreign agencies.

Sometimes these people are lawyers or translators who work in the adoption area. In other cases, these people did not start out as adoption specialists but fell into it due to circumstances. For example, a person may move to the United States from a Latin American country where he has friends working at an adoption agency. A co-worker interested in adopting from that country approaches him, and before too long this person is in business as an adoption facilitator.

Dealing with a facilitator can be risky. While some of these people are trustworthy and dedicated, others are out to make money and never actually plan to follow through with the adoption. There are many cases where couples paid large sums to facilitators and never received a baby.

A facilitator should be checked out thoroughly. If possible, the couple should get references from others the facilitator has helped. A check with local agencies, adoptive-parent groups, and even the local office of the U.S. Immigration and Naturalization Service is in order. One or all of these sources may know of the facilitator and be able to offer the couple guidance.

Even if the facilitator is approved by a local adoptive-parent group, an adoptive couple, or others, the prospective adoptive couple should be cautious. Any requirements for large outlays of cash should be considered very carefully. If possible, the couple should find out from the facilitator what this cash is for and who it will be going to. If they do not receive satisfactory answers, they should not use the facilitator.

Working Directly with a Foreign Agency. On occasion, a couple may find that they can work directly with a foreign agency. Many adoptive-parent groups here in the United States have lists of these agencies and can offer guidance on how to proceed. Some even sponsor workshops where they take the parents through the process step by step.

There are several challenges involved in using this approach. First, the couple must be very organized and must be prepared to double-check everything they do. There will be no social worker at a U.S. agency helping them over the rough spots. They may have to deal with language differences. At some point they will want to engage a translator to assist them in translating documents and may also want to use this person for phone calls or whatever else is needed.

These are the three ways international adoptions can be arranged. Perhaps it would help to understand these processes better and how they differ by looking at three real-life examples.

Working with an Agency. Naomi and Andrew's experience is an example of how the ideal international adoption should proceed. They adopted two infant girls at two different times from Chile after their independent adoption fell through. This disappointment made Naomi and Andrew determined to adopt. After talking with dozens of people in their city who either had adopted or knew something about adoption, they contacted LAPA (Latin American Parents Association in Seaford, New York; see listing on p. 221), which can assist a couple in dealing directly with orphanages in Latin America. They also heard about an agency in Washington, D.C., that placed children from Chile. "We had been very intimidated by all the paperwork and hassles," said Naomi. "To find a U.S. agency that would do this for us was great."

After meeting with people at the U.S. agency and educating themselves about foreign adoptions, Naomi and Andrew were very interested in adopting a baby from Chile. "To someone who feels they want a white infant, a Chilean child is very close in appearance," said Naomi.

Naomi recalled that their home study was completed in March. "Nine months to the day, our daughter was born," she said, and they traveled to Chile to pick up their daughter.

The couple had no idea what to expect, especially after hearing stories before they left. Some friends advised them to bring a large sum of money. "We thought we would go down a dark alley and put the money in a slot and a baby would roll out," said Naomi. "But everything was totally aboveboard. The social worker and lawyer that we worked with are well respected in their fields. We received receipts for everything."

The couple took some vacation time and stayed in Chile for ten days, although Naomi said that everything went so smoothly they could have flown in that morning and flown back to the United States that evening with their daughter. They had filled out a power of attorney authorizing the Chilean attorney to handle the case for them, and they let the attorney represent them at the court hearing in which the birthmother formally relinquished the child. All that was required of them was to go to the American consulate and pick up the baby's visa. "We had our daughter in our arms when she was only three and a half weeks old," said Naomi.

One should not assume, however, that all adoptions in Chile proceed as smoothly. It was obvious from listening to Naomi's story that they received the best guidance from the Chilean agency they were working with. "One must clear the international police at the airport before leaving the country," said Naomi. "Most of them don't speak English. The agency's secretary came to the airport with us." Naomi and Andrew were never stopped by the police.

Naomi later learned that another couple had been held up for several hours because of paperwork. A third couple, because of a misunderstanding, were placed under house arrest at their hotel until the police could verify that the couple had in fact received custody of the child that they were attempting to take out of the country. The matter eventually was straightened out, but one can just imagine what an ordeal that must have been for these adoptive parents.

Their Chilean adoption went so smoothly that Naomi and Andrew decided they would adopt another. They asked the U.S. agency to put them back on the list. "We thought it would take two years for us to get a second baby, but eleven months later we had another baby girl," said Naomi.

This time, Andrew traveled to Chile alone. "The lawyer and social worker down in Chile saw that he was well taken care of," said Naomi. "They took him out to dinner. Everything was just spectacular." Five days later, Andrew returned home with his new daughter.

Each Chilean adoption cost Naomi and Andrew about eight thousand dollars, which included airfare, hotel, and other expenses while Naomi and Andrew stayed in Chile. That cost also included reimbursing one birthmother a hundred dollars for a month's salary when she was unable to work because of the pregnancy, and buying the other birthmother, who had lost her job and was living in the streets, a plane ticket back home.

Working Through a Facilitator. Amy, a teacher, and Michael, an editor at a publishing house, who live in New Jersey, attended a general briefing on adoption at Spence-Chapin. They were discouraged by the waiting times for white infants and decided against a Korean adoption. Because Amy is of Italian extraction with dark hair and dark eyes, she and Michael felt that a child from South America would be a good choice because there was the chance he would resemble Amy.

Amy and Michael never checked with any of the U.S. agencies that handle South American adoptions. Instead, Amy talked with a woman she worked with whose neighbor recently adopted from Colombia. Through this neighbor Amy and Michael eventually were put in touch with Matilda, a woman who came from Colombia and had a friend at a small adoption agency there.

"Matilda always felt that these Colombian children would be well placed with homes in the United States," said Michael. "So she had set up a network of people that she was working with. She assured us that these people did not do it for the money."

That claim proved to be true. In fact, the cost was low for a foreign adoption—about $4,500. However, the entire process was, as Michael put it, "a nightmare."

Amy's neighbor called several months after the couple had talked with Matilda to tell them that there was a fifteen-month-old baby available for adoption. Were they interested? "We didn't really think about it," said Amy. "Here was a child coming our way." They said yes, not realizing they were facing seven months of unexplained delays before they could pick up their son Paul.

What was so frustrating to the couple was the lack of information they received while they were waiting. "I was never really confident that what was being done was being done fairly and expeditiously," said Michael. "But you don't know where to turn." The couple contacted an outside source—someone who had family in Colombia—and asked him to check out the situation for them. Their friend called the orphanage in Colombia, but did not manage to get very much information.

"Matilda was furious that we went above her head," recalled Amy. "It reinforced our feelings that we were not dealing with professionals."

If Michael and Amy had been dealing through a U.S. agency, they would have been kept fully informed as the adoption procedure progressed. (In fact, Mrs. Stowe at Spence-Chapin said that the agency spends six hundred dollars a month in overseas calls to check on the status of babies who have been selected by the agency's couples.)

Michael and Amy later found out the cause of the delays. At that time in Colombia, any child left for more than three months at an orphanage was considered abandoned. Michael and Amy were told about Paul before those three months were due to expire. Unfortunately for them, Paul's mother returned to claim him, and subsequently left him at the orphanage again. Officials at the orphanage were then required to wait until another three-month time period had passed before declaring Paul abandoned.

Shortly after Michael and Amy decided to adopt Paul, Amy found out that she was pregnant. That fact did not erase their commitment to Paul—if anything, they were more eager than ever to adopt him.

Amy's condition raised some concerns about her traveling, but her doctor okayed the trip after Amy said she was determined to go. If Michael and Amy had been working with an American agency, they might not have had to travel to South America to pick up Paul since most U.S. agencies have escort services. At the least, they might have been able to wait in a major city like Bogotá while an escort picked up Paul in his village and brought him to the couple.

Because they were doing the adoption through a facilitator, however, Michael and Amy had to go themselves to the small village where the orphanage was located. They described the town as primitive and hostile to Americans. "There were no showers," said Amy. "In order to bathe Paul we had to put a basin of water on the roof to warm it up. We weren't free to walk in the streets. Americans were not well received in this town. We were locked up there. It wasn't my idea of a vacation."

From the village, Michael and Amy were sent to Bogotá, where they had to finish the required paperwork before taking Paul out of the country. Often, a U.S. agency will have a representative in a major city to help a couple with this paperwork, since the language barrier can be a great hindrance. Michael and Amy completed this monumental bureaucratic task on their own with, as Michael put it, "nonstop running around and a lot of luck." They also used the excuse of Amy's pregnancy to avoid standing in line. In twenty-five hours, they managed to have Paul examined by a doctor, obtained his American visa, and had all other necessary documents, including Paul's birth certificate, authenticated and notarized.

Paul is nearly four years old now, and although Michael and Amy still get upset when talking about his adoption, mostly they focus on him and what a delightful addition he has been to their lives. Still, their negative experience in Colombia has affected their feelings about Paul's country. "We swore when we left the country that we were never going back," said Amy. "We would never stop him from going, though."

Working with a Foreign Agency. Nancy and Jeff, teachers from Long Island, adopted their daughter by working directly with an agency in Mexico. Their first step was to contact a local social worker for information on foreign adoptions. She put them in touch with an adoptive-parents group that held regular workshops on adopting internationally.

Jeff was shocked at the emphasis given in the discussion to the racial characteristics of the children, especially with regard to their skin color and facial features. "They were very blunt," Jeff said. "I was a little taken aback by that."

Of course, the group's intent was to prepare these prospective parents for what these children would really look like. Anyone who didn't think they could raise a child that had dark skin, for example, would be better off finding that out at an orientation meeting rather than when presented with the child.

Nancy and Jeff already had two adopted American children; the first was of Italian extraction like Nancy and Jeff, while the second was Italian and Mexican. The couple decided to adopt their third child from Mexico so that he or she would have something in common with their second child.

Because this was their third adoption, the couple were already familiar with the process, but adding the international element meant that they had to do some homework. Most of the information they gleaned was supplied by the adoptive-parents group, and someone from the group even served as an intermediary for them. Nancy and Jeff were given the name of the attorney in Mexico who would handle their case, but they didn't actually talk with him until they arrived in Guadalajara. With the help of the intermediary in the United States and the lawyer in Mexico, Nancy and Jeff were confident that they would be able to complete the process without using a U.S. agency.

Nancy and Jeff first attended the adoptive-parent group seminar in September, and in March they were flying to Mexico to pick up their new daughter. They decided to make a family vacation out of it and took their two sons and Nancy's mother. Ten minutes after they checked into the hotel, the Mexican lawyer arrived with the baby. She was only one week old.

After nine days in Guadalajara, the family flew on to Mexico City where they completed the necessary paperwork at the U.S. embassy. Nancy describes this stage as the worst part of the trip. They were eager to get home with their new daughter, but experienced one delay after another. "I came to tears when one fellow told me we wouldn't be getting home anytime soon," said Nancy.

The delay was caused by a relatively recent U.S. policy that requires that a child brought into the United States must be declared abandoned in his country. The U.S. action was taken after several instances in Latin America where babies were stolen from their mothers. If there is some question about whether the child has actually been abandoned, someone from the U.S. embassy may be required to visit the mother and get documented proof that she has chosen adoption, which happened in the case of Nancy and Jeff. This meant that they and their family had to wait in Mexico City while the U.S. investigator completed his check. Apparently this policy is not popular with U.S. embassy officials, either, who resent having to add these checks to their workload.

The adoption cost around ten thousand dollars, including all the travel expenses for the entire family. "It was a great vacation," said Jeff. "There was a certain amount of tension involved with the embassy. But aside from that one little incident, it was an enjoyable experience."

These are just three examples. Three other couples may have had totally different experiences. Yet some generalizations can be made. The Chilean adoptions proceeded smoothly because Naomi and Andrew worked with two agencies, one in the United States and one in Chile. If at all possible, the best arrangement is to have these two agencies working together with the couple to complete the adoption.

Adopting from a foreign country is a complicated procedure even when dealing with a U.S. agency that can give needed guidance at every step along the way. "It is almost impossible—and risky—to do it on your own," said Roger Toogood, of the Children's Home Society of Minnesota. "Even with all the experience our agency has, we often run into problems." Mr. Toogood's agency places children from South America, India, Korea, Hong Kong, and Greece with families both inside and outside Minnesota. In order to minimize problems when placing these children, Mr. Toogood said his agency works only with licensed agencies in the foreign countries.

Often the couple attempting an international adoption on their own are at the mercy of people thousands of miles away who speak a different language. There are many horror stories that come out of these attempts—babies arriving in the United States suffering from disease, a foreign lawyer or other official demanding a large sum of money, or the entire adoption falling through after the money has been paid and the intermediary has disappeared. Even those foreign adoptions that succeed under these circumstances can prove to be emotionally draining.

Those who succeed at foreign adoptions working on their own are highly organized, like Nancy and Jeff. This type of adoption places a large burden on the couple, who must be prepared to do much of the work by themselves. Nancy and Jeff did most of the work before they left for Mexico, and they had expert guidance from the adoptive-parent group they worked with. In addition, they were fortunate to have a Mexican attorney who handled many of the details for them.

Anyone intent on completing a foreign adoption should realize that, even with the help of an established agency, the bureaucratic machinery runs more slowly in other countries than it does in the United States. Many of the foreign adoption agencies in Korea and

South America have small staffs that are inadequate to handle the mounds of paperwork required with foreign adoption. And red tape—such as the requirement that the child be certified as abandoned before he is freed for adoption—further slows down the process.

What are the actual steps in beginning and completing a foreign adoption? Let's use the example of working through a U.S. agency.

1. *Inquiring About Foreign Adoption.* A couple's first job should be to learn more about the adoption agencies in their area that handle foreign adoptions. A good place to start would be with the state agency (see listings, p. 234), which should be able to put the couple in touch with these agencies. If the couple cannot find such an agency in their area (or if they are not accepted by those agencies) then they should look into agencies located in other states that handle foreign adoptions for families all over the United States.

2. *The Orientation Meeting.* An official who is experienced in foreign adoption will talk about the children available, waiting times, costs, whether travel to the country is necessary, paperwork requirements, and other factors. Time usually is allowed for questions. If a couple cannot locate an agency that holds such a meeting, then they should contact a local adoptive-parent group.

3. *Applying to the Agency.* Once the couple have made up their minds about foreign adoption, they can place a formal application with the adoption agency. They then would be required to undergo a home study that is required by the U.S. Immigration and Naturalization Service before any foreign child can be placed with the couple.

4. *Waiting for a Child.* Once the couple's home study is approved, it will be sent to foreign adoption agencies. The officials at those agencies review the home study and send to the U.S. agency biographical sketches and photographs of children they feel would be appropriate for the couple. This step in the process is called the referral.

5. *Freeing the Child for Adoption.* The couple can review these biographical sketches and with the help of their social worker decide on a child that they would like to adopt. This is called a match. Once a couple have decided on a child they wish to adopt, the foreign agency will be notified. The couple should then receive the child's birth certificate and proof that he has been relinquished by his biological parents.

The purpose of proof of relinquishment is to give the foreign child and the biological parents the same rights and protections that would be provided to an American child about to be adopted. However, in some cases, it may be difficult and time-consuming for the foreign agencies to obtain the necessary releases. Perhaps his birthmother did not sign the necessary release papers when she left the child at the agency; she must then be tracked down. If the biological father is known, he will have to sign the papers, too, which could involve further delays.

6. *Obtaining an I-600 Form.* Once the child has been freed, the couple would then contact their local office of the U.S. Immigration and Naturalization Service (INS) to obtain the I-600 form that classifies the child as an "immediate relative who is an orphan." The couple also will be required to submit their fingerprints, proof of U.S. citizenship, proof of marriage, and their home study. These forms are submitted to INS along with the child's birth certificate and relinquishment paper.

7. *Applying for the Child's Visa.* After INS approves the petition (in rare cases approval can be denied but the couple would then be within their rights to ask why), the couple can obtain a visa for the child from the State Department's Bureau of Consular Affairs. This visa would be issued by the U.S. consulate in the child's country. Once the visa has been granted, the child may leave his country and come to the United States.

8. *Travel to the Child's Country.* At some agencies, the adoptive couple will be given the choice of traveling to the country to pick up their new son or daughter or letting that responsibility be handled by an agency social worker who will serve as an escort. If the couple decide to go, then they will need to obtain valid passports.

9. *Finalizing the Adoption.* When the child arrives in the United States, he must be registered as an alien with INS. Even if the adoption was finalized abroad, it is a good idea to repeat the process in whichever state the child will reside. Agency officials will know how to proceed in their particular state.

10. *Medical Checkup.* The couple should arrange for the child to see a pediatrician as soon as possible. Some couples actually stop at the doctor's office on the way home from the airport.

A couple arranging a foreign adoption independently should be particularly diligent. What are some things they should consider? The couple must have a home study done by a social worker who is affiliated with a recognized U.S. adoption agency. (Some social workers have gotten around this requirement by having themselves registered as agencies. The couple should be sure to check on whether the social worker meets the necessary qualifications.) A home study is only good for a year, so the couple should make sure that they plan to adopt within the next twelve months.

The couple will want to make up a list of foreign agencies that they can send their home study to. Names of these agencies may be obtained from LAPA (Latin American Parents Association) or OURS in Minnesota (see listings, p. 217).

Once the couple have sent their home study to these agencies, they will wait to hear whether a child has been found for them. After receiving information on a particular child, they can decide whether the child is one they want to adopt.

As with an adoption through a U.S. agency, the couple would proceed with the same steps for obtaining proof of relinquishment, completing the I-600 form to submit to INS, and applying for the child's visa. The couple probably would have to travel to the country to pick up their child and to complete the paperwork that ordinarily would be completed by the U.S. agency there. To minimize problems, the couple should try to find out from the foreign agency ahead of time what will be required of them.

After they have returned to the United States, the couple will be required to have the child registered as an alien, and also will want to proceed with finalizing the adoption in their state.

One question many couples have when they begin to consider foreign adoption is where the children come from. More than just idle curiosity is involved—someday the parent will have to tell the adopted child something about his background. It helps if the adoptive couple know as much as possible about their child's biological parents and the circumstances that led to his adoption.

In Korea, a child often is abandoned when there is a breakdown in the biological family. The typical breadwinner in Korea does not have any job security. If he loses his job, he may not be able to find another one and will have no way to support his family. He might just desert his family.

For a time, the mother might try to hold the family together, but soon she will be faced with making a decision. In many foreign countries—and this includes Korea and most Latin American countries—there is a stigma attached to being a single mother. The biological mother knows that if she brings her children to an orphanage they will eventually be placed in adoption. Unless a child is abandoned, he cannot come to the United States.

When the Korean child is left at the orphanage, he may already be several months old. By the time this child is cleared to come to the United States, several more months may pass. What this means for the American couple is that adopting a Korean infant often means that the baby will be six months old or more when they finally take him home. For Latin American adoptions, it is possible that the babies will be younger.

Economic conditions are a prime reason a mother decides to place her child in an adoptive home in some Latin American countries. "There is no stigma attached to being a single parent in Chile," said Naomi. "A single mother can raise her child." However, unemployment is high in Chile, and it often is difficult for a single woman both to support and to care for a family. The birthmother of one of Naomi's adopted daughters was employed as a housekeeper, but she already had an eighteen-month-old son and— as harsh as it may seem—she was permitted to keep only one child with her at work. The birthmother of Naomi's second daughter had lost her job because of her pregnancy and was wandering the streets.

One of the positive aspects of dealing with a U.S. agency is that often the officials can give the couple some assurance that the child they are waiting to adopt is healthy—healthy, that is, by the standards of that country, not by American standards. It should be remembered that most of these countries are underdeveloped and the children do not receive regular monthly medical exams as they do in the United States. There are certain conditions endemic to the child's homeland that the adoptive parents should watch out for.

Korean children may have had hepatitis B and tuberculosis. Even though the children are regularly screened for these diseases, they may show the aftereffects. Asians also are susceptible to Mongolian spots, black and blue marks that may appear on all parts of the body. These marks will fade over time and the parents should not worry about them.

No matter where the child is from, it is more than likely he will have parasites—lice in the hair, scabies on the skin, and worms in his intestines. These conditions are treatable and probably will be detected by the doctor during his first exam. Until the child can be examined, it is advisable for the parents to wash his clothes separately and avoid bathing him in the kitchen sink.

For most of these children, there is an adjustment period. They may have difficulties adapting to the climate. Those from Korea suffer from frequent nosebleeds and dry skin. Babies from Korea are thrown off by the time change. Many of these babies cannot tolerate fat. "Eventually the child will eat hot dogs and hamburgers and love it," said Mrs. Stowe. "But in the beginning, it is hard." Mrs. Stowe's remedy to soothe the stomach is barley water made by toasting barley and then boiling it for 45 minutes.

The solutions are not so simple for some of the other adjustment problems the child may encounter later on. Because the child may look exotic, he will attract attention. Strangers can say cruel things, often talking as if the child were an inanimate object rather than a person. The adoptive parents need to consider their child's feelings when handling questions from bystanders. No one has a right to be told where the child is from, when he was adopted, who his biological parents are, etc. And the adoptive parents should feel free to refrain politely from entertaining these questions.

When the child is old enough to be told about his adoption, he naturally will have questions about his biological parents. It is wise not to play up the fact that the child was abandoned, if he indeed was. The adoptive parents should instead stress that the child's biological parents wanted him to be well taken care of and be able to take advantage of the opportunities that exist in a country like the United States. Never should the biological parents be talked about in a disparaging manner.

A teenager may have an identity problem if his race is different from that of his adoptive family. He is being raised as an American by American parents, and possibly with American siblings. Yet he may always look like a foreigner. Some teens react by rejecting their ethnic heritage. One adoptive mother said that her teenage Korean daughter rebelled after being taken by her adoptive parents to a party for adopted Korean children. "She told me, 'I'm not Korean, I'm American,'" the mother recalled. The best course is to remain patient and not pressure the child.

As with any adopted child, the adoptive parent should constantly work to develop the child's self-esteem. The child needs to understand that he is loved and accepted by his parents because of who he is. Part of what makes up his identity is his ethnic background and he should be proud of that fact.

During difficult times, adoptive parents may need to talk with others who have adopted foreign children. At this time, an adoptive-parents group, such as GIFT (Getting International Families Together) at Spence-Chapin, can be invaluable. "Part of what GIFT will do is make it clear that the child should feel good about being Korean," said Helen Kolsky, president of GIFT.

To create awareness at the schools, GIFT has prepared an information packet on Korea that parents can give to their children's teachers. Ms. Kolsky said that when Asia is studied in schools the emphasis often is on Japan and China with little or no attention given to Korea. "We are hopeful that teachers will be able to use our packet," she said. "We would like GIFT to become a source of Korean cultural information."

GIFT, like other adoptive-parents groups for those who have adopted foreign children, holds regular get-togethers where the children and their parents can learn more about Korea. Part of the celebration involves enjoying native foods.

Of course, many officials advocate traveling to the child's native land when he or she is old enough to understand such a trip. Some adoptive parents may be tempted to bring their foreign child home to the United States and never again mention the child's country. That would be a mistake. It is important for the child's development for him to understand and be proud of his ethnic background. This is also true when American parents adopt an American child of a different race. Parents should make an effort to include children of their child's race among his or her playmates. The adoptive couple need to understand that helping the child appreciate his heritage is all part of parenting a foreign child or an American child of another race.

For most adoptive couples, adopting a child from abroad is a rewarding and enriching experience. Rather than attempting to hide a child's ethnic background, those who adopt foreign children are more likely to rejoice in it. "Your child is different, and what's wrong with that?" asks Ms. Kolsky. "That's what's good about this country. It is becoming more international."

8

SPECIAL-NEEDS CHILDREN

L ydia's mother already had a one-year-old daughter when she found out she was pregnant. She wanted to have an abortion, but her husband threatened to kill her if she did. So she went ahead and had Lydia.

Lydia's parents divorced and for the first two years of her life she lived with her father. Lydia's father neglected her and eventually returned her to her mother.

Lydia's next two years were a nightmare of abuse. There were regular beatings, but some of the worst abuse Lydia suffered at her mother's hand was psychological. Lydia had an infected adenoid that caused her to wheeze when she breathed. Her mother would tell her she sounded like a pig. At dinnertime, her mother would put Lydia's plate on the floor and force her to eat her food like an animal.

When Lydia misbehaved, her mother would bring her to a nearby swamp that was infested with alligators. She would leave Lydia there for hours but not before terrifying Lydia with the threat that, if she moved, the snakes and alligators would eat her up.

After two years, Lydia's mother tired of her, too. She brought the little girl to a welfare agency and told them she didn't want her anymore. Lydia was placed in a foster care home while the local adoption agency waited for the right person to come along to adopt her.

That right person turned out to be Rebecca, a thirty-nine-year-old social worker who worked in a large northeastern city far from Lydia's southern town. Rebecca had been vacationing in Jamaica when she was struck by the sight of so many poor children. As a single person, Rebecca had not yet thought about being a mother, but now she was determined to adopt a needy child. Because she had a full-time job, she didn't want an infant. An older child—maybe a child five or six—would be perfect.

Rebecca inquired about adopting a Jamaican child but was disappointed to learn there was a six-month residency requirement. When she returned to her job she made some phone calls and discovered a southern agency that had young children ready for placement. Shortly after she contacted the agency, she received a phone call. The agency had a daughter for her, a five-year-old girl named Lydia. Three weeks later, Rebecca picked Lydia up at the airport.

Rebecca immediately realized that Lydia had a great deal of catching up to do. Her speech was so slurred that Rebecca could not understand most of what she said. She didn't know the basic things that most little children know—numbers, letters, colors. And she was very shy, almost withdrawn, especially around strangers.

Rebecca thought about placing Lydia in a special school or hiring a speech therapist. Her pediatrician agreed that the child needed help, but felt that since she had been through so much it would be better to let her settle in before exposing her to more stress.

For the next six months, Rebecca worked with Lydia by talking with her, reading her books, correcting her speech, and, most of all, giving her much of the love and affection she had never had as a baby. Under such care, she thrived.

That was two years ago. Lydia now is in the gifted class at her local elementary school. She plays the piano, is active in the Girl Scouts, and this past summer went away to camp. She is much more sociable and, according to Rebecca, "liable to talk a blue streak." She talks about her school, her friends, and most of all her new mom, Rebecca.

"It even surprised me how quickly Lydia took to me," Rebecca said. "You can't tell that this child is not my own. She looks like me, has allergies like me. She even wants to dress like me." Rebecca laughed. "She wants to wear a blazer to school!"

Adopting an older child like Lydia can be a rewarding experience, as well as a tremendous challenge. But it is a challenge that more couples and single parents are eager to try.

While there is a scarcity of healthy white infants available for adoption, there is an abundance of older children of all races—many of them with emotional or physical handicaps—waiting for homes. Because many of these children already are available, a couple or single parent may be able to adopt them within a short period of time.

In the early stages, the processes of adopting a special-needs child and an infant are similar. There will be a home study before the special child is placed. At a good agency, this time is used to prepare the parents for the special child who will soon be in their home. Once the home study has been approved, the matching process begins.

At this point the process becomes much different from adopting an infant. The agency begins by telling the parents about all the children they have available for adoption. Agencies like to have the parents do their own selecting, and may hold an adoption party to give the parents the opportunity to meet some of these children.

The issue of adoption is approached much more delicately with the children. "What we say to these children is that our job is not to find an adopter," said Kathryn S. Donley, of the New York Spaulding, one of a network of fifteen agencies around the United States that place special children. "Our job is to understand what has happened to these children and what will happen in the future. We begin to raise the issues of, 'Who are you going to live with until you're grown? Who are you going to bring good news home to?' Then we introduce the idea, 'If you cannot stay with this foster family, then we need to begin talking about a family for you.' "

Many older children are frightened by the concept of adoption. Often it is helpful to show these children photographs of other children and their adoptive families. Soon, the social worker will begin to get some input from the child. It is impossible to predict how a child will react when he meets his prospective adoptive parents. Sometimes a child agrees immediately; other times he is slow to make a commitment. Ms. Donley said that the adults have to walk a fine line, neither forcing a decision on the child nor leaving the decision entirely up to him. "Then the child will say no for all the wrong reasons," she said.

Anyone interested in adopting a special child should be realistic. There are success stories like Lydia. But there are also many disappointments. Ms. Donley said that many people underestimate the types of problems these children may have. "They may compare it to a niece who was a bedwetter," she said. "It's a completely different thing. It is often hard to convince a family that these difficulties can become so serious that a family might want to give up."

For that reason, an agency will be brutally honest with a couple or single parent who expresses an interest in adopting a special-needs child. It is not that agency officials want to discourage these adoptions—far from it. But they want the adoptive parents to be well informed so that they know what to expect and will be able to handle it.

When an agency official talks about special-needs or hard-to-place children, he is really talking about two groups of children. The first group consists of children of all ages, from infants to young teens, from the United States or foreign countries, who have serious physical problems such as Down's syndrome, mental retardation, or physical handicaps.

These children probably will need special care at home and, when old enough, will have to be sent to a special school. In most cases, the adoptive parent will be able to receive monetary help from the government to better provide for such a child. The agency that arranges the adoption also will offer support services as they become needed.

The second group of special-needs children are older children. They may be from a foreign country, but more often they are American children, many from poor families, who have been in the foster care system for a good part of their childhood. Many of these children have been physically or psychologically abused by their biological parents and some have been abandoned. The fact that they are older means that the agency had a hard time terminating the rights of the biological parents. Often there is a pattern. The child is abused by a parent, removed from that parent's care, and placed in a foster home. Yet before the agency can free that child for adoption, the parent may be declared rehabilitated by the court and the child returned home. Thereupon begins another round of abuse followed by foster care.

Several years of such traumatic events can permanently scar a child. By the time that child is available to be adopted, he may have serious psychological problems that the adoptive parent will have to deal with. "A ten-year-old does not come to you with a blank slate," said Ms. Donley. "When you take on that older child, you take on other parts of his history."

There has been a great effort to free a child for adoption before he can be seriously damaged by the system. "To free a child today is a snap," said Hertha Fischer, director of the Children, Youth and Families Division for the Federation of Protestant Welfare Agencies Inc. in New York City. Years ago, if a parent sent even a postcard, that was interpreted as the parent exhibiting interest in the child. Today, most states require a parent to show that he has had significant contact with the child. "It is a lot easier to terminate parental rights than it used to be," said Ms. Fischer.

However, another factor that may slow down the process is that the biological father's rights also must be terminated. "We used to be able to take the surrender of the mother without involving the father," said Ms. Fischer. "Now, by law, you have to make an attempt to find him."

According to a survey by the U.S. Department of Health and Human Services, in 1977 there were 502,000 children in foster care. By 1982, that figure had been reduced to 243,000. The remaining number of children became adults, and thus no longer came under child-care laws, or they were adopted.

Even though those figures are coming down, the rate isn't fast enough for some people. "We think these figures are conservative, and we use them because even in this conservative form they are a tragedy," said Roy Maurer, national director of the North American Council of Adoptable Children. In 1984, Mr. Maurer said, there were fifty thousand children who had been freed for adoption, and another fifty thousand who were very close to being freed.

The fact that social-work officials are critical of the foster care system does not mean that they are critical of foster parents. A good agency screens its foster parents as carefully as it screens its adoptive parents, and with good reason: A large percentage of foster parents end up adopting the children they care for. Mr. Maurer noted that more than 80 percent of the special children eventually are adopted by foster parents.

"We used to say that being a foster parent wasn't a back door to adoption," said Ms. Fischer. "Now, foster parents get first crack."

Years ago, agencies did not make a major effort to find permanent homes for special-needs children because it was assumed that they were unadoptable. Now their attitude has changed dramatically. Not only do they believe that these children deserve permanent homes, they also devote a great deal of their time and effort toward finding them such homes. "Any child able to live in a family is adoptable," said Jane Edwards, executive director of Spence-Chapin in New York City.

Hertha Fischer, who has worked with agencies for more than twenty years, has witnessed this change firsthand. "We're placing more of these children in adoption and not allowing them to grow up in the foster care system," she said. "Years ago, we wondered about someone who came in looking for a handicapped child to adopt. Now we go out and look for these people."

The public has had a great deal to do with changing the attitude of the agencies. When fewer infants became available for adoption, many couples decided to adopt toddlers. Now that there are fewer toddlers available, couples are deciding to adopt older or handicapped children.

Single parents also have had a great impact. Agency officials used to look askance at a single person who wanted to become a parent. Years of experience with these single parents has changed many an official's view. Single parents now are highly regarded by agencies; indeed, in some situations, agency officials believe that a single parent may be the best choice because in such a one-on-one situation the child will benefit from more attention.

Anyone seriously considering adopting a special-needs child should contact a local adoption agency. If that agency first contacted does not place special children, it can put the interested adoptive parent in contact with an agency that does.

Another choice is to contact one of the national adoption exchanges that list waiting children from all parts of the country. A listing of these exchanges is included at the back of the book (p. 237).

Agencies that work with special children frequently hold orientation meetings to inform the community of the children who are available, meetings that are also useful for those who are unsure about whether they can take on this responsibility.

Most agencies keep files of those children waiting for homes that interested people may browse through. Commonly called "blue books," these files often include a photograph of each child and a brief family history.

Many agencies also hold get-togethers where prospective adoptive parents can meet some of the special children. Officials like to keep these events low-key, because some children are scared by the very word *adoption*. It is hoped that if they get to meet some of the possible parents they can begin to develop a rapport before the subject is ever seriously discussed.

Evelyn Middelstadt, who worked with Lutheran Social Services in Kansas for twenty-five years, noted that those interested in adopting have always been encouraged to visit with adoptive families who had children similar to the ones being considered. "These adoptive parents were the ones making it, and they could talk about the joys and the struggles," she said.

What do agencies look for in prospective adoptive parents for special children?

Most important is the desire to parent one of these children. "We are looking for interest on the part of the adoptive parent," said

Ms. Donley. "We also look for experience in working with children." Those who express a preference for adopting a handicapped child might be asked about any experience they have with such children.

It is unlikely that someone who was sincerely interested in parenting a special child would be turned away. It is the prospective adoptive parent who would have to make the decision as to whether he would be able to meet this challenge. To assist the parent in making that decision, the agency will be candid with regard to the child being considered. "This is not a state secret," said Ms. Donley. "The families have to know what they are getting into."

Prospective parents will also be told about possible forms of assistance available to them. Subsidies exist through a federal program administered by the states that helps adoptive parents pay for the child's basic care as well as his medical bills. A good source of information on what help is available can be obtained from the North American Council on Adoptable Children in Washington, D.C. The council is an umbrella group that includes about six hundred parenting organizations around the United States.

The financial assistance is available as a result of the federal Adoption Assistance and Child Welfare Act (Public Law 96–272), passed by Congress in 1980 and aimed at encouraging the adoption of handicapped children. To be eligible for these federal funds each state must establish its own program, which includes providing some state money. Some states have failed to implement programs because they fear that the federal government will one day pull out its support, leaving the states alone to bear the entire burden. Mr. Maurer's group is active in lobbying state governments to implement these programs.

The council also is active in providing adoptive parents with the information they need to care for a handicapped child. "A parent may adopt a child, need a wheelchair, and not know where to get one," said Mr. Maurer. "It sometimes takes skill to get what the child deserves." Mr. Maurer explained that the subsidy is attached to the child, not the family. "If a family is willing to pull a child out of public care and give that child permanent nurturing, then we have an obligation to facilitate that." Mr. Maurer's parenting group also assists in finding the proper educational facility for a handicapped child.

Depending upon the child's handicap, it may be necessary to alter facilities in a home. These changes might include adding ramps, low sinks, or wide doorways.

An adoptive parent may find it easier to attend to a handicapped child's physical needs when compared with his emotional needs. If the child is severely retarded or brain damaged, it may be impossible to get any feedback that would make the adoptive parent feel he was having a positive impact. "In these cases, when looking for a parent, you need someone with patience and the willingness to get love back from other members of the family," said Mr. Maurer. "The child may not be capable of returning love."

That may also be true of an older child who has been battered by the system. What are the possible problems that could develop with an older child? Depending upon the child's history, there could be a behavioral problem. "When you adopt a youngster who is, say, age six, he has had six years to find out how to get what he wants," said Ms. Fischer. "If you had your own child, you would have had six years to work with him. If you adopt him when he is six and your systems mesh—great! If not, then you have to work at it."

With most older children, there is a "honeymoon" period after they are first placed when they are on their best behavior. "With some kids, the honeymoon period is over in an hour," said Ms. Fischer. "With others it takes a long time."

The child's intent is to test his new parents. "He wants to find out if you like him when he's bad," said Ms. Fischer. "Your own natural children do this when they're infants. Then it's easy to handle."

Relatives and friends can be another source of tension during the settling-in period. Because the child may appear to be normal and well adjusted, those outside the family may find it difficult to accept the fact that he is emotionally troubled and needs special care. Ms. Donley noted that, if the adoptive parents take this child to a restaurant and he misbehaves, those watching will wonder why the child is not being spanked. "He may have been abused in the past and that is not the way to deal with him," she said. Even under these pressures, the adoptive parents must stick to their own plan for disciplining the child.

There may be trouble in the classroom, too. The child may be making progress but, to his teachers and classmates, he is still disruptive. In this situation, the adoptive parents have a difficult decision to make. Do they share the child's history with the principal and teachers at the school, hoping that to do so will mean more sensitivity on their part when dealing with the child? Sometimes parents have shared information on the child and later regretted it. There have been occasions where a teacher has misused a child's history, possibly embarrassing him in front of his classmates.

Few of these older children are orphans. Their biological family will be part of their lives and must be dealt with by the adoptive parent. "Children often cling irrationally to someone who mistreated them," said Ms. Donley. "How do you live with a child that is having that sort of problem?"

If the biological parents are living in the area, it is possible the child will want to visit them. The smart parent is the one who shares these visits. In that way, the adoptive parent demonstrates to the child that he accepts his family yet remains in charge of the situation.

It is important that the adoptive parent not criticize the child's biological parents. "If we look down on his natural parents, we look down on him," said Ms. Fischer.

Rebecca noted that Lydia does not visit her biological parents, but she sometimes will talk about them. "She needs to be reassured that she isn't to blame for what her mother did," said Rebecca. "We talk about it in terms of people who have trouble managing their lives. But I tell her that her mother loved her enough not to hurt her anymore and that was why she gave her up."

The difficulties cannot be minimized; there are agonizing times for those who adopt older children. The feelings of anxiety may be intensified by the fact that they are going it alone. It may seem a long time between visits by the social worker. If the child has been legally adopted, the social worker may no longer be making these visits. "Adoptive parents are not unlike other parents in that they don't want to admit that they are tired or can't cope," said Ms. Fischer. Whatever the circumstances, it is advisable for the parents to seek out a professional for help, even if only for the assurance that they are doing all that is humanly possible to make the situation work.

Unfortunately there are situations that don't work—in those cases, a couple or single parent must admit that the child they have chosen is not right for them. Conceding defeat is never easy and, for the adoptive parents, the entire experience can be paralyzing. They may be wary about attempting another adoption, believing that *they* are the problem, not the child.

Often, however, the agency may have warned the adoptive parents about the child's limitations. Ronny Diamond, assistant director of the adoption department at Spence-Chapin in New York City, recalled one such situation where a couple wanted to adopt an eight-year-old boy. "This couple was head over heels about this child," said Ms. Diamond. The agency was frank with the couple, telling them the child was emotionally disturbed. "They wouldn't hear us," she said. "They were focused on the child having a learning disability." After a year, the child became violent and the couple were forced to admit they couldn't handle him.

Norma, a single adoptive parent who today has three Korean children and one from Vietnam, recalled that her earlier attempt to adopt a brother and sister from El Salvador had failed miserably. "It took me a year to get my emotions back together," she said.

However, Norma said she was never advised by the agency that placed the children—a twelve-year-old girl and nine-year-old boy—that they had serious problems. It turned out that the two had been living on the streets in El Salvador for three years until they were picked up by the police and brought to a shelter. In New York, both children refused to learn English. "The girl took an instant dislike to me and I disliked her," said Norma. "I had tremendous guilt feelings over this. How could I dislike someone who needed me so much?"

Norma placed the children in a Catholic school, but hardly a day went by that she didn't receive a call from the school secretary. "They stole everything that wasn't nailed down," she said. "They stole a lot of jewelry. I used to frisk them every chance I got." Norma kept the children for seven months before finally admitting defeat.

Of course, adopting a special-needs foreign child presents other problems since the child also must be assimilated into American culture. But whatever the situation, the prospective parents should ask for and receive as much background material on the children as possible. It also is wise to develop a trusting relationship with a good agency, and to consider seriously any advice offered by the agency professionals.

Agencies do want to find homes for hard-to-place children but not at the expense of driving away qualified adoptive parents. It is easy to become attached to a child because of his appearance or personality. But if a social worker raises questions about adopting such a child, the prospective parent should take a more objective look.

When the agency hits upon a perfect match, it does much to boost the morale of everyone involved. "The success stories are all around you—the child placed last year who is in a regular classroom doing very well," said Ms. Donley. "With these families, there is a different yardstick to measure success by. Here's the bottom line: Is this child better off than he would have been if he had not joined this family? The answer becomes, 'Absolutely.'"

9
ADOPTION BY A SINGLE PARENT

Being infertile is one reason a person may not be able to have a child. Being single may be another.

Years ago, people thought that marriage came first and then children. But today, more single people who have either ruled out marriage voluntarily or have failed to meet the right person have decided that they shouldn't be deprived of the joys of parenting. These people are deciding to adopt.

Single women may reach the decision to adopt sooner than single men. The reason is easy to see. A woman's biological clock runs out much sooner than a man's. Any woman who is still single by the time she is thirty-five may begin to wonder about whether she will ever have children. She has three choices: Sit and wait hoping that Mr. Right will come along and that she will get pregnant without any trouble; try to get pregnant, either with a partner or through artificial insemination; or adopt.

Some women opt for the second alternative, only to discover that they have fertility problems, which may lead them to decide to adopt.

Any single person thinking about adoption should realize certain facts. There is virtually no chance of adopting a healthy white infant, since agencies prefer to place these infants with couples. The same would hold true with an independent adoption because it is unlikely that the birthmother would choose a single parent for the child.

With some agencies, there is a chance of adopting an infant from a minority background. But, again, if a couple came forward to adopt this baby, they would be the agency's first choice.

115

In any case, an infant might not be the best choice for a single parent. Because the single parent would probably continue on his or her job, having a school-age child could work out the best, for the single parent would not have to worry about finding someone to care for the baby during the day. Instead, the parent would find a good school conveniently located between home and work.

The major obstacle for a single parent is that he or she must carry the entire parenting burden twenty-four hours a day. There is no respite, no saying, "Wait until your father gets home," no one to share the parenting responsibilities with.

Of course, single-parent households are no longer an oddity these days, when more and more children are being raised in homes with only one parent. No one ever said that two parents were needed to create a loving and warm home for a child. A single parent can do that, too, provided he or she has the energy, determination, and common sense.

In fact, there are some instances where an agency would choose to place a special child with a single parent rather than a couple. If the child had been abused by his mother, for example, it might be better to place the child with a single man. If the child had been neglected, a one-on-one situation, where the child would get all the attention of a single parent, could be very beneficial.

Most important is that the single parent receive help from relatives and close friends. "With a single parent, we look for a strong person with a great deal of family support," said Jane Edwards, executive director of Spence-Chapin in New York City.

Not too long ago, agencies were not so eager to place children in single-parent homes. "Some agencies viewed single men in particular with suspicion," said one official. "They thought, 'Is this man a homosexual looking for someone to have sex with?' "

But several events have caused the agencies to change their attitude about single people as parents. In the past two decades, the number of couples having trouble conceiving has increased. More than twenty years ago, there was a shortage of couples who wanted to adopt infants. At that time, a child became difficult to adopt when he turned one. So some agencies decided to make a real effort to place these infants, if not with couples, then with single parents. Hertha Fischer, of the Federation of Protestant Welfare Agencies in New York City, was involved in an effort to recruit single women for these children.

"We sat these women down and said, 'This is a new experience,' " Ms. Fischer recalled. "I told them, 'We're going to learn and you're going to learn. We're going to see what it takes to care for these infants.' "

Ms. Fischer said that the project was such a success that the agency she was working with continued to do single-parent adoptions. The situation has changed drastically over the past twenty years with regard to the children who are being adopted by single parents, however. Now that there are so few infants available—and so many couples eager to adopt them—singles have little chance of adopting an infant.

Like Ms. Fischer's agency, many others had positive experiences with single parents and today regard them as top candidates for adopting older children and those with handicaps. Richard Zeilinger, of the Children's Bureau of New Orleans, said his agency has completed over three hundred single-parent adoptions since 1970.

"Almost all of them have worked out very well," Mr. Zeilinger reported. "It takes extra care and extra work on the part of everybody. When you have an older child and you place him with a single parent, it is because it is indicated—perhaps the child has difficulty relating to a parent of one sex. Even so, most children want a mommy and a daddy and it takes some getting used to."

Being both a mother and father to a child takes dedication. But when the situation works, it often works very well. A good example is Rebecca, who adopted five-year-old Lydia. Rebecca's decision to adopt was something that built up over time. Although Rebecca was satisfied with her career as a social worker, she had never married and was eager to have a child. Seeing the children in Jamaica looking for homes gave impetus to Rebecca's desire to adopt.

Her family was not supportive of her idea. "My family was ambivalent about it because I was single," she said. "They couldn't understand that marriage was not in my immediate plans."

Even if she did marry, Rebecca knew that she would probably never have a biological child. Years earlier she had discovered that she had serious fertility problems and would have difficulty conceiving. "That fact never bothered me because I never really wanted to be pregnant," she said. "I never had the desire to have my own child. I just kept thinking of all the children out there who needed homes."

Rebecca also knew that, because of the demands of her job, it would be difficult for her to care for an infant. "I wanted an older child, but one that was still young enough that I could mold," she said.

Once Lydia was in Rebecca's home, Rebecca found that her

family's attitude toward the adoption changed. Lydia has become very close to Rebecca's father. "She relates to my father as her daddy," said Rebecca. "She knows that he's really her grandfather, but to her he's also her daddy."

Rebecca recognized right away Lydia's need to have a strong male figure in her life because her father had figured so prominently in her early childhood, before returning Lydia to her mother. Rebecca was grateful that her father was so enthusiastic about fulfilling this role.

Rebecca also was overwhelmed by the enthusiasm shown by many of her friends. "My friends have really come through," she said. "They have been very supportive and excited right from the start. It's like Lydia is their kid, too. Many of my single friends who do not have children, and haven't had the nerve to adopt, were thrilled to be able to share Lydia with me."

Many of Rebecca's friends have been available to babysit or to take Lydia to the doctor's office or to school when Rebecca has had work commitments. "I would never have been able to do this alone," Rebecca said.

Rebecca has been very fortunate in that she and Lydia have meshed so well. "Everyone kept saying, 'Wait until the honeymoon period is over,'" Rebecca said. "But I haven't seen any of that acting out that I had been told to expect." Lydia's one behavioral problem is that she can be very stubborn. But Rebecca recognized right off that this was the result of her treatment by her biological parents. "Being stubborn for her was a defense because everything she owned always was taken from her," she said.

Lydia also still has a fear that Rebecca will abandon her or mistreat her the same way that her biological mother did. "She is very fearful if I'm out late at night, especially if I'm still out when it's time for her to go to sleep," said Rebecca. "She will insist on waiting up for me and will constantly ask the babysitter when I'm coming home."

Having a five-year-old in her apartment definitely changed Rebecca's life, probably more than she had ever imagined. "I can no longer be spontaneous; there is more structure in my life now," she noted. "In the beginning I resented it. But now I've worked it out."

Mornings are, according to Rebecca, the part of the day she hates the most. "I was used to having a nice quiet time in the morning and enjoyed having the bathroom all to myself," she laughed. "Now it's constant hustle and bustle. Getting Lydia up sometimes means fighting with her and I hate that. But I soon found out that mornings are the same with most families." Rebecca solved Lydia's wake-up problem with a simple gimmick—an alarm clock. She loves the fact that it's hers and she now takes the responsibility of getting herself up and dressed on time very seriously.

Along the way, Rebecca has found comfort in the support of her family and friends, and also in a local single adoptive-parent group. "I speak to these other parents—just about the common everyday things—and I find their comments to be very helpful," Rebecca said.

Like Rebecca, Norma discovered that she could not have biological children. In the past ten years, Norma, a nurse who lives in New Jersey, has adopted four children, one from Vietnam and three from Korea. Throughout all this time, she has continued to undergo artificial insemination in an attempt to have a baby.

Norma is convinced, however, that even if she had given birth early on she would still have wanted to adopt. "I'm from a very large family in the Midwest which included several adopted American children and several foster children," she recalled. "Since my early twenties, I have always known that even if I had a biological child, I would also end up being someone's stepmother or adoptive mother."

Norma adopted her first child—a twelve-year-old girl from Vietnam—in 1975. Norma was told when she adopted Susie that she was ten. It turned out that the Vietnamese government was only allowing children under ten to leave the country. And so Susie and several other children lied about their ages in order to come to America.

When she found out about the age disparity, Norma was not angry, especially after learning the reason for Susie's lie. Susie, however, had grown very close to her adoptive mother and was upset by the idea that she had hidden her true age. "Susie has always considered me her mother," said Norma. "She has family, but she doesn't know whether any of them are living." Today Susie is married and the mother of a four-month-old baby. Norma said they continue to have a close relationship and visit frequently.

In 1978, Norma tried to adopt two children from El Salvador, but the placement didn't work out. That experience was so traumatic she waited another year before pursuing adoption again. She contacted the agency she had worked with before and expressed interest in another adoption. She didn't expect a call back for months. Twelve days later the social worker called her with news. Was Norma interested in adopting three children from Korea, a sister and two brothers? Norma immediately said yes.

"It has been a good placement," Norma said. "These three children are extremely bright and intelligent." When Norma received the children, Daniel was six, Nan was five, and Justin was twenty-seven months. Their father had died and their mother had walked out, and they had spent ten months in an orphanage.

Norma made good use of her training as a registered nurse. She took two months off from her job to stay home and care for her new family. Her immediate concern was for their health. The children arrived from Korea with head lice and parasites in their intestines, which Norma believes was the result of eating improperly cooked food. In addition, they were all suffering from bronchitis. "The oldest child still has a cough in the winter and I suspect at one time he might have had tuberculosis," said Norma.

After taking care of their sicknesses, Norma got down to the other tasks involved with mothering her new brood. "They needed a lot of nurturing," she recalled. "They needed to be taught basic things like nutrition and hygiene. But most of all they needed to be cuddled and held. A social worker visited us and after seeing the children crawl all over me like puppy dogs, she said that they were starved for affection. I felt that they had had a great deal of affection at one point, but then had it taken from them."

Norma believes that her four adoptions went so well not only because of her nursing background, but because she is good at caring for adopted children. She is still trying to adopt more children, from Korea, India, or Latin America. "I'm not aiming to be the next Mother Teresa," she said. "I'm not aiming for sainthood. I just happen to believe in large families. My feeling is you can always manage somehow. Some of the happiest families are the large ones with few material things and a lot of emotional give-and-take."

As much as she enjoys her children, Norma takes time each day to get out of the house, walk around, and clear her head. She calls it her sanity walk. When she comes back, she is refreshed and ready once again to take charge of her children.

Rebecca, Norma, and others have given up many of the freedoms associated with the single life-style. There are no more spontaneous dinners with friends. No more drinks after work. A weekend in the country with a friend must be arranged to include the children. Theirs is a more structured life, a structure dictated by the addition of children. None of these single parents complains, however. Each feels that what they have given up has been returned to them tenfold in the relationships they enjoy with their new families. "It was the best thing I ever did," concluded Rebecca.

10

GETTING THROUGH IT EMOTIONALLY

A doption is a wonderful way to start a family, but there is no denying that, until that wonderful event actually occurs, the entire process—first, coping with infertility, and then, arranging an adoption—can be a difficult one. At times, the prospective adoptive couple may feel they are on an emotional roller coaster.

What are these high and low points? Here are the experiences of John and Esther, two lawyers from New York City:

- Low point—John and Esther discover that they have fertility problems.
- High point—They visit a fertility expert who identifies their problem and says it can be treated.
- High point—Treatment is started and prognosis is good.
- Low point—Months pass and Esther cannot achieve pregnancy.
- High point—Doctor offers other treatment.
- High point—Esther becomes pregnant.
- Low point—Pregnancy turns out to be ectopic. Esther begins to hemorrhage when the tube ruptures.
- Low point—Doctor suggests John and Esther look into adoption.
- High point—The couple talk with others who have adopted. They are encouraged.
- High point—John and Esther research adoption and collect a list of agency names.
- Low point—They visit an agency where the social worker is very discouraging about their chances of adopting a white infant.
- Low point—They give up on the agencies.
- High point—They are put in touch with a woman who wants to

place her infant for adoption. Their lawyer makes the necessary arrangements.

- Low point—Birthmother changes her mind and decides to keep the baby.
- Low point—John and Esther have difficulty seeking another independent adoption. Family members encourage them to continue.
- High point—They begin their search with renewed energy. They advertise in newspapers and receive several inquiries.
- High Point—They carry through with their plan and eventually adopt an infant girl. John and Esther finally are parents.

John's and Esther's experiences are not unusual. Many of the couples interviewed for this book had been through as much or more in their quest to start a family.

How do a couple cope with these emotional ups and downs?

It is not easy, but it can be done. The most important thing to remember is that becoming emotional can only impede a couple's efforts to adopt. If the couple hope to adopt through an agency, displaying intense emotions during the interview and home study could place their application in jeopardy. The social worker doing the interviews will be prepared to witness some tears, of course. But if either partner were to become so distraught that he or she could not be consoled, then the social worker may begin to wonder whether the couple are ready to adopt.

Showing emotions can hurt in independent adoptions, too. In the beginning, the couple might be talking with the birthmother, who could misinterpret an emotional conversation with the husband or wife. She may believe this couple to be unprepared to care for an infant.

Then, of course, there are other individuals who might take advantage of a couple who appeared so desperate to become parents. These people might hope to profit from an adoption.

It is easy to see why it is important to the couple to keep a close rein on their feelings. It will not advance their case any and most likely will hamper their efforts.

That said, how do a couple adjust? Everyone has their own method for coping with a stressful situation—prayer, exercise, new activities, a change of scenery. The couple should try whatever works for them. Consider the case of Darlene and Chris.

Darlene, an interior decorator, and Chris, a teacher, live in Minneapolis. They have been married for three years and for the past two have been trying to have a baby. They have been to several specialists, but none has been able to find a reason for the couple's inability to have children.

Every day for three months, Darlene left work early to drive fifty miles to a medical center for treatment. The doctors wanted to determine whether Darlene was ovulating. Once at the center Darlene would often wait two hours before she even got into the doctor's office. By the time she returned to work, it was often too late—and she was too exhausted—to do any work. Before too long, Darlene was forced to leave her job. "Infertility," she said, in what could be *the* understatement of the year, "affects your whole life."

Darlene and Chris were determined that infertility was not going to wreck their lives. So they devised their own plan to cope. As a first step, Darlene decided not to seek another full-time job but to set up her own business working out of her home. In this way she was able to continue to produce an income, yet could still keep her schedule flexible enough to make her doctor's appointments.

Both felt committed to continuing Darlene's medical treatments. At the same time, Darlene began to research adoption. Within a few months, the couple had submitted their application to an adoption agency. Darlene and Chris now regard their childlessness as a temporary state. They feel certain that within the next few years they will become parents, whether through pregnancy or adoption.

In the meantime, Darlene and Chris have begun to relax and enjoy their married life together. They have taken up some new hobbies, spent money on redecorating their home, and treated themselves to a luxurious European vacation.

On weekends, they often will visit Darlene's sister, who has a two-year-old girl. Rather than finding these visits depressing, Darlene and Chris rejoice in spending time with their niece. For the present, being close to her fulfills their desire to relate to a child. Both are confident that, sometime soon, they will have that experience with their own baby.

Linda and her husband Ed, a policeman, from New Jersey, suffered fertility problems for five years. During that time, she had five major operations, each one necessitating a week-long stay in the hospital. In addition, she also endured a battery of in-office tests, some simple, others more complicated and painful.

"I was at such a low point that I was paralyzed emotionally," Linda recalled. "I couldn't go to a baby shower or see a pregnant woman. I was a schoolteacher, and sometimes I couldn't even face that. I couldn't stand it when parents didn't show up for school meetings. It made me so mad. Why should they be able to have children and I couldn't?"

Linda's method of coping was to devote herself even more to her job, to the children whose lives she could influence. She never told anyone at work about her infertility struggle. As a result, she could leave her problem behind when the school bell rang each morning. No one knew about it, so she never talked about it during the day.

In her off hours, Linda did her homework on adoption. Eventually her studying paid off when she and Ed adopted an infant boy. They are thrilled with their new role as parents. Linda still hopes she will be pregnant one day, but she is not obsessed with achieving that goal. "For me it was motherhood, not being pregnant," she said.

John and Esther, the two lawyers from New York City used in the example at the beginning of the chapter, struggled for five years to have a baby. John said that their lowest point was the period following Esther's ectopic pregnancy. "It was almost like dying," said John. "That was really how I felt."

"Looking back today, we realize how depressed we were during that whole time," John continued. "It affected everything. I put off a job search." And Esther added, "I used it as an excuse not to leave my job. If I had an appointment with a doctor or an adoption agency, that meeting—not my job hunt—always came first."

After they adopted their baby, both John and Esther changed jobs. Their lives are back on course.

These three couples represent those who survived the struggle. Other couples may find the adjustment more difficult. Here is some advice to help these couples through those tough times.

Coming to Terms with Infertility—Before the Adoption

There was a time when infertile people were thought to have mental problems. In some way, that helped to explain their inability to reproduce. Medical information now proves otherwise, but for some infertile people this myth turns into a self-fulfilling prophecy. Infertile people may not start out with psychological problems, but over time the strain of the situation may indeed lead to a mental breakdown.

In some ways the pendulum has swung too far in the other direction. Today infertility is regarded as a medical problem, yet when compared to other medical problems it is not the worst thing that could happen to someone. Except in extreme situations, the condition is not life-threatening. But it can be emotionally debilitating, making it impossible for a man or woman to function within a marriage, profession, or society.

Yet little or no attention is given to infertility as a major emotional crisis. And that's exactly what infertility is. Marriages break up, friendships are ended, relationships with parents are strained, career performance suffers. Unless the individual is well adjusted to begin with, having to grapple with the unwanted (and always undeserved) state of childlessness may put someone over the edge.

In every other regard, the infertile couple may represent the American dream. They may both be specimens of health, admired for their achievements at work, and surrounded with all the elements necessary for happiness and success. They also may be hiding their infertility from family and friends. Thus the couple may have reduced their chances that anyone will talk seriously with them about their problem. Unless the couple are strong enough to confront the situation early on—as Darlene and Chris did—they may not recognize their crisis until it is too late.

The infertile couple should be aware that they may not be able to handle all the repercussions on their own. They should not feel embarrassed to seek out professional help.

If going to a psychologist or other professional seems too big a step, then the infertile couple should look into a support group like RESOLVE. It is important that they realize they are not the only couple going through this trauma. There are others, and their advice and experience could prove invaluable.

"We've found that peer support with people who have been through infertility isn't a depressing experience; it's an uplifting experience," said RESOLVE's executive director, Beverly Freeman. "You have a chance to see that other people who are infertile are attractive. You see that they also have strong feelings. Those strong feelings then begin to become much less frightening."

There can be no doubt that talking about infertility can be a catharsis for the infertile couple. No one should attempt to downplay what they have been through. Both partners should have someone—either a friend or a professional—that they can talk to about their suffering.

Coming to Terms with Infertility—During the Adoption

The infertile couple should try to keep their emotions in check while pursuing adoption. Often during the adoption process, one partner will be more positive and more able to handle affairs than the other. Days later, the situation may be reversed and the stronger partner will falter and need support.

It is important that the couple always appear to those in a position to judge them as parents as united, strong, and able to cope. That holds true whether they are talking on the phone to agencies or birthmothers, or going through interviews and a home study at the agency. So if one partner is stronger for a period of time, then that partner should be the one doing the phone calling, research, or whatever is necessary.

If one partner is having a bad day and the couple are scheduled for a home study interview, then perhaps it would be best for them to make an excuse and try to reschedule the appointment. It is better to experience a slight delay than to place their application in jeopardy.

During agency interviews, the couple should try to keep their answers relating to their infertility short. While they may feel the need to unburden themselves to the social worker, it is not a good idea. The social worker needs to come away with the impression that the couple have come to terms with their situation. It is unlikely he or she will feel that way if the couple launch into a lengthy discussion of their infertility.

Most couples find it emotionally difficult only when adoption appears to be an elusive goal. Once a couple have been accepted by an agency or are on the verge of adopting independently, the entire process becomes easier.

Coming to Terms with Infertility—After the Adoption

Even after an infertile couple adopt, they may still have feelings of anger and resentment that stem from their failure to conceive. If so, they should definitely seek help. "Grief and sadness don't entirely leave, but infertility can be placed in perspective," said Ms. Freeman. "Through peer support infertility takes its place among other things in a couple's lives instead of becoming the focus of attention."

Feelings of resentment, if allowed to persist, could affect the parents' relationship with an adopted child. If these feelings have not been laid to rest they may hinder the process of telling the child he is adopted. How can a parent expect a child to accept these facts if the parent still cannot accept them?

If the adoptive mother still feels inadequate because she was never able to give birth, she may find herself unduly threatened by her adopted child's desire to search for his biological mother. Her resistance to his search could damage their relationship.

Preserving the relationship with the adopted child is perhaps the best reason the infertile couple could have for coming to terms with their infertility. But there are other reasons. The infertile couple do not exist in a vacuum. They have to continue to live with parents, friends, and business associates who do not understand what it is like to struggle for so many years to become parents.

Even after becoming adoptive parents, the memory of that struggle does not go away. Thus, a casual comment from a friend ("Believe me, childbirth is no picnic; adoption is the easy way to do it.") can send the infertile adoptive mother into a rage. Venting that rage may mean losing a friend. But a tactful response ("Mary, please don't say that. Harry and I struggled for eight years to have a child. Twenty-four hours of labor would have been a picnic compared to that.") will serve not only to reprimand but also to sensitize.

It is unlikely that the friend would make that comment again. (If she did, then no one could blame the adoptive mother for an angry response.) More than likely the friend was hoping to make the woman feel better by making it seem that she hasn't missed anything by not being pregnant. However, both women know that is not true. And it is best to get that fact out in the open.

Many women who have adopted and enjoy their roles as mothers still feel a pang of regret when they see a pregnant woman. Clare, who has two adopted children now in their twenties, tells this story: "I am very happy with my children, and usually don't think about my infertility. But when I went through menopause I found myself falling to pieces every time I saw a baby carriage. I finally realized that I would never experience pregnancy and it made me very sad."

Clare has adjusted to her situation; most infertile women will do likewise. The best tactic is to recognize that it is a major disappointment not to experience pregnancy, and go on from there. To dwell on the situation cannot possibly make it better. It may even begin to damage relationships with adopted children, husband, other relatives, and friends.

Younger women and their husbands are more likely to be discussing pregnancy and their experiences in the delivery room. Once a couple's children are in school, they will be more focused on other challenges facing them as parents. So if it will help the adoptive parents adjust in the beginning, they should know that these discussions of childbirth will be short-lived.

In the meantime, if discussions on childbirth bother the infertile woman, then perhaps she should let her friends know that and they can conduct these discussions when she is not there. Of course, a better approach would be for this adoptive mother to join in the discussion by telling of her experience in seeing her adopted child for the first time.

Waiting for the Baby

The normal gestation period is nine months. How do a couple cope with a gestation period of fifteen months? Twenty-four months? Or longer?

Some couples go all out, decorating a nursery, buying furniture and clothes, telling the good news to all their relatives and friends. While this obviously fills some sort of need in these couples, I cannot recommend this course. Too often, the wait stretches on and the completed nursery only acts as a constant reminder of what isn't there. Facing a completely outfitted crib each day can only increase a couple's anxiety.

As for telling so many people, the couple should remember that once the news is out that they are planning to adopt they could be besieged with questions. All the attention will probably add to their nervousness. There will be plenty of time to tell everyone after the baby arrives. Beforehand, they should give the information to as few people as possible.

While they are waiting for their baby, the couple may find it difficult being around their friends who have children. There is nothing wrong with a couple considering their own feelings and perhaps avoiding certain social situations that might make them feel uncomfortable. Often a couple are almost masochistic about keeping up their commitments, even if it means these encounters are upsetting to them. They should not feel reluctant to tell friends and relatives how they feel if they must decline an invitation. Good friends will understand.

For example, an infertile woman should not feel compelled to visit in the hospital a friend who has just had a baby. There is nothing more depressing to a woman having trouble getting pregnant than a maternity ward, except for the nursery where she may be faced with a dozen adorable newborns. Better that she save her visit for when her friend has come home from the hospital. Facing just one newborn will be hard on her, but that task is at least manageable.

A couple should also not feel bad about refusing to attend a gathering where everyone but them will be bringing their children.

These times may include children's birthday parties. "Kiddie birthday parties are always the worst," said one woman. "Do I sit with the boys and talk about baseball, or do I sit with the girls who are going to talk about children?"

After the Adoption—Getting Back in Touch with Each Other

It may take a long time for an adoptive couple to reestablish the sex life they enjoyed before their infertility problems. One woman had this to say: "Before my husband and I had trouble having a baby, we used to enjoy sex. It wasn't unusual for us literally to spend the entire weekend in bed. On Saturday we would get a bottle of champagne and spend the afternoon in bed. Then we would get up and broil some steaks, eat them in the bedroom, have more champagne, and go back to bed. On Sunday we would rise late. This was a big weekend for us. Our adopted son is almost three now, and it has just been within the last six months that we have once again started to enjoy each other."

There is no doubt that trying so hard to have a baby can threaten to destroy a couple's sexual relationship. "Making love by the calendar for four years isn't the best thing for a marriage," says one husband. In most cases, a couple will be able to reestablish a normal sex life over time. They should be patient with each other and not be afraid to talk about what they are feeling.

If one spouse has fertility problems, then he or she may feel responsible for the couple's inability to reproduce. "I kept thinking that if my husband had married someone else, he would have had a family by now," said Linda, the teacher from New Jersey. Carrying these guilt feelings around can be damaging for that partner.

In some marriages, the healthy partner may begin to resent the other. This may be particularly true if the woman suffers from pelvic inflammatory disease, which may have been caused by having too many sexual partners. Her husband's anger may be real and her guilt unbearable.

It is important for a couple to keep the lines of communication open during these trying times. If they cannot talk to each other, then perhaps they need to seek professional help, either individually or together.

Coping is what it is all about. Those who survive the infertility battle do so because they find ways to live with the problem. Life goes on, and for most infertile couples, that life can still be filled with all the things that are worthwhile—a good marriage, loyal friends, and, of course, children.

11

THE ADOPTED CHILD

E ureka! It's done. The couple have adopted a baby. Is raising an adopted child any different from raising a biological child? Well, yes—and no.

When caring for an adopted infant, there are some differences. The adoptive mother would not be able to nurse the baby like a biological mother, for example. But for most of the time, the adoptive couple could easily forget that their baby was not biological. One woman I contacted to interview for this book expressed some hesitancy about discussing her infant son's adoption. "For years now, I've talked about adoption constantly," she told me. "For a while I just want to enjoy being a mother and forget that my son is adopted."

That attitude is understandable. No one could blame a couple for wanting to enjoy totally the parenting experience without having to think about adoption. However, that attitude cannot go on indefinitely. An adopted child *is* different from a biological child. And no amount of pretending on the part of his adoptive parents will make it otherwise.

When agencies did a superlative job of physically matching adoptive parents and adopted children, it was possible for the parents never to tell a child he was adopted. We have all heard stories of an adopted child finding out late in life that he was adopted. Often that fact is discovered after his adoptive parents have died and he sorts through their papers only to discover his adoption certificate.

In many cases, this news can be a shock and can create serious psychological problems for this adopted adult. He may feel anger toward his parents, intensified if they are dead and cannot explain their actions. He may feel that his adoption was something they wanted to hide from him because they were ashamed of it. If they are dead, it is unlikely he will ever be able to put together all the pieces.

These days, it is more difficult to hide from the child that he is adopted. For one thing, many adopted children look so unlike their adoptive parents that the fact becomes obvious. If a Caucasian couple walk down the street with their adopted Korean child, everyone will know he is adopted. Even if the child is of the same ethnic background as his adoptive parents, their features may be dissimilar enough to raise questions in the minds of onlookers.

But aside from physical appearance, many of the couple's relatives and friends will probably know that the child is adopted. No doubt some of these people served as a great support system as the couple grappled with infertility and went through the adoption process. Unless all these people can be sworn to secrecy—an almost impossible task—then it is unlikely that the adoption will be forever kept from the child.

Times have changed a great deal since adoption was regarded as something that should be kept under wraps. It no longer is considered a stigma to be adopted. Look at some of the celebrities who openly admit either to being adopted or to having adopted children. Elizabeth Taylor, Barbara Walters, and President Ronald Reagan all have adopted children. Some of the stars of the 1984 Olympic games—including skating star Scott Hamilton and diving champion Greg Louganis—are adopted. All these people have talked about adoption in glowing terms.

Sociological change has drastically altered family life. The typical American family exists only on TV. Sure, there are families consisting of a father, mother, and children. But the rising divorce rate has presented new answers to the question, "Who is minding the children?" In some cases it's the mother, a single woman living alone. Or it is the father, a divorced man who manages with a housekeeper or help from a relative. Then there are children being raised by two women living together, two men, or a woman and man living together but not married. Also, there are grandparents raising children, as well as aunts, uncles, other relatives, and friends. Compared to all this, the adopted child being brought up by an adoptive father and mother appears to have the most normal home life of all.

What this means is that the adopted child no longer must worry that his home situation is different from those of his classmates.

Everyone's situation is unique and no one should be ostracized because of that.

In the past adoptive parents may have kept the truth from their children simply because it was easier than telling them. It does seem like an awesome task. How does an adoptive parent tell his child that he is adopted? How does he explain the adoption? Do both parents participate in the telling or just the parent who spends more time with the child? How old should the child be when he is told? Will one explanation satisfy him, or will he keep coming back for more details?

There are no easy answers to any of these questions. The situation will be different for every family. But because the telling process is such an important duty for the adoptive parent, it is worth it to spend some extra time researching the issue.

As a start, here are answers to some of the most commonly asked questions concerning the telling process.

What can we do to prepare ourselves for telling our child about the adoption?

The adoptive couple should not feel embarrassed to ask for help with this issue. It is a well-known fact that just the thought of the child asking, "Where did I come from?" is enough to give the shakes to even the most confident adoptive parent.

The best strategy for preparation is to read everything available on the subject. The parents should also talk with other adoptive parents, especially those who have recently tackled the task of telling their children. Others who may have good advice include pediatricians, social-work professionals, and child psychologists.

When should we tell the child about his adoption?

This is perhaps the most controversial question with regard to the telling process.

Many years ago, some parents never told their children they were adopted. Then popular opinion went in the opposite direction. Not only did parents tell their children, but they told them early and often. Thus, even before a child knew what "adoption" meant he was continually exposed to the word. This process might start with a toddler. "Let's adopt the cat," his mother might tell him, and then include a short definition. "Now we can adopt the plant," etc., etc.

Parents also were encouraged to use the word "adopted" in conjunction with the child. A father might say to his two-year-old, "When we adopted you, we lived in an apartment." When driving past the adoption agency the father might say, "That's where we adopted you."

At the time, this strategy seemed like a good one. It made the adoptive parents feel better because they could use the word "adoption" openly and freely. The parents also felt that the child was being helped by this process because he was gradually learning about adoption, and doing so in a positive way.

However, there are many social-work professionals who now disagree with this approach, believing not only that it is useless, but also that it can actually confuse the child. Joan Spector, a clinical social-work psychotherapist in Great Neck, New York, has done research on children and the telling process. According to Ms. Spector, children who do not understand what adoption is begin to interpret it in terms they can grasp. So when told they are adopted, they instead think they are being told they are "dotted" or a "doctor."

That does not mean that the parents should avoid using the word "adoption," or try to hide the fact from the child. They should merely try to act normal about the situation. In this way the child will be exposed to the word and will feel able to raise questions whenever he likes. Yet he will not constantly be bombarded with the fact that he is adopted before he knows what that means.

So when is the proper time to begin the adoption discussion? In most cases, the child himself will initiate this discussion. Some psychologists maintain that, until a child is old enough to understand sex, he is not old enough to understand adoption. These experts believe that a three- or four-year-old is incapable of absorbing the concept of adoption. Even a five-year-old may be too young to comprehend the meaning of this discussion. One researcher actually found that children younger than six and a half years did not understand adoption.

Parents should be careful, however, in how they explain the adoption to the child. Introducing another woman—the birthmother—may actually be damaging to the child. The question, "Mommy, where did I come from?" from a three-year-old might precipitate a whole discussion on how the child grew in another woman's belly who couldn't keep him but found a nice mommy and daddy who could. To a young child who still cannot understand adoption, being told that there is another woman out there who somehow has a claim to him can frighten him.

Ms. Spector said she counseled one child who had been told this story and had recurring nightmares that a woman was trying to take him from his home. "Children need to feel they belong to their parents," said Ms. Spector. "To introduce a concept to a little child that there is another woman whose belly he grew in risks confusing the child."

Some parents rush into a discussion of adoption simply because they feel they should be the first ones to broach the subject with the child. A parent's worst fear is that the adopted child may be taunted by a classmate at school. But experts say this early discussion will be useless if the child still does not understand the concept. These experts also believe that any situation can be handled, even the case of the child hearing the word "adopted" from a classmate.

Reuben Pannor, of Vista Del Mar Child Care, said one adoptive mother he counseled had her six-year-old girl come home crying after a classmate told her she was adopted. The little girl had even dragged the little boy home with her and said to her mother, "You tell him I'm not adopted."

It turned out that the little boy didn't even know what the word adoption meant. "In a situation like that, the mother should hug her little girl and say, 'You're home now where your family will always be and that's what's important,' " said Mr. Pannor. "To the little boy she should say, 'She is part of our family and we love her very much,' and then to explain adoption to both children, she should add, 'Adoption is how we built our family.' "

This incident brings up an important point. Even if the child comes home and says, "John told me I'm adopted," it might not necessarily mean that the child is ready for a full-scale explanation of adoption. Rather, the parent should try to determine what the child thinks adoption means and try to answer his questions.

The parent should remember that discussing adoption is not a one-shot deal. The telling process is ongoing, stretching over years. It is possible the child will be satisfied with a simple explanation on one occasion, go away to think about it, and come back the next day with more questions.

In all these discussions, the parent should not give the child more information than he is ready for. Oftentimes adoptive parents are too quick to jump the gun. If a child sees a pregnant woman and comments on her fat stomach, he is not asking for a full discussion on sex or adoption. The adoptive parent must be sensitive to what he is asking and try to give him an answer that is appropriate for his age.

The important thing is that any information given to the child be conveyed in a warm and loving manner. He may not understand everything he is being told, but he should feel comfortable coming back and taking up the discussion again in the future.

When the child is old enough to understand adoption fully, it is possible that he will go through a period when he will be depressed as he tries to absorb what has happened to him. The adoptive parents should be sensitive to his feelings throughout this period and be there to comfort and support him.

Should both parents participate in the telling process?

Definitely. The child should feel comfortable broaching the subject with either parent at any time.

The husband and wife should discuss what they plan to tell the child. It would not do for the child to wind up with two very different stories.

Obviously each parent will have a different approach to the subject. It may be more difficult for the mother because she must deal with the existence of a birthmother and the fact that she did not carry the adopted child in her womb.

What should the child be told?

In the beginning, a simple explanation is best. If the child comes to the parent and says, "John says I'm adopted. What does that mean?" the parent might respond, "Daddy and I wanted to start a family and so we went to talk with a nice lady about bringing home a baby. So she brought you to us and we were so excited because you were so beautiful. And we took you home and that was how we became a family."

The child will no doubt enjoy this story. The parent may even find herself repeating it to him again and again. One day, however, the child will begin to ask questions about sex and where babies come from. When he receives an explanation, he will begin to wonder how the adoption agency fits into this scenario. Then the parent will offer a simple answer. "Yes, babies grow in women's tummies. But I wasn't able to get a baby to grow in my tummy. You grew in another lady's tummy and then she brought you to the agency and we brought you home."

Soon to follow will be the child's questions on why the lady whose tummy he grew in didn't keep him. "I'm sure she wanted to keep you," the parent might answer. "But she knew that she wouldn't be able to take good care of you and she wanted you to have a nice home and two parents who would love you very much, and that's why we became your family."

This explanation will establish a good basis for dealing with any future questions about the child's birthparents. It is important that the adoptive parents always talk about the child's birthparents in positive terms. The child may misinterpret any criticism of his birthparents to be criticism of him, too. Also, the adoptive parents should be careful to stress to the child that his birthmother decided on adoption because she cared about him, not because she wanted to get rid of him. Especially if the child was an infant when he was placed in an adoptive home, this probably was the case. With abortion being so available, a birthmother would have to care about the child and want to give him life if she decides on adoption.

Should the adopted child be told that he was chosen or that he is special in some way?

This was a common theme years ago when adoptive parents told their children about adoption. "We went into the nursery, and out of all the children there we chose you because you were so special." Throughout his childhood, he might hear that story in different ways. "You are very special because we chose you out of all the babies in the world."

I once attended a panel discussion where two adult adoptees told about their experiences. Both of them had been told early on that they were adopted, and both were told that they were special. These two adults, one a man, the other a woman, agreed that being told they were special added to their self-esteem. "I loved it," said the man.

Current thinking, however, is against stressing to the adopted child that he is special. Some professionals feel it may set up unreasonable goals for the child. Others are against telling an adopted child he is special for a simple reason: It isn't true. It is unlikely that an adoptive couple would actually get to choose their adopted child, whether they go through an agency or adopt privately. There is nothing wrong with the tale in the previous example that says that the agency official brought out the child and the couple were thrilled with him because he was so beautiful. That probably is true and enough to make the child feel very special.

What should the child be told about his biological parents?

Once the child is old enough to understand adoption, he obviously will begin to ask questions about his biological parents. Some adoptive parents instinctively regard this as a threat to their own security. They fear that what will follow will be the child's desire to search for his biological parents.

The adoptive parents must realize that it is only natural that the child will want to learn more about his background. His curiosity about his biological parents is healthy and natural. In some ways, it is similar to the curiosity the adoptive parents had—or may still have—about biological children. Didn't the adoptive parents wonder what their biological children would look like? Wasn't that curiosity the major thrust behind their continuing attempts to have a child? But that fact did not affect their love for this adopted child. Even if they had a biological child, they would love their adopted child as much.

For the adopted child, looking for his biological parents may answer some questions he may have about his origins. He may even develop a friendship with his biological mother or father, or both. But chances are that even those friendships would not affect his relationship with his adoptive parents. He will still consider them his parents, the mother and father who raised him.

In this context then, the adoptive parents should try to satisfy their child's interest in learning about his biological parents. When he is old enough, they should share with him any information they received from the agency or the lawyers if it was an independent adoption. For some children, receiving this information is enough. They may never be strongly motivated actually to meet their biological parents.

Should other adults who have contact with the child be advised of the telling process?

If there are adults who have a great deal of contact with the child—babysitters, grandparents, aunts, or friends—it probably would be a good idea to educate them about the telling process. Especially if one of these adults has a close relationship with the child, the child may feel he can ask this adult questions he is reluctant to ask his parents.

These adults should be informed of what the parents have told the child. They should be encouraged to act naturally and positively whenever they engage in a discussion on adoption with the child. If they are evasive or nervous, the child may begin to feel that certain facts are being kept from him. Other relatives may go in the opposite direction and over-stress adoption to the child. A grandparent may introduce the child as his "adopted grandchild." Needless to say, this behavior should not be permitted.

*Can others outside the immediate circle of family and friends be help-
ful in the telling process?*

Of course, the adoptive parents will need to tell their pediatrician
that the child is adopted. If the child develops a close relationship
with this doctor, then he could be helpful in the future if the child
seeks out someone to talk to.

What about the child's teachers? Should they be told that the
child is adopted?

Some teachers feel strongly on being given such information.
They feel it would help in the future if, for instance, another child
makes a comment to the child.

Many adoptive parents worry, however, that some teachers may
use the fact that the child is adopted as the reason for his misbe-
havior. "Schools still tend to have a tracking system," said Mr.
Pannor. "A teacher is told that the child is adopted and then everything is hung on that." In most cases, the parents will have to make
their own decision on what—if anything—to tell the child's teacher.

*Are there other things, outside the actual telling process, that will
affect the child's attitude about adoption?*

Once the child understands adoption, he may begin to look at
certain things in his life in a new light. During this transition
period, it is important that the parents continue to function as
usual, even if the child acts out his frustrations at times.

For example, the child one day may use his new information to
attack his parents with the comment, "You can't tell me what to
do. You're not my real parents." Or, "I wish you never adopted
me." Or, "Someday I'll find my real parents and then I won't have
to live here anymore."

What the adoptive parent must remember is that all children at
one time or another make hurtful comments to their parents. A
biological child may say, "I wish I had never been born. Why did
you have me anyway?" Or, "I wish you weren't my father. I wish
Mommy had married someone else."

The adopted child's comments may cut deeper because they
strike at the adoptive parents' most vulnerable spot. There may
have been times when the adoptive mother didn't feel like the
child's *real* mother. Hearing him say that just reinforces her own
insecurity.

What the adoptive parents must guard against, however, is making any retaliatory remark to reinforce the child's own insecurity.

Deep down, the adopted child may fear that he was abandoned by his biological parents and that he may one day be abandoned by his adoptive parents. Therefore a remark like, "I hope you do find your real parents and then we won't have to take care of you anymore," may never be forgotten by the child. As difficult as it may be to keep cool during an argument, the adoptive parent must make the effort. "We are your real parents and we love you," the adoptive parent should say. "But that doesn't mean that you can keep a messy room."

In addition to the telling process, probably the greatest challenge the adoptive parents will face will occur when the child is an adult and decides that he wants to search for his biological parents. How does the adoptive parent handle this situation?

First, the parents should understand that the child's desire to locate his birthmother and perhaps birthfather is natural. We live in an era when people are intent on tracing their roots. An individual might make this search for many reasons, normal curiosity for one. Beyond that, the person may believe that by finding out who his relatives are, where they came from, and how they lived he may uncover some hidden traits in himself. He may want to answer the question, "If my relatives didn't come to America, where would I be now? How would I be living? What would I be doing?"

For an individual who knows who his biological parents are, this search begins with his grandparents, and his great-grandparents. He wants to know the country his relatives came from and perhaps to look up any relatives still living there.

Biological parents may not only assist in this search, but may also applaud it. They might also be curious but never had the opportunity to do such research.

The adoptive parents, however, may not be as thrilled with such a search. Their feelings may range from tolerance to actual anger. At the core of this issue is the adoptive parents' fear that their relationship with their adopted child will be forever changed by what he finds out.

That may be. But showing disapproval for the child's search will only serve to drive him away from the adoptive parents. The best policy is to support him in his mission, offer assistance if needed, and accept the fact that the outcome may be that the child will establish a relationship with his biological parents.

Some adoptive parents have actually planned for the day when their child will search. Several couples I interviewed who had adopted infants through independent adoptions made it their job to meet the birthmother or to get as much information as possible on her so that the child would be able to find her in the future.

In most states, adoption records are sealed by the courts. Some states have now passed laws so that an adopted adult and the birthparents may register their interest in meeting. If both parties express the desire to meet, then such a meeting is arranged.

So far, there has not been a rush by adoptees to locate their biological parents, or by biological parents to find their children. That may change in the future as more states set up registries and the system receives more publicity.

No one knows how the next generation of adopted children will feel about this issue. The desire to trace one's roots may intensify or diminish. But the adoptive parents should be prepared either way.

It is possible that the search may turn up information that is disturbing to the adoptee. He may be upset to learn that his mother was a drug addict, a prostitute, or spent some time in prison. He may believe that somehow these newly discovered facts will affect his own life. If he cannot get through this trauma on his own, then perhaps he will need to seek professional counseling.

It also is possible that the adopted adult will be hurt by the fact that his birthmother seems indifferent to his existence. She may have her own family now, and want to forget about that early part of her life. The support of his own family—his adoptive parents—will be very important to him at that point.

Unfortunately, much of the publicity given to adopted people searching for their biological parents has been negative. That is perhaps because those who are unhappy with being adopted and have unhappy experiences finding their biological parents have been given the most publicity. There are probably just as many adopted children who search with happy results.

In any event, the adoptive parents should not be unduly troubled about this issue. The odds are great that the adopted adult will not want to search for his biological parents. If he does, the results will most likely be positive and enhance not only his own self-confidence but also his relationship with his adoptive parents.

12

CAMPAIGNING FOR ADOPTION

O nce someone has become an adoptive parent it is very easy to become an outspoken advocate for adoption. Sometimes this advocacy is done informally, with the adoptive parent talking more about adoption to relatives, friends, and business associates.

Other adoptive parents decide to become more active and join adoptive-parent groups in order to campaign for change. While public perception of adoption has come a long way in the last twenty years, there is still much that needs to be done, and adoptive parents are in a better position to address these challenges than anyone else.

Adoptive-parent groups are forming all over the United States, ranging widely in size and goals. Some are support groups where adoptive parents and adopted children can go for help and information. Often these groups plan social events.

These get-togethers can be very important for the adopted child as he is growing up. Within such a group, he is exposed to many other adopted children, and even if he is the only adopted child in his school he will be reminded that there are many other children like him who are healthy and happy. Most of these groups tend to be small and local. The best way to locate one of these groups is to check with local adoption agencies. (Also check the listings at the back of this book, p. 203.)

Other adoptive-parent groups actually have become involved in disseminating information on adoption. Some of these groups act as middlemen for couples arranging foreign adoptions. These organizations usually are state, regional, or national in their memberships, and may hold annual meetings where delegates can attend workshops and exchange information.

Many of these adoptive-parent groups—whether local or national—are concerned about issues that will affect their adopted children as they grow up and are working to improve the adoption process.

What follows is a list of what needs to be done. Already, many adoptive parents are campaigning for adoption. Anyone who adopts has a stake in joining this effort.

Young, unwed mothers need to know that there is an alternative to abortion or raising the baby alone.

That alternative is adoption and, unfortunately, it is given less attention today by Planned Parenthood and other groups than it should be given.

No one can minimize the trauma involved with carrying a baby for nine months and then agreeing to adoption. That waiting time can be made easier once the birthmother goes to a good agency and is given a comfortable place to live. She will know that her medical and legal expenses will be paid for.

She will go through the physical aspects of pregnancy and it will take her some time to regain her figure. No doubt she will suffer from the separation. That feeling may never go away. For years she may think about the child on his birthday or around holidays.

But there is so much about adoption that will give her peace of mind. She gave the baby the opportunity to go out and contribute his skills and talents to society. The agency probably allowed her to participate in selecting the couple who would adopt her baby, so she is reassured that he will be well taken care of.

There are no easy answers to an unplanned pregnancy. And ultimately the unwed mother must make that decision herself. What needs to be done is for more of these women to hear about the adoption alternative.

Many agencies do advertise their services; others simply do not have the funds. This is one area where adoptive-parent groups can help by getting out into the community and publicizing adoption. They can make sure that these young women know what services are available to them before they make their choice.

Adoption agencies need to improve their services and their sensitivity toward the birthmother and adoptive couple in order to encourage more people to come to them.

Many social-work professionals advocate banning independent adoptions. There are several states that now prohibit these adoptions; more are sure to follow. Ultimately, what could happen is that a national law will be passed making independent adoption illegal anywhere in the United States.

That is a drastic step that should never happen. There are many problems involved in independent adoptions, but the solution is for the agencies to convince people to come to them because they are doing a better job, not because they have been granted a monopoly by the federal government. At present, many agencies are not doing a good job, which leads an increasing number of couples to arrange adoptions on their own.

Nevertheless, many agency officials have buried their heads in the sand, pushing to outlaw independent adoptions while at the same time doing nothing to improve their own services. What do agencies need to do?

- Advertise their services to encourage young women to come to them.
- Offer to meet these young women in less intimidating surroundings than a bureaucratic-looking agency building. A restaurant, the birthmother's home, or a friend's apartment are good alternatives.
- Allow the birthmother to play a major role in selecting the adoptive couple for the child. If she wants to talk with them or meet them, every effort should be made to meet her request.
- Provide training for all employees who answer inquiries from the public. No one who calls to ask about adoption should receive a rude response. In addition, any letter from an adoptive couple inquiring about adoption should be answered promptly, even if the answer is that the agency is not accepting applications.
- Demystify the application and home study process. Couples or individuals who are refused for placement should be given a reason for this decision. Home studies should be cosigned by the social worker and the couple.
- Eliminate age requirements. It is a simple fact that people—and that means all people, not just infertile people—are living longer and starting families later in life. It is unreasonable to eliminate a couple because one partner is older than thirty-five or forty.
- Avoid measuring all adoptive parents against some unreasonable standard for perfect parents. No one can be a perfect parent, but there are many people who want to adopt who will be good parents.
- Work to become involved in the independent adoption process. Agencies should be available for counseling and home study in

cases where a couple come to them after they have already identified a baby they wish to adopt. The agency should be willing
to counsel the birthmother and the couple, and to complete a
home study if needed.

*All states should establish registries so that birthparents and adopted
children can locate each other if they so desire.*

Not all adopted adults want to find their birthparents, and not all
birthparents want to locate their grown children. But for those
that do, the process should be made easy. A registry system is the
best method. In this way, if one party does not want to be found,
by not registering with the state he or she can be sure that his or
her privacy will be protected.

For those who do want to search, it is a disheartening experience
to be told that the information cannot be released to them.
In some cases, adopted adults have gone through other methods
to find birthparents with upsetting results. Setting up a system
whereby both parties can meet if they are agreeable is the best
method.

If independent adoptions continue to increase, then this entire
question of open records versus closed records may be irrelevant.
In independent adoption, as in agency adoption, the records are
sealed by the court. But in some independent adoptions, the adoptive couple have met the birthmother, know her name, and perhaps
even correspond with her. So in the future, those who were adopted
independently may have a freedom denied to those who were adopted
through agencies.

Adoptive couples should be given financial assistance for the adoption.

At present, the adoptive couple cover the cost of medical and
legal expenses for the birthmother. This is true whether the couple
adopt through an agency or independently. There are very few
agencies these days that can afford to pay for these items themselves.

The cost of an adoption today can range from five thousand to
twenty thousand dollars, depending upon the birthmother's sheltering cost, ease of delivery, and time spent in the hospital. In most
cases, any medical insurance that an adoptive couple carry cannot
be applied toward the birthmother's medical expenses. If the birthmother's parents have insurance, they may be reluctant to use it

because everyone in their office will find out about their daughter's pregnancy.

Insurance companies need to change their policies to cover some of these medical expenses. If costs continue to rise, then eventually only the wealthy will be able to afford adoption.

As it is, some couples are being driven to desperate means to work around these high costs. There have been instances where the husband checked the birthmother into a hospital claiming that she was his wife. His medical plan covered the cost of the delivery and his name and his wife's appeared on the birth certificate. When the baby was released from the hospital, the birthmother handed him over to the couple.

Corporations are doing some things to help employees who want to adopt. At least a dozen corporations—including Pitney Bowes, Hallmark Cards, IBM, Time, Pfizer, Procter & Gamble, Control Data, G.D. Searles, Syntex, Smithkline, and Eli Lilly—will pay their employees around one thousand dollars toward the cost of an adoption. Foote, Cone & Belding, a New York advertising agency, has one of the most generous programs, which covers 80 percent of the costs incurred by an employee who adopts. Other corporations need to implement these programs.

Adoptive-parent groups can work to change the minds of insurance companies and corporations. Since these companies are apt to look at the issue in dollars and cents, it should be pointed out to them that we are not talking about a great deal of money. There were an estimated eighteen thousand infant adoptions in the United States in 1982. Even if insurance companies footed the medical bills for all those adoptions, it would cost them only about $180 million. While that amount may seem high, it is a drop in the bucket compared to the total health care costs in the United States, which reached $355 billion in 1983.

As for the corporations, how many employees would adopt each year? Whatever the number, the amount spent would be small compared to the good will and public relations it would buy.

Another area where corporations can help out is in granting adoptive mothers maternity leave. Most companies grant biological mothers paid leave for periods that range from several weeks to several months. Yet adoptive mothers must use personal leave or take the time off without being paid.

The explanation for this disparity usually is that the biological mother needs to recover physically while the adoptive mother does not. But we all know women who have had babies and gone back to work days or weeks after giving birth. The truth is that maternity leave is not just a recuperation period for the mother. It also is a time for her to get to know her baby. An adoptive mother deserves that opportunity, too.

There is much that needs to be done to publicize adoption for what it is: a beautiful way to have a family. The adoptive couple and their adopted children who love each other and enjoy their lives together are the best advertisement ever for adoption.

APPENDIXES

PUBLIC AND PRIVATE ADOPTION AGENCIES

T he following list of adoption agencies was gathered by contacting the state agency in each state. Remember that this list should only be a starting point. Because agencies open and close every year, the state agency is usually the best source for up-to-date information on adoption agencies that are in operation. The state agency also will be able to identify county or other local offices closest to you that are part of the state network.

Most agencies—whether public or private—serve specific geographical areas. Be sure to ask when you make contact with them what these restrictions might be.

Public agencies will be most helpful in locating special-needs and older children who are available for adoption. For infant adoptions, private agencies will be where you will want to concentrate your efforts.

Alabama

State Agency

State Department of Pensions and
  Security
Administrative Building
64 North Union Street
Montgomery, AL 36130
(205)261-3409

Private Agencies

Association for Guidance, Aid, Placement and Empathy (AGAPE)

P.O. Box 11558
Montgomery, AL 36111
(205)272-9466

Association for Guidance, Aid, Placement and Empathy (AGAPE)
2733 Mastin Lake Road
Huntsville, AL 35810
(205)859-4481

Association for Guidance, Aid, Placement and Empathy (AGAPE)
P.O. Box 16414

149

Mobile, AL 36601
(205)660-5002

Catholic Social Services
2164 11th Avenue South
Birmingham, AL 35265
(205)324-6561

Catholic Social Services
1010 Church Street
Huntsville, AL 35801
(205)536-0041

Catholic Social Services
137 Clayton Street
Montgomery, AL 36104
(205)269-2387

Catholic Social Services
404 Government Street
Mobile, AL 36601
(205)471-1305

Children's Aid Society
3600 8th Avenue, South
Birmingham, AL 35222
(205)251-7148

Children's Services International, Inc.
14 Office Park Circle, Suite 106
Birmingham, AL 35223
(205)871-8092

Lifeline Children's Services
2908 Pumphouse Road
Birmingham, AL 35243
(205)967-0811

United Methodist Children's Home
1712 Broad Street
Selma, AL 36701
(205)875-7283

Alaska

State Agency

Department of Health and Social Services
Division of Family and Youth Services
Pouch H-05
Juneau, AK 99811
(907)465-3631

Private Agencies

Adoption Advocates International
P.O. Box 566

Girdwood, AK 99587
(907)783-2589

Catholic Social Services
3935 Reka Drive
Anchorage, AK 99508
(907)277-2554

Fairbanks Counseling and Adoption
   Agency
Box 1544
Fairbanks, AK 99707
(907)456-4729

Latter Day Saints Social Services
201 East 56th #225
Anchorage, AK 99504
(907)563-6522

WACAP, Washington Association of
   Concerned Parents
1709 South Bragaw, Suite S
Anchorage, AK 99508
(907)276-3691

Arizona

State Agency

Department of Economic Security
P.O. Box 6123
Phoenix, AZ 85005
(602)255-3981

Private Agencies

All God's Children
P.O. Box 37637
Phoenix, AZ 85069
(602)863-4944

Arizona Children's Home
2700 South 8th Avenue
Tucson, AZ 85713
(602)622-7611

Black Family and Children Services
2615 North 7th Street
Phoenix, AZ 85006
(602)285-0961

Catholic Community Services of
   Southern Arizona
18 Howell Avenue
P.O. Box 86
Bisbee, AZ 85603
(602)458-3530

Catholic Community Services of
Yuma
301 South 2nd Avenue
Yuma, AZ 85364
(602)783-3308

Catholic Social Services of Flagstaff
5 West Cherry
Flagstaff, AZ 86001
(602)774-1911

Catholic Social Services of Phoenix
1825 West Northern Avenue
Phoenix, AZ 85021
(602)997-6105

Catholic Social Services of
Tri-City
610 East Southern
Mesa, AZ 85204
(602)964-8771

Catholic Social Services of Tucson
155 West Helen
P.O. Box 5746
Tucson, AZ 85703-5746
(602)623-0344

Catholic Social Services of Yavapai
116 North Summitt
Prescott, AZ 86301
(602)778-2531

Christian Family Care Agency
222 West Thomas, Suite 104
Phoenix, AZ 85013
(602)234-1935

Dillion Southwest
P.O. Box 3535
Scottsdale, AZ 85257
(602)945-2221

Family Service Agency
1530 East Flower
Phoenix, AZ 85014
(602)264-9891

Globe International
6220 West Monte Vista Road
Phoenix, AZ 85035
(602)247-3038

House of Samuel
11777 South Old Nogales Highway
Tucson, AZ 85706
(602)294-1997

Jewish Family and Children's Service
2033 North 7th Street
Phoenix, AZ 85006
(602)257-1904

Jewish Family Service of Tucson
102 North Plumber Avenue
Tucson, AZ 85719
(602)792-3641

Latter Day Saints Social Services
235 South El Dorado
Mesa, AZ 85204
(602)968-2995

Latter Day Saints Social Services of
Snowflake
P.O. Box 856
Snowflake, AZ 85937
(602)536-4118

Southwest Adoption Agency
4327 North Scottsdale Road, Suite 200
Scottsdale, AZ 85251
(602)234-2229

Arkansas

State Agency

Department of Human Services
BC/BS Building
7th and Gaines Streets
P.O. Box 1437-ADOPTION
Little Rock, AR 72203
(501)371-2207

Private Agencies

Catholic Social Services
Division of Adoption Services, Inc.
2415 North Tyler
Little Rock, AR 72207
(501)664-0340

Children's Homes, Inc.
5133 Children's Homes Circle
Paragould, AR 72450
(501)239-4031

Friends of Children, Inc.
2024 Arkansas Valley Drive, Suite 804
Little Rock, AR 72212
(501)224-5900

California

State Agency

Department of Social Services
744 P Street
Sacramento, CA 95814
(914)445-3146

California Department of Social Services District Offices

1625 Shattuck Avenue, Room 101
Berkeley, CA 94709
(415)540-2028

520 Cohasset Road, Suite 11
Chico, CA 95926
(916)891-1986

107 South Broadway, Room 6027
Los Angeles, CA 90012
(213)620-4365

2400 Glendale Lane
Sacramento, CA 95825
(914)920-6897

P.O. Box 6694
2350 Professional Drive
Santa Rosa, CA 95406
(707)576-2205

320 F Street
Eureka, CA 95501
(707)445-8864

Private Agencies

AASK (Aid to Adoption of Special Kids)
3530 Grand Avenue
Oakland, CA 94610
(415)451-1748

Adoptions Horizons
P.O. Box 247
Arcata, CA 95521
(707)822-2660

Adoptions Unlimited
4471 Suite R, Riverside Drive
P.O. Box 462
Chino, CA 91710
(714)591-0391

Bal Jagat, Inc.
9311 Farralone Avenue

Chatsworth, CA 91311
(213)709-4737

Bethany Christian Service
115D Mark Randy Place
Modesto, CA 95350
(209)522-5121

Black Adoption Placement and Research Center
952 Magnolia Street
Oakland, CA 94607
(415)839-3678

Catholic Social Service of San Francisco
2045 Lawton Street
San Francisco, CA 94122
(415)665-5100

Children's Bureau of Los Angeles
2824 Hyans Street
Los Angeles, CA 90026
(213)384-2515

Inglewood District Office:
    4632 West Century Boulevard
    Inglewood, CA 90304
    (213)678-5045

San Fernando Valley District Office:
    6851 Lenox Avenue
    Van Nuys, CA 91405
    (213)785-8861

Children's Home Society of California (Headquarters)
2727 West 6th Street
Los Angeles, CA 90057-3198
(213)389-6750
(Branch offices are located throughout the state)

Christian Adoption and Family Services
17150 Norwalk Boulevard, Suite 117
Cerritos, CA 90701
(213)860-3766

Family Connections
1528 Oakdale Road
Modesto, CA 95355
(209)524-8844

Holt International Children's Services
California Branch Office (North)
1684 East 14th Street, Suite 205
San Leandro, CA 94577
(415)351-4996

Holt International Children's Services
California Branch Office (South)
5230 Clark Avenue, Suite 32
Lakewood, CA 90713
(213)920-0803

Holy Family Services—Counseling
and Adoptions
357 Westlake Avenue
Los Angeles, CA 90057
(213)484-1441

Santa Ana Office:
1403 South Main Street
Santa Ana, CA 92707
(714)835-5551

San Fernando Valley Office:
6851 Lennox Avenue
Van Nuys, CA 91405
(213)785-8861

Infant of Prague
3510 East Ventura
Fresno, CA 93702
(209)237-0851

Latter Day Saints Social Services (Headquarters Office)
501 North Brodhurst Avenue,
Suite 300
Anaheim, CA 92801
(714)520-0525

Partners in Adoption
927 Cherry Street
P.O. Box 2791
Santa Rosa, CA 95405
(707)578-0212

Sierra Adoption Services
Mt. St. Mary School
Churchhand Chapel Streets
P.O. Box 361
Nevada City, CA 95939
(916)265-3314

Vista Del Mar Child Care Services
3200 Motor Avenue
Los Angeles, CA 90034
(213)836-1223

Colorado

State Agency

Department of Social Services
1575 Sherman Street
Denver, CO 80203
(303)866-5270

Private Agencies

The Adoption Option
7625 West 5th Avenue, Suite 110-D
Lakewood, CO 80226
(303)233-2328

Alternative Homes for Youth
3000 Youngfield, Suite 155-A
Wheat Ridge, CO 80033
(303)233-0041

Archdiocese of Denver
Ministry to the Handicapped
1050 South Birch Street
Denver, CO 80222
(303)759-5150

Attention, Inc.
1406 Pine Street
Boulder, CO 80302
(303)447-1206
Mail: P.O. Box 907
Boulder, CO 80306

Bethany Christian Services (Colorado Branch Office)
2150 South Bellaire Street,
Suite 201
Denver, CO 80222
(303)758-4484

Brentwood Home, Inc.
6559 Van Gordon Court
Arvada, CO 80004
(303)424-7768
Mail: P.O. Box 149,
Wheat Ridge, CO 80034

Catholic Community Services
Social Services of Pueblo United
302 Jefferson
Pueblo, CO 81005
(303)544-4234

Center for Therapeutic Learning—
Annex
549 East 8th Street
Loveland, CO 80537
(303)669-7550

Chatfield School and Littleton Academy, Inc.
6170 South Bemis Street
Littleton, CO 80120
(303)798-5961

Mail: P.O. Box 1039
    Littleton, CO 80160

Chicago Creek Roads
998 Highway 103
Idaho Springs, CO
(303)567-2909
Denver phone: (303)825-8703
Mail: Rt. 1, Box 50
    Idaho Springs, CO 80452

Christian Home for Children, Inc.
6 West Cheyenne Road
Colorado Springs, CO 80906
(303)632-4661

Colorado Baptist Family Services,
    Inc.
615 West Uintah
Colorado Springs, CO 80905
(303)634-1692

Colorado Boys' Ranch Founda-
    tion
28071 Highway 109
La Junta, CO 81050
(303)384-5981

Colorado Christian Home
4325 West 29th Avenue
Denver, CO
(303)433-2541
Mail: P.O. Box 12295
    Denver, CO 80212

Colorado Christian Service
4796 South Broadway
Englewood, CO 80110
(303)761-7236

Denver Academy
235 South Sherman
Denver, CO 80209
(303)777-5870

Denver Alternative Youth Services
    (The Family Connection)
1240 West Bayaud
Denver, CO 80223
(303)698-2300

Denver Catholic Community Ser-
    vices
200 Josephine Street
Denver, CO 80206
(303)388-4411

Excelsior Youth Center, Inc.
15001 East Oxford Avenue

Aurora, CO 80014
(303)693-1550

Family Builders by Adoption
726 East 16th Avenue, Suite 108
Denver, CO 80230
(303)832-7098

Family Tree Inc.
3805 Marshall Avenue, #100
Wheat Ridge, CO 80033
(303)422-2133

Friends of Children of Various Nations
600 Gilpin Street
Denver, CO 80218
(303)321-8262

Hand in Hand
4965 Barnes Road
Colorado Springs, CO 80917
(303)596-1589

Human Services, Inc.
838 Grant
Denver, CO 80203
(303)830-2716

Jefferson Hall Residence, Inc.
7695 West 59th Avenue
Arvada, CO 80004
(303)421-4870

Jewish Family and Children's Service
    of Colorado
300 South Dahila Street, Suite 101
Denver, CO 80222
(303)321-3115

Latter Day Saints Social Services
9590 West 14th Avenue, Suite 1
Lakewood, CO 80215
(303)238-8169

The Lane Children's Foundation Place-
    ment Agency
Box 96
Ramah, CO 80832
(303)541-2375

Lutheran Social Services of Colorado,
    Inc.
2695 Alcott Street, Suite 3385
Denver, CO 80211
(303)433-8811

Randell-Moore Accelerated Schools
2160 South Cook
Denver, CO 80210
(303)758-2003

Special Child Placement Agency
1300 Vrain Street
Denver, CO 80204
(303)825-3651

Synthesis, Inc.
720 Kipling Street, Suite 13-15
Lakewood, CO 80215
(303)233-8025

Thaddeus House Placement
Agency
1131 South Routt Way
Lakewood, CO 80226
(303)988-1587, (303)988-1990

Volunteers of America
1865 Larimer
Denver, CO 80202
(303) 297-0408

Walk on Water Adoption Agency
1000 Driftwood
Fort Collins, CO 80525
(303)484-0950

Wallace Village for Children
8405 West 100th Avenue
Broomfield, CO 80020
(303)466-7391
Mail: Box 345
    Broomfield, CO 80020

Youth Behavior Program, Inc.
27972 Meadow Drive, Suite
    200
P.O. Box 2764
Evergreen, CO 80439
(303)674-1910

Youth Benefits Unlimited, Inc.
7901 Zenobia Street
P.O. Box 970
Westminster, CO 80030
(303)426-9783

Connecticut

State Agency

Department of Children and Youth
    Services
170 Sigourney Street
Hartford, CT 06105
(203)566-8742

Private Agencies

The Casey Family Program East
    (Administrative Offices)

191 Boston Post Road
Westport, CT 06880
(203)334-6991

Southwestern Connecticut Division:
    102 Bank Street
    Bridgeport, CT 06604
    (203)334-6991

Northeastern Connecticut Division:
    36 Woodland Street
    Hartford, CT 06105
    (203)727-1030

Catholic Charities Inc.
Diocese of Norwich
11 Bath Street
Norwich, CT 06360
(203)889-8346

Catholic Charities of the Diocese of
    Bridgeport, Inc.
238 Jewett Avenue
Bridgeport, CT 06606
(203)372-4301

Catholic Charities–Catholic Family
    Services, Inc.
Archdiocese of Hartford
896 Asylum Avenue
Hartford, CT 06105-1991
(203)522-8241

Child and Family Agency of Southeast-
    ern Connecticut, Inc.
255 Hempstead Street
New London, CT 06320
(203)443-2896

Child and Family Services, Inc.
1680 Albany Avenue
Hartford, CT 06105
(203)236-4511

Northeast District Office:
    110 Main Street
    Manchester, CT 06040
    (203)643-2761

The Children's Center
1400 Whitney Avenue
Hamden, CT 06514
(203)248-2116

The Children's Home
60 Hicksville Road
Cromwell, CT 06416
(203)635-6010

Curtis Home Corp., Children's Pro-
    gram

380 Crown Street
Meriden, CT 06450

Family and Children's Aid of Greater
  Norwalk, Inc.
138 Main Street
Norwalk, CT 06851
(203)846-4203

Family and Children's Services, Inc.
60 Palmer's Hill Road
Stamford, CT 06902
(203)324-3167

The Family Life Center
79 Birch Hill
Weston, CT 06833
(203)222-1468

Family Service, Inc.
92 Vine Street
New Britain, CT 06052
(203)223-9291

Bristol District Office:
29 High Street
Bristol, CT 06010
(203)583-9225

Franciscan Family Care Center, Inc.
267 Finch Avenue
P.O. Box 417
Meriden, CT 06450
(203)237-8084

Hall Neighborhood House, Inc.
52 Green Street
Bridgeport, CT 06608
(203)334-3900

Highland Heights (St. Francis Home
  for Children, Inc.)
651 Prospect Street
Box 1224
New Haven, CT 06505
(203)777-5513

International Adoptions, Inc.
96 Chapel Street
Stratford, CT 06497
(203)377-7927

International Alliance for Children,
  Inc.
23 South Main Street
New Milford, CT 06776
(203)354-3417

Jewish Family Service Inc.
2370 Park Avenue

Bridgeport, CT 06604
(203)366-5438

Jewish Family Service of Greater
  Hartford
740 North Main Street
West Hartford, CT 06117
(203)236-1927

Jewish Family Service of New Haven,
  Inc.
152 Temple Street, Room 318
New Haven, CT 06510
(203)777-6641

Latter Day Saints Social Services
57 Quornhunt Road
West Simsbury, CT 06092
(203)889-0148

Lutheran Child and Family Services of
  Connecticut, Inc.
74 Sherman Street
Hartford, CT 06105
(203)236-0679

Professional Counseling Center
79 South Benson Road
Fairfield, CT 06433
(203)259-5300

Thursday's Child, Inc.
227 Tunxis Avenue
Bloomfield, CT 06002
(203)242-5941

Wheeler Clinic, Inc.
91 Northwest Drive
Plainville, CT 06062
(203)527-1644

Delaware

State Agency
Division of Child Protective Services
824 Market Street, Seventh Floor
Wilmington, DE 19801
(302)571-6410

Private Agencies
Catholic Social Services
1200 Broom Street
Wilmington, DE 19806-4297
(302)655-9624

Child and Home Study Associates
101 Stonecrop Road
Wilmington, DE 19810
(302)475-5433

Children's Bureau of Delaware, Inc.
2005 Baynard Boulevard
Wilmington, DE 19802
(302)658-5177

Welcome House
146 Brackenville Road
Hockessin, DE 19707
(302)239-2102

District of Columbia

Private Adoption Agencies

Adoption Service Information Agency
(ASIA)
7720 Alaska Avenue, N.W.
Washington, D.C., 20012
(202)726-7193

American Adoption Agency
1228 M Street
Washington, D.C., 20005
(202)797-3756

The Barker Foundation
4545 42nd, N.W., Suite 207
Washington, D.C., 20016
(202)363-7751

Catholic Charities—Archdiocese of
District of Columbia
2800 Otis Street, N.E.
Washington, D.C., 20018
(202)526-4100

Children's Adoption Resource
Exchange
1039 Evarts Street, N.E.
Washington, D.C., 20017
(202)526-5200

Family and Child Service of Washington, D.C.
929 L Street, N.W.
Washington, D.C., 20001
(202)289-1510

Lutheran Social Services of the National Capital Area
5121 Colorado Avenue
Washington, D.C., 20011
(202)829-7605

Pierce-Warwick Adoption Service
5229 Connecticut Avenue, N.W.
Washington, D.C., 20015
(202)966-2531

Saint Sophia Greek Orthodox Adoption Service
36th Street and Massachusetts Avenue,
N.W.
Washington, D.C., 20007
(202)333-4730

Florida

State Agency

Department of Health and Rehabilitative Services
1317 Winewood Boulevard
Tallahassee, FL 32301
(904)488-1060

Private Agencies

Adoption Services, Inc.
3767 Lake Worth Road, Suite 109
Lake Worth, FL 33461
(305)969-0591

Advent Christian Home for Children
Dowling Park, FL 32060
(904)776-1009

Baptist Home for Children
2332 Bartram Road
Jacksonville, FL 32207
(904)721-2711

Boys Village of San Antonio, Inc.
Group Home Project
P.O. Box 505
San Antonio, FL 33576
(904)588-3786

Camelot Care Center, Inc.
Route 1, Box 656
Lutz, FL 33549
(813)949-5515

Catholic Charities Bureau
P.O. Box 14375
Gainesville, FL 32604
(904)372-0294

Catholic Charities Bureau
700 Arlington Road
P.O. Box 1931

Jacksonville, FL 32211
(904)725-9119

Catholic Charities Bureau
P.O. Box 543
St. Augustine, FL 32084
(904)892-6300

Catholic Community Services, Inc.
1300 South Andrews Avenue
Fort Lauderdale, FL 33334
(305)522-2513

Catholic Service Bureau, Inc.
1010 Windsor Lane
Key West, FL 33040
(305)296-8032

Catholic Service Bureau, Inc.
4949 Northeast Second Avenue
Miami, FL 33137
(305)754-2444

Catholic Service Bureau, Inc.
319 Davis Boulevard
Naples, FL 33962
(813)774-6483

Catholic Service Bureau of Palm
 Beach County
900-45th Street
West Palm Beach, FL 33407
(305)655-6342

Catholic Social Services
319 Riveredge Boulevard
Cocoa, FL 32922
(305)636-6144

Catholic Social Services, Inc.
40 Beal Parkway, SW
Fort Walton Beach, FL 32548
(904)244-2581

Catholic Social Services, Inc.
901 Marble Arcaid Building
129 South Kentucky Avenue
Lakeland, FL 33801
(813)686-7153

Catholic Social Services, Inc.
3191 Maguire Boulevard
Orlando, FL 32803
(305)894-8888

Catholic Social Services, Inc.
714 North Cove Boulevard
Panama City, FL 32401
(904)763-0475

Catholic Social Services, Inc.
218 East Government Street
P.O. Box 285
Pensacola, FL 32502
(904)438-8564

Catholic Social Services, Inc.
6412 Central Avenue
St. Petersburg, FL 33707
(813)345-9126

Catholic Social Services, Inc.
855 West Carolina Street
Tallahassee, FL 32309
(904)222-2180

Catholic Social Services, Inc.
730 South Stirling Boulevard
Tampa, FL 33609
(813)870-6220

Catholic Social Services, Inc.
513 Lee Avenue Northwest
Winter Haven, FL 33880
(813)299-7983

Children's Home, Inc.
10909 Memorial Highway
Tampa, FL 33615
(813)855-4435

Children's Home Society
2517-2nd Street
Fort Myers, FL 33901
(813)334-2008

Children's Home Society of Florida
201 Osceola Avenue
Daytona Beach, FL 32014
(904)255-7407

Children's Home Society of Florida
105 Northeast Third Street
Fort Lauderdale, FL 33301
(305)763-6573

Children's Home Society of Florida
 (State Office)
P.O. Box 10097
Jacksonville, FL 32207
(904)396-4084

Children's Home Society of Florida
3027 San Diego Road
Jacksonville, FL 32207
(904)396-2641

Children's Home Society of Florida
800 Northwest 15th Street

Miami, FL 33136
(305)324-1262

Children's Home Society of Florida
212 Pasadena Place
Orlando, FL 32803
(305)422-4441

Children's Home Society of Florida
5375 North Ninth Avenue
Pensacola, FL 32504
(904)476-3133

Children's Home Society of Florida
9721 Executive Center Drive North,
   Suite 140
St. Petersburg, FL 33702
(813)576-2383

Children's Home Society of Florida
P.O. Box 3474
Tallahassee, FL 32302
(904)877-5176

Children's Home Society of Florida
3600 Broadway
West Palm Beach, FL 33407
(305)844-9785

Children's Home Society of Mid-
   Florida
409 SE 19th Avenue
Ocala, FL 32670
(904)629-7597

Children's Home Society—Polk County
842 South Missouri Avenue
Lakeland, FL 33801
(813)688-7968

Christian Family Services, Inc.
2720 Southwest Second Avenue
Gainesville, FL 32607
(904)378-1471

Christian Home and Bible School
P.O. Box 896
Mt. Dora, FL 32757
(904)383-2155

Daniel Memorial
3721 Belfort Road
Jacksonville, FL 32216
(904)737-1677

Family Counseling Center Project CAN
2960 Roosevelt Boulevard
Clearwater, FL 33520
(813)531-0481

Florida Baptist Children's Home
177 Lake Hunter Drive
Lakeland, FL 33802
(813)688-4981

Florida Baptist Children's Home (State
   Office)
P.O. Box 1653
Lakeland, FL 33802
(813)687-8811

Florida Baptist Children's Home
7748 Southwest 95th Terrace
Miami, FL 33156
(305)271-4121

Florida Baptist Children's Home
8415 Buck Lake Road
Tallahassee, FL 32301
(904)878-1458

Florida Sheriff's Boys Ranch
Boy's Ranch, FL 32060
(904)842-5501

Florida Sheriff's Girls Villa
P.O. Box 1380
Bartow, FL 33830
(813)533-0371

Florida Sheriff's Youth Ranch
3180 County Road 102
Clearwater, FL 33519
(813)725-4761

Florida United Methodist Children's
   Home
P.O. Box 8
Enterprise, FL 32763
(305)688-4486

Jewish Family and Children's Service,
   Inc.
1415 La Salle Street
Jacksonville, FL 32207
(904)396-2941

Jewish Family and Children's Services
1790 Southwest 27th Avenue
Miami, FL 33145
(305)445-0555

Jewish Family and Children's Services
2411 Okeechobee Boulevard
West Palm Beach, FL 33409
(305)684-1991

Jewish Family Services, Inc., of
   Broward County
1909 Harrison Street, Suite 109

Hollywood, FL 33020
(305)927-9288

Latter Day Saints Social Services
2300 Maitland Center Parkway,
  Suite 326
Maitland, FL 32751
(305)660-2471

Our Mother's Home
4612 Bellview Avenue
Pensacola, FL 32506
(904)944-4885

Suncoast International Adoptions, Inc.
1016 Ponce de Leon Boulevard
Bellair, FL 33516
(813)586-5015

United Family and Children's Services
2190 Northwest Seventh Street
Miami, FL 33135
(305)643-5700

United Methodist Children's Home
2824 Desert Street
P.O. Box 15310
Pensacola, FL 32514
(904)478-8950

Universal Aid for Children, Inc.
P.O. Box 610246
North Miami, FL 33161
(305)757-9057

Youth Haven
5867 Whitaker Road
Naples, FL 33942
(813)262-3327

Georgia

State Agency

Department of Human Resources
Residential Child Care Section
878 Peachtree Street, N.E.
Atlanta, GA 30309
(404)894-5294

Private Agencies

Catholic Social Services, Inc., Adoption Program
680 West Peachtree Street, N.W.
Atlanta, GA 30308
(404)881-6571

Child Service and Family Counseling
1105 West Peachtree Street
Atlanta, GA 30309
(404)873-6916

Children's Service International
Suite 408, 3109 Maple Drive, N.E.
Atlanta, GA 30305
(404)261-6992

Family Counseling Center—CSRA, Inc.
718 Greene Street
Augusta, GA 30901
(404)722-8264

Friends of Children
5064 Roswell Road, Suite B-201
Atlanta, GA 30342
(404)256-2121

Illien Adoptions International
1254 Piedmont Avenue, N.E.
Atlanta, GA 30309
(404)872-6787

In His Care
4650 Flat Shoals Road
Decatur, GA 30034
(404)243-5020

Jewish Family Services, Inc.
1605 Peachtree Road, N.E.
Atlanta, GA 30309
(404)873-2277

Latter Day Saints Social Services Corporation
4832 North Royal Atlanta Drive
Tucker, GA 30084
(404)939-2121

Lutheran Ministries of Georgia
726 West Peachtree Street, N.E.
Atlanta, GA 30308
(404)875-0201

The New Beginning Adoptions and Counseling Agency
3564 Forrest Road
Columbus, GA 31907
(404)561-7954

Parent and Child Development Services, Inc.
535 East 54th Street
Savannah, GA 31405
(912)355-9471

Hawaii

State Agency

Department of Social Services and
Housing, Family, and Children's
Services
P.O. Box 339
Honolulu, HI 96809
(808)548-2211

Private Agencies

Catholic Social Services
250 South Vineyard Street
Honolulu, HI 96809
(808)537-6321

Child and Family Services
200 North Vineyard Boulevard
Honolulu, HI 96809
(808)521-2377

Hawaii International Children Placement
P.O. Box 263
Hawi, HI 96719
(808)889-5122

Idaho

State Agency

Department of Health and Welfare
State-House Mail
Boise, ID 83720–9990
(208)334-3554

Private Agencies

AID, Inc.
P.O. Box 742
Post Falls, ID 83854
(208)773-0526

America's Children, Inc.
P.O. Box 1000
Boise, ID 83701
(208)384-1006

Catholic Counseling Services of
Idaho, Inc.
2316 North Cole Road, Suite F
Boise, ID 83704
(208)322-1262

Franciscan Family Care Center
892 McKiney
Pocatello, ID 83201
(208)233-9383

Idaho Youth Ranch Adoption Services
1417 Main Street
Boise, ID 83702
(208)342-6375

Latter Day Saints Social Services
10740 Fairview, Suite 100
Boise, ID 83704
(208)376-0191

Latter Day Saints Social Services
920 Deon Drive, Suite D
Pontello, ID 83201
(208)323-7780

Latter Day Saints Social Services
1420 East 17th, Suite B
Idaho Falls, ID 83401
(208)522-0061

North Idaho Children's Home
P.O. Box 319
Lewiston, ID 83501
(208)743-9404

Illinois

State Agency

Adoption Information Center of Illinois
201 North Wells Street, Suite 1342
Chicago, IL 60606
(312)346-1516

Private Agencies

The Baby Fold
108 East Willow Street
Normal, IL 61761
(309)452-1170

Bensenville Home Society
331 South York Road
Bensenville, IL 60106
(312)766-5800

Bethany Home
220 11th Avenue
P.O. Box 638
Moline, IL 61265
(309)797-7700

Catholic Charities of Chicago
126 North DesPlaines
Chicago, IL 60606
(312)236-5172

Catholic Charities—Joliet Diocese
411 Scott Street
Joliet, IL 60432
(815)723-3405

Catholic Charities of Lake County
1 North Genessee, Room 203
Waukegan, IL 60085
(312)249-3500

Catholic Social Services—Diocese of
    Belleville
220 West Lincoln Street
Belleville, IL 62221
(618)277-9200

Catholic Social Services—Peoria
    Diocese
413 N.E. Monroe
P.O. Box 817
Peoria, IL 61652
(309)671-5700

Catholic Social Services—Rockford
    Diocese
556 West Galena Boulevard
Aurora, IL 60506
(312)892-4366

Catholic Social Services—Springfield
    Diocese
108 East Cook Street
Springfield, IL 62704
(217)523-4551

Central Baptist Family Services
201 North Wells
Chicago, IL 60606
(312)782-0874

Chicago Child Care Society
5467 South University Avenue
Chicago, IL 60615
(312)643-0452

Children's Home and Aid Society
730 North Main Street
Rockford, IL 61103
(815)962-1043

Children's Home and Aid Society of
    Illinois
1002 College Avenue
Alton, IL 62002
(618)462-2714

Children's Home and Aid Society of
    Illinois
307 West University Avenue
Champaign, IL 61820
(217)359-8815

Children's Home and Aid Society
Homes Now for Black Children
2151 West 95th Street
Chicago, IL 60643
(312)238-3203

Counseling and Family Service
1821 North Knoxville Avenue
Peoria, IL 61603
(309)685-5287

The Cradle Society
2049 Ridge Avenue
Evanston, IL 60204
(312)475-5800

Evangelical Child and Family Agency
1530 North Main
Wheaton, IL 60187
(312)653-6400

Family Care Services of Metropolitan
    Chicago
234 South Wabash Avenue
Chicago, IL 60604
(312)427-8790

Family Counseling Clinic, Inc.
19300 West Highway 120
Grayslake, IL 60030
(312)223-8107

Family Service of Decatur
151 East Decatur Street
Decatur, IL 62521
(217)429-5216

Family Service Center of Sangamon
    County
1308 South Seventh Street
Springfield, IL 62703
(217)528-8406

Jewish Children's Bureau of Chicago
1 South Franklin
Chicago, IL 60606
(312)346-6700

Latter Day Saints Social Services
1809 North Mill Street, Suite H
Naperville, IL 60540
(312)369-0486

Lutheran Child and Family Services
2408 Lebanon Avenue
Belleville, IL 62221
(618)234-8904

Lutheran Child and Family Services,
Chicago South Branch
6127 South University
Chicago, IL 60637
(312)753-0600

Lutheran Child and Family Services
7620 Madison Street
River Forest, IL 60305
(312)771-7180, (312)287-4848

Lutheran Child and Family Services
220 East Cook Street
Springfield, IL 62704
(217)544-4631

Lutheran Social Services of Illinois
4840 West Byron Street
Chicago, IL 60641
(312)282-7800

Lutheran Social Services of Illinois—
Galesburg
167 North Kellogg
Galesburg, IL 61401
(309)343-7681

Lutheran Social Services of Illinois—
Moline
3401-16th Street, Suite 1B
Moline, IL 61265
(309)797-2226

Lutheran Social Services of Illinois—
Nachusa
P.O. Box 100
Nachusa, IL 61057
(815)284-7797

Lutheran Social Services of Illinois—
Peoria
815 North Western Avenue
Peoria, IL 61604
(309)676-2151

Lutheran Social Services of Illinois—
Rockford
1311 Parkview Avenue
Rockford, IL 61107
(815)399-8832

St. Mary's Services
5725 North Kenmore Avenue
Chicago, IL 60660
(312)561-5288

Sunny Ridge Family Center
2 South 425 Orchard Road
Wheaton, IL 60187
(312)668-5117

Travelers Aid Society International
327 South LaSalle Street, Suite 1500
Chicago, IL 60604
(312)435-4500

Indiana

State Agency

Department of Public Welfare, Child
Welfare, Social Services Division
141 South Meridian Street, 6th Floor
Indianapolis, IN 46225
(317)232-5613

Private Agencies

Adoptions Unlimited, Inc.
218 South Third Street
Elkhart, IN 46514
(219)295-8985

Baptist Children's Home
354 West Street
Valparaiso, IN 46383
(219)462-4111

Bethany International Adoptions
9595 Whitley Drive, Suite 210
Indianapolis, IN 46240
(317)848-9518

Catholic Charities
3104 West 100 North
Kokomo, IN 46901
(317)457-1172

Catholic Charities Bureau
603 Court Building
Evansville, IN 47708
(812)423-5456

Catholic Family Services of Lake
County
5252 Hohman Avenue, Room 7
Hammond, IN 46320
(219)933-0696

Catholic Family Services of Michigan
City
524 C Franklin Square
Michigan City, IN 46360
(219)879-9312

Catholic Social Services
919 Fairfield Avenue
Fort Wayne, IN 46802
(219)422-7511

Catholic Social Services
120 South Taylor Street
South Bend, IN 46617
(219)234-3111

Children's Bureau of Indianapolis
426 English Foundation Building
615 North Alabama Street
Indianapolis, IN 46204
(317)634-6481

Chosen Children Adoption Services,
  Inc.
305 Bank Street
New Albany, IN 47150

Homes for Black Children
3131 East 38th Street
Indianapolis, IN 46218
(317)545-5281

Indiana Agency for LDS Social Services
5151 West 84th Street
Indianapolis, IN 46268
(317)875-0046

Indiana Agency of LDS Social Services
100 West Court Avenue, Suite 202
Jeffersonville, IN 47130
(812)288-9779

Jewish Family and Children's Services
1717 West 86th Street
Indianapolis, IN 46260
(317)872-6641

Lutheran Child and Family Services
1525 North Ritter Avenue
Indianapolis, IN 46219
(319)359-5467

Lutheran Family Services of Northwest Indiana
Southlake Professional Building
8127 Merrillville Road, Suite 1
Merrillville, IN 46410
(219)769-3521

Lutheran Social Services
330 Madison Avenue
Fort Wayne, IN 46802
(219)426-3347

St. Elizabeth's Home
2500 Churchman Avenue
Indianapolis, IN 46203
(317)787-3412

Shults-Lewis Children and Family
  Services
P.O. Box 471
Valparaiso, IN 46383
(219)462-0513

South-Central Christian Children's
  Home, Inc.
2420 Highway 62
Jeffersonville, IN 47130
(812)282-8248

Suemma Coleman Agency
1100 West 42nd Street
Indianapolis, IN 46208
(317)926-3891

The Villages, Inc.
3050 North Meridian Street
P.O. Box 55721
Indianapolis, IN 46220
(317)924-1474

The Villages, Inc.
P.O. Box 994
Bedford, IN 47421
(812)275-7539

Iowa

State Agency

Department of Human Services
Hoover State Office Building
Des Moines, IA 50319
(515)281-5658, (515)281-6074

Private Agencies

American Home Finding Association
217 East Fifth Street
Box 656
Ottumwa, IA 52501
(515)682-3449

Bethany Christian Services
322 Central Avenue
P.O. Box 143
Orange City, IA 51041
(712)737-4831

Bethany Home
122 East 17th Street
Davenport, IA 52803
(319)324-9169

Catholic Charities of Dubuque
1229 Mt. Loretta
P.O. Box 1309
Dubuque, IA 52001
(319)556-2580

Catholic Charities of Sioux City
1825 Jackson Street
Box 2025
Sioux City, IA 51104
(712)252-4545

Catholic Council for Social Concern,
    Des Moines Diocese
818 Fifth Avenue
P.O. Box 723
Des Moines, IA 50303
(515)244-3761

Family Resources, Inc.
115 West Sixth Street
Box 190
Davenport, IA 52803
(319)323-1853

Florence Crittenton Home
1105 28th Street
Sioux City, IA 51104
(712)255-4321

Hillcrest Family Services
1727 First Avenue S.E.
Cedar Rapids, IA 52402
(319)362-3149

Holt International Children's Services
105 North Jefferson
P.O. Box 399
Indianola, IA 50125
(515)961-3920

Iowa Children's and Family Services
1101 Walnut
Des Moines, IA 50309
(515)288-1981

Keys to Living
5300 North Park Place, N.E.
Cedar Rapids, IA 52402
(319)373-1301

Lutheran Family Service
230 Ninth Avenue, North
Fort Dodge, IA 50501
(515)573-3138

Lutheran Social Services of Iowa
3116 University
Des Moines, IA 50311
(515)277-4476

Tri-County Counseling Service
1514 Mulberry
Muscatine, IA 52761
(319)263-6943

Kansas

State Agency

Department of Social and Rehabilita-
    tion Services
2700 West 6th Street
Topeka, KS 66606
(913)296-3284

Private Agencies

The Adam Center
6000 High
Mission Hills, KS 66208
(816)444-4545

Adoption and Counseling Services, Inc.
5400 Lackmon Road
Shawnee, KS 66217
(816)753-4333

Catholic Charities
2546 20th Street
Great Bend, KS 67530
(316)792-1393

Catholic Charities
229 South 8th
Kansas City, KS 66102
(913)621-1804

Catholic Charities
Box 1366
Salina, KS 67401
(913)725-0208

Catholic Charities
306 Van Buren
Topeka, KS 66603
(913)233-6300

Catholic Social Services
P.O. Box 659
437 North Topeka
Wichita, KS 67202
(316)264-8344

Child Placement Services
15520 South Ridgeview
Olathe, KS 66062
(913)782-4678

Family and Children's Services of
Kansas City, Inc.
6300 West 95th
Overland Park, KS 66214
(913)642-4300

Family Life Services
115 East Chestnut Avenue
Arkansas City, KS 67005

Gentle Shepherd Placement Services,
Inc.
304 South Clairborne
Olathe, KS 66062
(913)764-3811

Highlands Child Placement Services,
Inc.
201 North 7th
Kansas City, KS 66101
(816)924-6565

Inserco, Inc.
445 North Dellrose
Wichita, KS 67207
(316)681-2129

Jewish Family and Children's Services,
Inc.
4550 West 90th Terrace
Shawnee Mission, KS 66207
(913)649-1056

Kansas Children's Service League
1503 Fulton Terrace
Garden City, KS 67846
(316)276-3232

Kansas Children's Service League
Black Adoptions Project
710 Minnesota
Kansas City, KS 66101
(913)621-2016

Kansas Children's Service League
2053 Kansas Avenue
Topeka, KS 66605
(913)232-0543

Latter Day Saints Social Services
7100 Hadley
P.O. Box 12392
Shawnee Mission, KS 66212
(816)461-5512

Lutheran Social Services—Spaulding
Midwest Inc.
1855 North Hillside
Wichita, KS 67214
(316)686-6645

Maude Carpenter Children's Home
1501 North Meridan
Wichita, KS 67203
(316)942-3221

Professional Consulting Services
112 South Main, Suite 125
El Dorado, KS 67042
(316)321-0392

The Villages, Inc.
P.O. Box 1695
Topeka, KS 66601
(913)273-5900

Kentucky

State Agency

Department for Social Services
Cabinet for Human Resources
275 East Main Street
Frankfort, KY 40621
(502)564-2134

Private Agencies

Catholic Charities Agency
2911 South 4th Street
Louisville, KY 40208
(502)637-9786

Catholic Social Services Bureau
3629 Church Street
Covington, KY 41011
(606)581-8974

Chosen Children Adoption Services,
Inc.
4010 Dupont Circle
Louisville, KY 40207
(502)897-0318

Holt International Children's Services
2911 South 4th Street
Louisville, KY 40208
(502)636-2291

Kentucky Baptist Board of Child Care
10801 Shelbyville Road
Middletown, KY 40243
(502)245-2101

Lutheran Social Services of Miami
Valley Inc.
7529 Sussex Drive
Florence, KY 41043
(606)525-8750

South Central Christian Family
Services
6105 Outer Loop
Louisville, KY 40219
(502)969-0977

Louisiana

State Agency

Department of Health and Human
Resources
Office of Human Development
State Office Adoption Program
333 Laurel Street, Room 704
Baton Rouge, LA 70801
(504)342-4040, (504)342-4028

Regional Agencies

Department of Health and Human
Resources, Office of Human
Development

900 Murray Street
P.O. Box 832
Alexandria, LA 71301
(318)487-5202

2843 Victoria Drive, Watkins Building
P.O. Box 15393
Baton Rouge, LA 70895
(504)925-4532

302 Jefferson Street
Lafayette, LA 70501
(318)264-5255

710 Ryan Street
P.O. Box 1807
Lake Charles, LA 70602
(318)491-2186

122 St. John Street, 4th Floor
State Office Building
Monroe, LA 71201
(318)261-3351

625 St. Charles Street
P.O. Box 30779
New Orleans, LA 70190
(504)568-7413

801 State Office Building
1525 Fairfield Avenue

Shreveport, LA 71130
(318)226-7100

1000A Marble Street
P.O. Box 797
Thibodaux, LA 70301
(504)447-7277

Private Agencies

Associated Catholic Charities Archdiocese of New Orleans, Inc.
2929 South Carrollton Avenue
New Orleans, LA 70118
(504)821-5390

Catholic Community Services, Dioceses
of Alexandria–Shreveport
2315 East Texas Avenue
P.O. Box 7417
Alexandria, LA 71306
(318)445-2401

Catholic Family Services, Diocese of
Alexandria–Shreveport
3109 Alexander Avenue
Shreveport, LA 71104
(318)869-3241

Catholic Social Services, Inc.
Catholic Community Life Office, Diocese of Baton Rouge
1800 South Acadian Thruway
P.O. Box 1668
Baton Rouge, LA 70821
(504)344-0427, (504)387-0561

Catholic Social Services, Diocese of
Houma–Thibodaux
1220 Aycock Street
P.O. Box 883
Houma, LA 70361
(504)876-0490

Catholic Social Services, Diocese of
Lafayette, Inc.
601 West St. Mary Boulevard
Lafayette, LA 70506
(318)235-5218

Children's Bureau of New Orleans
226 Carondelet Street, Suite 801
New Orleans, LA 70130
(504)525-2366

Jewish Children's Regional Service of
Jewish Children's Home
5342 St. Charles Avenue
P.O. Box 15225

New Orleans, LA 70175
(504)899-1595

Jewish Family and Children's Service,
Inc.
107 Camp Street, Suite 400
New Orleans, LA 70130
(504)524-8475

Louisiana Child Care and Placement
Services, Inc.
9080 Southwood Drive
Shreveport, LA 71118
(318)686-2243, (318)686-2274

Lutheran Social Services of the South,
Inc. (Home Office)
4430 Bundy Road
New Orleans, LA 70127
(504)241-1337

Sellers Baptist Home and Adoption
Center
2010 Peniston Street
New Orleans, LA 70115
(504)895-2088

Volunteers of America
3720 Prytania Street
New Orleans, LA 70115
(504)891-3908

Volunteers of America
354 Jordan Street
Shreveport, LA 71101
(318)221-2669

Maine

State Agency

Department of Human Services
Bureau of Social Services
State House, Station 11
Augusta, ME 04333
(207)289-2971

Department of Human Services Regional Offices

Capitol Shopping Center
Augusta, ME 04333
(207)289-3271

396 Griffin Road
Bangor, ME 04401
(207)947-0511

41 Washburn Street
Caribou, ME 04736
(207)498-8151

200 Main Street
Lewiston, ME 04240
(207)783-9151

509 Forest Avenue
Portland, ME 04101
(207)774-4581

Private Agencies

Coastal Adoption Placement Service
P.O. Box 85
Addison, ME 04606
(207)497-2441

Community Counseling Center
622 Congress Street
P.O. Box 4016
Portland, ME 04101
(207)774-5727

Good Samaritan Agency
160 Broadway
P.O. Box 319
Bangor, ME 04401
(207)942-7211

Growing-Thru-Adoption
P.O. Box 7082
Lewiston, ME 04240
(207)786-2597

International Christian Adoption
Agency
60 West River Road
Waterville, ME 04901
(207)872-2156

Maine Adoption Placement Service
P.O. Box 772
Houlton, ME 04730
(207)532-9358

Maine Children's Home for Little Wan-
derers
34 Gilman Street
Waterville, ME 04901
(207)873-4253

St. Andre's Home, Inc.
283 Elm Street
Biddeford, ME 04005
(207)282-3351

Maryland

State Agency

Department of Human Resources
Social Services Administration
300 West Preston Street
Baltimore, MD 21201
(301)576-5313

Private Agencies

Adoption and Unmarried Parents
1302 Park Avenue
Baltimore, MD 21217

Associated Catholic Charities
320 Cathedral Street
Baltimore, MD 21201
(301)547-5498

Baltimore Family Life Center
101 West Read Street
Baltimore, MD 21201
(301)837-5755

Bethany Christian Services
114-B Annapolis Street
Annapolis, MD 21401
(301)263-7703

Board of Child Care
3300 Gaither Road
Baltimore, MD 21207
(301)922-2100

Boys and Girls Homes of Montgomery
County, Inc.
Child Placement Agency
9601 Colesville Road
Silver Spring, MD 20901
(301)598-8444

Family and Children's Society of
Baltimore, Inc.
204 West Lanvale Street
Baltimore, MD 21217
(301)669-9000

Family and Children's Society Group
Home—Jane Egenton House
708 Park Avenue
Baltimore, MD 21201
(301)699-9006

Jewish Family and Children's Service
5750 Park Heights Avenue

Baltimore, MD 21215
(301)466-9200

Jewish Social Service Agency
6123 Montrose Road
Rockville, MD 20852
(301)881-3700

Latter Day Saints Social Services—
East Coast
198 Thomas Johnson Drive, Suite 13
Frederick, MD 21701
(301)428-4988

Lutheran Social Services of Maryland,
Inc.
5000 York Road
Baltimore, MD 21212
(301)532-9600

Martin Pollak Project
1214 West Street
Annapolis, MD 21401
(301)269-1966

Maryland Children's and Family
Services, Inc. (Administrative
Offices)
303 West Chesapeake Avenue
Towson, MD 21204
(301)825-3700

Woodbourne Center Adolescent Foster
Care and Child Placement Services
1301 Woodbourne Avenue
Baltimore, MD 21239
(301)433-1000

Youth Resources Center, Inc.
Starting Over—Independent Living,
Skills Program
6201 Belcrest Road
Hyattsville, MD 20782
(301)779-1257, (301)779-1946

Massachusetts

State Agency

Department of Social Services
150 Causeway Street
Boston, MA 02114
(617)727-0900

Private Agencies

Alliance for Children, Inc.
P.O. Box 369

Needham Heights, MA 02194
(617)449-1277

Berkshire Center for Families and
Children
472 West Street
Pittsfield, MA 01201
(413)448-8281

Boston Adoption Bureau, Inc.
14 Beacon Street, Suite 620
Boston, MA 02108
(617)277-1336

Boston Children's Services Association
867 Boylston Street
Boston, MA 02216
(617)267-3700

Cambridge Adoption and Counseling
Association, Inc.
P.O. Box 190
Cambridge, MA 02142
(617)491-6245

Cambridge Family and Children's
Service
99 Bishop Allen Drive
Cambridge, MA 02139
(617)876-4210

Catholic Charitable Bureau
99 Bishop Allen Drive
Cambridge, MA 02139
(617)547-9566

Catholic Charities
430 North Canal Street
Lawrence, MA 01840
(617)685-5930

Catholic Charities
70 Lawrence Street
Lowell, MA 01852
(617)452-1421

Catholic Charities
79 Elm Street
Southbridge, MA 01550
(617)765-5936

Catholic Charities
16 Main Street
Uxbridge, MA 01569
(617)278-2424

Catholic Charities of Cambridge and
Somerville
Box 457
270 Washington Street

Somerville, MA 02143
(617)625-1920

Catholic Charities Center
686 North Main Street
Brockton, MA 02401
(617)587-0815

Catholic Charities Family and Children's Services
15 Ripley Street
Worcester, MA 01610
(617)798-0191

Catholic Family Services
55 Lynn Shore Drive
Lynn, MA 01902
(617)593-2312

Catholic Social Services
P.O. Box M, South Station
Fall River, MA 02724
(617)674-4681

Children's Aid and Family Services
47 Holt Street
Fitchburg, MA 01420
(617)345-4147

Children's Aid and Family Services
8 Trumbull Road
Northampton, MA 01060
(413)584-5690

Concord Family Services
Community Agencies Building
Old Road to 9 Acre Corner
Concord, MA 01742
(617)369-4909, (617)259-8556

DARE Family Services
3 Monument Square
Beverly, MA 01915
(617)927-1674

DARE, Inc.
186A South Street
Boston, MA 02111
(617)423-3737

DARE, Inc.
189 Deane Street
Taunton, MA 02780
(617)824-6606

Downey Side Homes
999 Liberty Street
Springfield, MA 01104
(413)781-2123

ECHO
29 Devonshire Road
P.O. Box 14222
Cheshire, MA 01228
(413)743-9240, (413)743-9241

Family and Children's Services
111 North Common Street
Lynn, MA 01902
(617)598-5517

Family and Children's Services of
    Catholic Charities
53 Highland Avenue
Fitchburg, MA 01420
(617)422-6918

Family Services Association
430 North Canal Street
Lawrence, MA 01840
(617)683-9505

Florence Crittenton League
119 Hall Street
Lowell, MA 01854
(617)452-9671

Hermandad of Guadeloupe Adoption
    Services, Inc.
185 Meadow Lane
West Barnstable, MA 02668
(617)362-3142

International Adoptions, Inc.
218 Walnut Street
Newton, MA 02160
(617)965-2320

Italian Home for Children
1125 Centre Street
Jamaica Plain, MA 02130
(617)524-3116

Jewish Family and Children's Service
31 New Chardon Street
Boston, MA 02114
(617)227-6641

Jewish Family Service
184 Mill Street
Springfield, MA 01108
(413)737-2601

Jewish Family Services
646 Salisbury Street
Worcester, MA 01609
(617)755-3101

Jewish Family Services of Greater
    Framingham

873 Concord Street
Framingham, MA 01701
(617)879-3953

Jewish Family Services of the North
    Shore
564 Loring Avenue
Salem, MA 01970
(617)745-9760

La Alianza Hispana, Inc.
409 Dudley Street
Roxbury, MA 02119
(617)427-7175

Latter Day Saints Social Services, Inc.
150 Brown Street
Weston, MA 02193
(603)889-0148 (New Hampshire)

Love the Children of Massachusetts
P.O. Box 334
Cambridge, MA 02238
(617)576-2115

Nazareth Child Care Center
420 Pond Street
Jamaica Plain, MA 02130
(617)522-4040

New Bedford Child and Family
    Services
141 Page Street
New Bedford, MA 02740
(617)996-8572

New England Home for Little
    Wanderers
161 South Huntington Avenue
Boston, MA 02130
(617)232-8600

North Shore Catholic Charities
3 Margin Street
Peabody, MA 01960
(617)532-3600

Our Lady of Providence Children's
    Center
2112 Riverdale Road
West Springfield, MA 01089
(413)788-7366

Project Impact
25 West Street
Boston, MA 02111
(617)451-1472

Protestant Social Service Bu-
    reau

776 Hancock Street
Wollaston, MA 02170
(617)773-6203

Roxbury Children's Services,
Inc.
22 Elm Hill Avenue
Dorchester, MA 02121
(617)445-6655

Southeastern Adoption Services,
Inc.
P.O. Box 356
Marion, MA 02738
(617)748-2979

Springfield Home for Friendless
Women and Children, Inc.
Children's Study Home
44 Sherman Street
Springfield, MA 01109
(413)739-5626

Western Massachusetts Office of
Cambridge Adoption and Counseling
Associates
145 Lake Buel Road
Framingham, MA 01230
(413)528-2749
Mail: P.O. Box 190
Cambridge, MA 02142

Worcester Children's Friend Society
21 Cedar Street
Worcester, MA 01609
(617)753-5425

World Adoptions Services, Inc.
161 Auburn Street
Newton, MA 02166
(617)332-3307

Michigan

State Agency

Department of Social Services
P.O. Box 30037
Lansing, MI 48909
(517)373-8383

Private Agencies

The Adoption Cradle
2 West Michigan Mall

Battle Creek, MI 49016
(616)963-0794

Adventist Adoption and Family
125 College, Box C
Berrien Springs, MI 49103
(616)473-4541

Americans for International Aid and
Adoptions
877 South Adams Street
Birmingham, MI 48011
(313)645-2211

Baptist Family Services
214 Mill Street
St. Louis, MI 48880
(517)681-2171

Bethany Christian Service
901 Eastern N.E.
Grand Rapids, MI 49503
(616)459-6273

Catholic Family Services
1819 Gull Road
Kalamazoo, MI 49001
(616)381-9800

Catholic Family Service of Bay City
1006 South Wenona Avenue
Bay City, MI 48706
(517)892-2504

Catholic Family Services of Midland
4809 Jefferson Avenue
Midland, MI 48640
(517)631-4711

Catholic Family Services of Saginaw
710 North Michigan
Saginaw, MI 48602
(517)753-8446

Catholic Social Services
347 Rock Street
Marquette, MI 49855
(906)228-8630

Catholic Social Services, Inc.
300 North Washington
Lansing, MI 46933
(517)372-4020

Catholic Social Services of the Diocese
of Muskegon
313 West Webster
Muskegon, MI 49440
(616)726-4735

Catholic Social Services of Flint
202 East Boulevard
Flint, MI 48503
(313)234-1681

Catholic Social Services of Kent
  County
300 Commerce Building
Grand Rapids, MI 49502
(616)456-1443

Catholic Social Services of Macomb
  County
235 South Gratiot
Mount Clemens, MI 48043
(313)468-2616

Catholic Social Services of Monroe
  County
16 East Fifth
Monroe, MI 48161
(313)242-3800

Catholic Social Services of Oakland
29625 Inkster Road
Farmington Hill, MI 48024
(313)851-7180

Catholic Social Services of St. Clair
2601 Thirteenth
Port Huron, MI 48060
(313)985-8162

Catholic Social Services of Washtenaw
117 North Division
Ann Arbor, MI 48108
(313)662-4534

Catholic Social Services of Wayne
  County
9851 Hamilton
Detroit, MI 48202
(313)883-2100

Child and Family Services
904 Sixth Street
Bay City, MI 48706
(517)895-5932

Child and Family Services
205 East Boulevard Drive
Flint, MI 48503
(313)234-3671

Child and Family Services
12451 James Street
Holland, MI 49423
(616)399-9166

Child and Family Services
3075 East Grand River
Howell, MI 48843
(517)546-7530

Child and Family Services
109 Harlow, Drawer A
Marquette, MI 49855
(906)226-2516

Child and Family Services
Box 763
1101 Military
Port Huron, MI 48060
(313)984-2647

Child and Family Services of Michigan
P.O. Box 516
Alpena, MI 49707
(517)356-4567

Child and Family Services of Michigan
9880 East Grand River
Brighton, MI 48116
(313)227-1191

Child and Family Services of Michigan
210 Beaumont Place
Traverse City, MI 49684
(616)946-8975

Child and Family Services of Muskegon County
Michigan Building, 2nd Floor
Muskegon, MI 49440
(616)726-3582

Child and Family Services of Saginaw
  County
1226 North Michigan
Saginaw, MI 48602
(517)753-8491

Child and Family Services of St. Joseph
2000 South State
St. Joseph, MI 49085
(616)983-5545

Child and Family Services of Washtenaw
2301 Platt Road
Ann Arbor, MI 48108
(313)971-6528

Children and Youth Services
801 West Baltimore
Detroit, MI 48202
(313)876-6010

Children's Aid and Family Services of
  Macomb County
57 Church Street
Mount Clemens, MI 48043
(313)468-2656

Children's Aid Society
7700 Second Avenue
Detroit, MI 48202
(313)875-0020

Christian Family Services of Oakland
17105 West 12 Mile Road
Southfield, MI 48076
(313)557-8390

Community, Family and Children's
  Services
202 West Mitchell
Gaylord, MI 49735
(517)732-5313

Community Family Child Services
614 West Old Field Road
Alpena, MI 49707
(517)354-2050

Community Family Services
1000 Hastings Street
Traverse City, MI 49684
(616)947-8110

D.A. Blodgett Homes for Children
805 Leonard N.E.
Grand Rapids, MI 49503
(616)451-2021

Ennis and Associate Counseling
P.O. Box 3098
Flint, MI 48502
(313)235-0683

Family and Child Services
213 Toledo Street
Adrian, MI 49221
(517)265-5352

Family and Child Services
182 West Van Buren Street
Battle Creek, MI 49014
(616)965-3247

Family and Child Services of the
  Capitol Area, Inc.
300 North Washington
Lansing, MI 48933
(517)484-4455

Family and Children Services
50 Wayne Street

Pontiac, MI 48050
(313)332-8352

Family and Children's Services of
  Midland
P.O. Box 2086
Midland, MI 48640
(517)631-5390

Family and Children of the Kalamazoo
  Area
1608 Lake Street
Kalamazoo, MI 49001
(616)344-0202

Family Service and Child Aid of
  Jackson County
906 West Monroe
Box 1468
Jackson, MI 49204
(517)782-8191

Foreign Adoption Consultation
1223 Hillcrest Avenue
Kalamazoo, MI 49008
(616)381-9234

Homes for Black Children
2340 Calvert
Detroit, MI 48206
(313)869-2316

Jewish Family Services
24123 Greenfield
Southfield, MI 48075
(313)559-1500

Latter Day Saints Social Services
37634 Enterprise Court
Farmington Hill, MI 48018
(313)553-0902

Lutheran Adoption Services
8131 East Jefferson
Detroit, MI 48214
(313)864-4200

Methodist Child Placing
26645 West 6 Mile
Detroit, MI 48240
(313)531-4060

Spaulding for Children
3660 Waltrous
Chelsea, MI 48118
(313)475-2500

Teen Ranch
2861 Gurdon T. Wolfe

Marlette, MI 48453
(517)635-7511

Whaley Children's Center
1201 North Grand Traverse
Flint, MI 48503
(313)234-3603

Minnesota

State Agency

Department of Public Welfare
Centennial Office Building
St. Paul, MN 55155
(612)296-3740

Private Agencies

Bethany Christian Services
901 Eastern Avenue, N.E.
Grand Rapids, MN 49503
(616)459-6273

Caritas Family Services
Suite 100, 305 7th Avenue N.
St. Cloud, MN 56301
(612)252-4121

Catholic Charities of the Archdiocese
of Minneapolis–St. Paul (Minneapolis Area Office)
404 South 8th Street
Minneapolis, MN 55404
(612)340-7500

St. Paul Area Office:
215 Old 6th Street
St. Paul, MN 55102
(612)222-3001

Catholic Social Service Diocese of Winona, Inc.
P.O. Box 829
Winona, MN 55987
(507)454-2270

Catholic Social Service Association
P.O. Box 610
1200 Memorial Drive
Crookston, MN 56716
(218)281-4224

Children's Home Society of Minnesota
2230 Como Avenue
St. Paul, MN 55108
(612)646-6393

Crossroads, Inc.
7703 Normandale Road, 100B
Edina, MN 55435
(612)831-5707

Hennepin County Bureau of Social
Services
12601 Ridgedale Drive
Minnetonka, MN 55343
(612)546-0533

Hope International Family Services,
Inc.
421 South Main Street
Stillwater, MN 55082
(612)439-2446

Jewish Family Service of St. Paul
1546 St. Clair Avenue
St. Paul, MN 55105
(612)698-0767

The Lutheran Home
611 West Main Street
Belle Plain, MN 56011
(612)873-2215

Lutheran Social Service of Minnesota
2414 Park Avenue
Minneapolis, MN 55404
(612)871-0221

New Life Homes and Family Services
3361 Republic Avenue
St. Louis Park, MN 55426
(612)920-8117

Ramsey County Community Human
Services
160 East Kellogg Boulevard
St. Paul, MN 55101
(218)298-5361

St. Louis County Social Service Department
422 West 3rd Street
Duluth, MN 55806
(218)727-8231

Wilde Foundation Children's Placement Service
919 Lafond
St. Paul, MN 55101
(612)642-4008

Mississippi

State Agency

Department of Public Welfare
P.O. Box 352
515 East Amite Street
Jackson, MS 39205
(601)354-0341

Private Agencies

Bethany Christian Services
3000 Old Canton Road
Room 360, Woodland Hills Building
Jackson, MS 39216
(601)366-4282

Catholic Charities
748 North President Street
P.O. Box 2248
Jackson, MS 39205
(601)355-8634

Catholic Social and Community
  Services
P.O. Box 1457
Biloxi, MS 39533
(601)374-8316

Mississippi Children's Home Society
P.O. Box 1078
1801 North West Street
Jackson, MS 39205
(601)352-7784

Missouri

State Agency

Department of Social Services
Division of Family Services
Broadway State Office Building,
  P.O. Box 88
Jefferson City, MO 65103
(314)751-2981

Private Agencies

APLACE
246 Grand Avenue
St. Louis, MO 63122
(314)965-5600

Bethany Christian Services
7750 Clayton Road

St. Louis, MO 63117
(314)644-3535

Catholic Charities
1112 Broadway
Kansas City, MO 64111
(816)221-4377

Child Placement Services
201 West Lexington, Suite 300
Independence, MO 64050
(816)461-3488

Christian Family Services
8812 Manchester Boulevard
St. Louis, MO 63144
(314)968-2216

Family Adoption and Counseling
  Services
221-A South Kirkwood Road, Office C
St. Louis, MO 63122
(314)822-7693, (314)772-1398

Family and Children's Service of
  Kansas City, Inc.
3515 Broadway
Kansas City, MO 64111
(816)753-5280

Highlands Child Placement Service
5506 Cambridge Avenue
Kansas City, MO 64131
(816)924-6565

Jewish Family and Children Services
1115 East 65th Street
Kansas City, MO 64131
(816)649-1056

Latter Day Saints
517 West Walnut
Independence, MO 64050
(816)461-5512

Lutheran Family and Children's Services
4625 Lindell, Suite 501
St. Louis, MO 63108
(314)739-2121

Worldwide Love for Children
1031 East Battlefield, Suite 219
Springfield, MO 65807
(417)881-1044

Montana

State Agency

Department of Social and Rehabilitation Services
P.O. Box 4210
Helena, MT 59604
(406)444-3865

Private Agencies

Catholic Social Services
530 North Ewing
Box 907
Helena, MT 59601
(406)442-4130

Lutheran Social Services of Montana
P.O. Box 1345
Great Falls, MT 59403
(406)761-4341

Montana Children's Home and Hospital
840 Helena Avenue
Helena, MT 59601
(406)442-1980

Montana Intercountry Adoption, Inc.
26 West Babock
Bozeman, MT 59715
(406)587-5101

Nebraska

State Agency

Department of Social Services
Box 95026
Lincoln, NE 68509-5026
(402)471-3121

Private Agencies

Catholic Social Services Bureau, Inc.
303 West 4th Street
Hastings, NE 68901
(402)423-6555
Mail: P.O. Box 2723
Lincoln, NE 68502

Child Saving Institute
115 South 46th Street
Omaha, NE 68132
(402)553-6000

Holt International Children's Services
P.O. Box 12153
2582 Redick
Omaha, NE 68112
(402)457-6323

Jewish Family Service
333 South 132 Street
Omaha, NE 68154
(402)334-8200

Lutheran Family and Social Services
120 South 24th Street
Omaha, NE 68102
(402)342-7007

Nebraska Children's Home Society
3549 Fontenelle Boulevard
Omaha, NE 68104
(402)451-0787

United Catholic Social Services
2132 South 42nd Street
Omaha, NE 68105
(402)558-3533
Mail: P.O. Box 6236
Omaha, NE 68106

Nevada

State Agency

State Welfare Division
Department of Human Resources
251 Jeanell Drive
Carson City, NV 89710
(702)885-4771

Private Agencies

Catholic Community Services
P.O. Box 5415
Reno, NV 89503
(702)322-7073

Catholic Community Services
P.O. Box 1926
Las Vegas, NV 89125
(702)385-2662

Latter Day Saints Social Services
1966 Santa Paula Drive
Las Vegas, NV 89015
(702)735-1072

Latter Day Saints Social Services
507 Casazza Drive, Suite C
Reno, NV 89502
(702)323-7376

New Hampshire

State Agency

Department of Health and Welfare
Division for Children and Youth
Hazen Drive
Concord, NH 03301
(603)271-4451

Private Agencies

Adoptive Families for Children
26 Fairview Street
Keene, NH 03431
(603)357-4456

Child and Family Services of New
  Hampshire
99 Hanover Street
P.O. Box 448
Manchester, NH 03105
(603)668-1020

Latter Day Saints Social Services
New Hampshire Nashua
  Agency
131 Route 101A
Amherst Plaza, Suite 204
Amherst, NH 03031
(603)889-0148

New Hampshire Catholic Charities
215 Myrtle Street
P.O. Box 686
Manchester, NH 03105
(603)669-3030

New Jersey

State Agency

Division of Youth and Family Services,
  Operations Support
1 South Montgomery Street
Trenton, NJ 08625
(609)292-9642

Adoption Resource Center Regional Offices

RD #2, Box 37-A
392 North White Horse Pike
Hammonton, NJ 08037
(609)567-0010

Adoption Resource Center, Central Regional Office
719 Alexander Road
Princeton, NJ 08540
(609)452-7611

1180 Raymond Boulevard, 17th Floor
Newark, NJ 07102
(201)648-4550

100 Hamilton Plaza
Paterson, NJ 07505
(201)977-4100

Private Agencies

Adoption Placement Services
RD #2
375 Fergeson Avenue
Franklin, NJ 08322
(609)728-8744

Associated Catholic Charities of the
  Archdiocese of Newark
Agency of Catholic Community
  Services
17 Mulberry Street
Newark, NJ 07102
(201)596-3958

Bethany Christian Services, Branch
  Office of Bethany
475 High Mountain Road
North Haledon, NJ 07508
(201)427-2566

Better Living Services, Inc.
116 High Street
Hackettstown, NJ 07840
(201)850-0947

Catholic Charities, Diocese of
  Metuchen
288 Rues Lane
East Brunswick, NJ 08816
(201)257-6100

Catholic Family and Community Services
476-17th Avenue
Paterson, NJ 07504
(201)523-2666

Catholic Social Services of the Diocese
of Camden, Inc.
1845 Haddon Avenue
Camden, NJ 08103
(609)541-2100

Catholic Welfare Bureau, Diocese of
Trenton
47 North Clinton Avenue
P.O. Box 1423
Trenton, NJ 08607
(609)394-5181

Children's Aid and Adoption Society of
New Jersey
360 Larch Avenue
Bogota, NJ 07603
(201)487-2022

Children's Home Society of New
Jersey
929 Parkside Avenue
Trenton, NJ 08618
(609)695-6274

Christian Home for Children
1512 Palisade Avenue
Box 228
Fort Lee, NJ 07024
(201)944-0023

Family and Children's Counseling and
Testing Center
40 North Avenue
P.O. Box 314
Elizabeth, NJ 07207
(201)352-7474

Family and Children's Services, Inc.,
of Monmouth County
191 Bath Avenue
Long Branch, NJ 07740
(201)222-9100

Holt International Children's Services,
Holt Adoption Program (Branch Office of Holt, Oregon)
413 Hillcrest Avenue
P.O. Box 7608
West Trenton, NJ 08628
(609)882-4972

Homestudies, Inc.
695 Larch Avenue
Teaneck, NJ 07666
(201)836-2874

Lutheran Social Services of New Jersey
189 South Broad Street

P.O. Box 30
Trenton, NJ 08601
(609)393-3440

Spaulding for Children
36 Prospect Street
Westfield, NJ 07090
(201)233-2282

United Family and Children's Society
305 West Seventh Street
Plainfield, NJ 07060
(201)755-4848

New Mexico

State Agency

Department of Human Services, Adoption Services
PERA Building, P.O. Box 2348
Santa Fe, NM 87503
(505)827-4058

Private Agencies

Catholic Social Services, Inc.
223 Cathedral Place
Santa Fe, NM 87501
(505)982-0441

Chaparrel Home and Adoption Services
4401 Lomas, N.E., Suite C
Albuquerque, NM 87110
(505)266-5837

Families for Children (A Division of
New Mexico Boys' Ranch)
1024 Eubank, N.E.
Albuquerque, NM 87112
(505)292-5445

Latter Day Saints Social Services
7800 Marble, N.E., Suite One
Albuquerque, NM 87110
(505)262-2639

New Mexico Christian Children's
Home
West Star Route, Box 48
Portales, NM 88130
(505)356-8414

Rainbow House International
RFD 1, Box 2340-E
Belen, NM 87002
(505)864-3325

New York

State Agency

Department of Social Services
40 North Pearl Street
Albany, NY 12243
(518)473-1509

Private Agencies

Abbott House
100 North Broadway
Irvington, NY 10533
(914)591-7300

Adoption and Counseling Services, Inc.
One Fayette Park
Syracuse, NY 13202
(315)471-0109

Angel Guardian Home
6301 12th Avenue
Brooklyn, NY 11219
(718)232-1500

Astor Home for Children
36 Mill Street
Rhinebeck, NY 12572
(914)876-4081

Brooklyn Home for Children
67-35 112th Street
Forest Hills, NY 11375
(718)263-0740

Brookwood Child Care
363 Adelphi Street
Brooklyn, NY 11238
(718)783-2610

Cardinal Hayes Home
North Avenue
Millbrook, NY 12545
(914)677-6363

Cardinal McCloskey School and Home
2 Holland Avenue
White Plains, NY 10603
(914)997-8000

Catholic Charities of Buffalo
525 Washington Street
Buffalo, NY 14203
(716)856-4494

Catholic Charities of Malone
105 West Main Street
Box 385

Malone, NY 12953
(518)483-1460

Catholic Charities of Ogdensburg
716 Carolina Street
Box 296
Ogdensburg, NY 13669-0296
(315)393-2660

Catholic Charities of Ogdensburg/
   Plattsburgh
151 South Catherine Street
Plattsburgh, NY 12901
(518)561-0470

Catholic Charities of Oswego
26 West Bridge Street
Fulton, NY 13126
(315)343-9540

Catholic Charities of Syracuse, Family
   Division
1654 West Onondaga Street
Syracuse, NY 13204
(315)424-1871

Catholic Charities of Syracuse/Rome
227 West Dominick Street
Rome, NY 13440
(315)337-8600

Catholic Charities of Watertown
380 Arlington Street
Watertown, NY 13601
(315)788-4330

Catholic Family Center
50 Chestnut Street
Rochester, NY 14604
(716)546-7220

Catholic Guardian Society of Brooklyn
191 Joralemon Street
Brooklyn, NY 11201
(718)596-5500

Catholic Guardian Society of N.Y.
1011 First Avenue
New York, NY 10022
(212)371-1000, Ext. 2337

Catholic Home Bureau
1011 First Avenue
New York, NY 10022
(212)371-1000, Ext. 2240

Catholic Social Services of Broome
   County
232 Main Street

Binghamton, NY 13905
(607)729-9166

Catholic Social Services of Utica/Syracuse
1408 Genesee Street
Utica, NY 13502
(315)724-2158

Cayuga Counseling Service
46 South Street
Auburn, NY 13021
(315)253-9795

Child and Family Services
678 West Onondaga Street
Syracuse, NY 13204
(315)474-4291

Child and Family Services of Erie
330 Delaware Avenue
Buffalo, NY 14202
(716)842-2750

Children's Aid Society
150 East 45th Street
New York, NY 10017
(212)949-4854

Children's Home of Kingston
26 Grove Street
Kingston, NY 12401
(914)331-1448

Children's Home of Poughkeepsie
91 Fulton Street
Poughkeepsie, NY 12601
(914)452-1420

Children's Village
Dobbs Ferry, NY 10522
(914)693-0600

Community Maternity Services
29 North Main Avenue
Albany, NY 12203
(518)438-2322

Edwin Gould Services for Children
41 East 11th Street
New York, NY 10003
(212)598-0050

Episcopal Mission Society
1331 Franklin Avenue
Bronx, NY 10456
(212)589-1435, (212)589-1434

Evangelical Family Services
201 South Main Street

North Syracuse, NY 13212
(315)458-1415

Family and Children's Services
204 North Cayuga Street
Ithaca, NY 14850
(315)458-1415

Family and Children's Services of
Albany
12 South Lake Avenue
Albany, NY 12202
(518)462-6531

Family and Children's Service of
Broome County
257 Main Street
Binghamton, NY 13905
(607)729-6206

Family and Children's Service of
Ithaca
204 North Cayuga Street
Ithaca, NY 14850
(607)273-7494

Family and Children's Services of
Schenectady
246 Union Street
Schenectady, NY 12305
(518)393-1369

Family Service of Utica
107 Genesee Street
Utica, NY 13501
(315)735-2236

Family Services of Westchester, Adoption and Children's Service Division
470 Mamaroneck Avenue
White Plains, NY 10605
(914)948-9004

Graham-Windham
One Park Avenue
New York, NY 10016
(212)889-5600

Green Chimneys
Putnam Lake Road
Brewster, NY 10509
(212)892-6810

Greer-Woodycrest Services
Hope Farm
Millbrook, NY 12545
(914)677-5041

Harlem Dowling Children's Services
2090 Seventh Avenue

New York, NY 10027
(212)749-3656

Hillside-Northhaven (Hillside Children's Center)
150 Floverton Street
Rochester, NY 14610
(716)482-3992

Infants Home of Brooklyn
1358 56th Street
Brooklyn, NY 11219
(718)851-8000

Jewish Board of Family and Children
Services
130 West 57th Street
New York, NY 10019
(212)851-6570

Jewish Child Care Association
345 Madison Avenue
New York, NY 10017
(212)490-9160

Jewish Family Services of Erie County
775 Main Street
Buffalo, NY 14203
(716)853-9956

Kennedy Child Study Center
151 East 67th Street
New York, NY 10021
(212)988-9500

Lakeside School
South Main Street
Spring Valley, NY 10977
(914)356-7000

Latter Day Saints Social Services of
New York
105 Main Street
Fishkill, NY 12524
(914)896-8266

Leake and Watts Children's Home
463 Hawthorne Avenue
Yonkers, NY 10705
(914)963-5220

Little Flower Children's Services
200 Montague Street
Brooklyn, NY 11201
(718)858-1212

Louise Wise Services
12 East 94th Street
New York, NY 10028
(212)431-7470

Lutheran Community Services
33 Worth Street
New York, NY 10013
(212)431-7470

Lutheran Service Society of New York
2500 Kensington Avenue
Buffalo, NY 14226
(716)839-3391

Malone Catholic Charities
105 West Main Street
Malone, NY 19253
(518)483-1460

McMahon Services for Children
225 East 45th Street
New York, NY 10017
(212)986-3418

Mercy Home for Children
273 Willoughby Street
Brooklyn, NY 11205
(718)622-5842

Mishon B'nai Yisrael
4105 16th Avenue
Brooklyn, NY 11204
(718)851-6570

Mission of the Immaculate Virgin
6581 Highland Boulevard
Staten Island, NY 10309
(718)984-1500

New York Foundling Hospital
1175 Third Avenue
New York, NY 10021
(212)472-2233

New York Spaulding for Children
22 West 27th Street, 10th Floor
New York, NY 10001
(212)696-9560

Ohel Children's Home
4423 16th Avenue
Brooklyn, NY 11204
(718)851-6300

Our Lady of Victory
790 Ridge Road
Lackawanna, NY 14218
(716)827-9611

Parsons Child and Family Center
845 Central Avenue
Albany, NY 12206
(518)438-4571

Pius XXII Youth/Family Services
369 East 149th Street
New York, NY 10455
(212)993-3650

Praca Child Care
853 Broadway
New York, NY 10003
(212)673-7320

St. Cabrini Home
West Park, NY 12493
(914)384-6500

St. Christopher's Home of Brooklyn
50 Court Street
Brooklyn, NY 11201
(718)855-0330

St. Christopher's Home of Glen Cove
12 Pearsall Avenue
Glen Cove, NY 11542
(516)759-1844

St. Christopher's Home of Jamaica
90-04 161st Street
Jamaica, NY 11432
(718)526-7533

St. Christopher's/Jennie Clarkson
71 South Broadway
Dobbs Ferry, NY 10522
(914)693-3030

St. Dominic's
535 East 138th Street
Bronx, NY 10454
(212)993-5765

St. John's Residence for Boys
150-111 Street
Rockaway, NY 11694
(212)945-2800

St. Joseph's Children's Services
345 Adams Street
Brooklyn, NY 11201
(718)858-8700

St. Mary's of the Angels
Convent Road
Syosset, NY 11791
(516)921-0808

St. Vincent's Hall
66 Boerum Place
P.O. Box 174
Brooklyn, NY 11202
(718)522-3700

Salvation Army Foster Home Services
233 East 17th Street
New York, NY 10003
(212)505-4200

Sheltering Arms Children's Services
122 East 29th Street
New York, NY 10016
(212)679-4242

Society for Seaman's Children
26 Bay Street
Staten Island, NY 10301
(718)447-8338

Spence-Chapin Adoption Services
6 East 94th Street
New York, NY 10028
(212)369-0300

Talbot-Perkins Children's Services
116 West 32nd Street, 12th Floor
New York, NY 10001
(212)736-2510

Wyndham Lawn Children's Home
6395 Old Niagara Road
Lockport, NY 14094
(716)433-4487

North Carolina

State Agency

Department of Human Resources,
  Division of Social Services
325 North Salisbury Street
Raleigh, NC 27611
(919)733-3055

Private Agencies

Bethany Christian Services
25 Reed Street
P.O. Box 15436
Asheville, NC 28813-0436
(704)274-7146

Catholic Social Ministries
400 Oberlin Road, Suite 350
Raleigh, NC 27605
(919)832-0225

Catholic Social Services of the Diocese
  of Charlotte, North Carolina, Inc.
1524 East Morehead Street
P.O. Box 35523

Charlotte, NC 28235-5523
(704)333-9954

The Children's Home Society of North
  Carolina, Inc.
740 Chestnut Street
P.O. Box 6587
Greensboro, NC 27405
(919)274-1538

Family Services, Inc.
610 Coliseum Drive
Winston-Salem, NC 27106-5393
(919)722-8173

Latter Day Saints Social Services
5624 Executive Center Drive, Suite 109
Charlotte, NC 28212
(704)535-2436

North Dakota

State Agency

Department of Human Services
State Capital
Bismarck, ND 58505
(701)224-2316

Private Agencies

Building Families through Adoption
1802 North 20th Street
Bismarck, ND 58501
(701)258-9650

Catholic Family Service
P.O. Box 686
Fargo, ND 56107
(701)258-4457

Lutheran Social Services of North
  Dakota
1325 South 11th Street
P.O. Box 389
Fargo, ND 58107
(701)235-7341

New Horizons Foreign Adoptions
  Service
2876 Woodland Place
Bismarck, ND 58501
(701)223-0651

South American Resource Center, Inc.
1136 West Divide Avenue
P.O. Box 2344

Bismarck, ND 58502
(701)222-3960

The Village Family Service Center
1721 South University Drive
Fargo, ND 58103
(701)235-6433

Ohio

State Agency

Department of Human Services
30 East Broad Street
Columbus, OH 43215
(614)466-8510

Ohio Department of Human Services District Offices

117 Walnut Avenue, N.E.
Canton, OH 44702
(216)453-7729

100 East Eighth Street
Cincinnati, OH 45202
(513)852-3280

Frank J. Lausche Building
615 West Superior Avenue, 9th Floor
Cleveland, OH 44113
(216)622-3404

899 East Broad Street
Columbus, OH 43205
(614)466-4456

One Government Center, Room 913
Toledo, OH 43604
(419)245-2855

Private Agencies

The Bair Foundation
3645 State Route 5
P.O. Box 95
Cortland, OH 44410
(216)638-5694

Baptist Children's Home and Family
  Ministries, Inc.
2150 South Center Boulevard
Springfield, OH 45506
(513)322-0006

Beech Brook
3737 Lander Road

Pepper Pike, OH 44124
(216)831-2255

Berea Children's Home
202 East Bagley Road
Berea, OH 44017
(216)234-2006

Bethany International Adoptions/
Bethany Christian Services
1655 West Market Street, Suite 340
Akron, OH 44313
(216)867-2362

Catholic Community League of Canton
609 Cleveland Avenue, N.W.
Canton, OH 44702
(216)455-0374

Catholic Community Services, Inc.,
of Trumbull County
2354 Youngstown Road, S.E.
Warren, OH 44484
(216)369-4254

Catholic Service Bureau, Inc., Colum-
biana County
964 North Market Street
Lisbon, OH 44432
(216)424-9509

Catholic Service Bureau of Lake
County
8 North State Street
Painesville, OH 44077
(216)352-6191

Catholic Service League of Ashtabula
County
4631 Main Avenue
Ashtabula, OH 44004
(216)998-7221

Catholic Service League of Geauga
County
10771 Mayfield Road
Chardon, OH 44024
(216)285-3537

Catholic Service League of Summit
County
640 North Main Street
Akron, OH 44310
(216)762-7481

Catholic Service League of Western
Stark County, Inc.
1807 Lincoln Way East
Massillion, OH 44646
(216)833-8516

Catholic Service League of Youngstown, Inc.
5385 Market Street
Youngstown, OH 44512
(216)788-8726

Catholic Social Services Bureau
of Ashland, Medina and Wayne
Counties
246 Northland Drive
Medina, OH 44256
(216)725-4923

Catholic Social Service Bureau of Lo-
rain County
2136 North Ridge Road
Elyria, OH 44035
(216)324-2614

Catholic Social Services, Inc.
197 East Gay Street
Columbus, OH 43215
(614)221-5891

Catholic Social Services of Cuyahoga
County
3409 Woodland Avenue
Cleveland, OH 44115
(216)881-1600

Catholic Social Services of the Miami
Valley
922 West Riverview Avenue
Dayton, OH 45407
(513)223-7217

Catholic Social Services of Southwest
Ohio
100 East Eighth Street
Cincinnati, OH 45202
(513)241-7745

Catholic Social Services of Toledo
1933 Spielbusch Avenue
Toledo, OH 43624
(419)244-6711

Child and Family Services, Inc.
616 South Collett Street
Lima, OH 45805
(419)225-1040

Children and Family Service
5035 Marmion Avenue
Youngstown, OH 44502
(216)782-5664

The Children's Home of Cincinnati
5051 Duck Creek Road

Cincinnati, OH 45227
(513)272-2800

Children's Services
1001 Huron Road
Cleveland, OH 44115
(216)781-2043

Family and Community Services of
Catholic Charities
302 North Depeyster Street
Kent, OH 44240
(216)678-3911

Family Counseling and Crittenton
Services
185 South Fifth Street
Columbus, OH 43215
(614)221-7608

Family Counseling Services of Central
Stark County
618 Second Street, N.W.
Canton, OH 44703
(216)454-7066

Family Counseling Services of Western
Stark County, Inc.
11 Lincoln Way West, Suite 612
Massillion, OH 44646
(216)832-5043

Family Service Association
184 Salem Avenue
Dayton, OH 45406
(513)222-9481

Family Service Association
1704 North Road, S.E. Heaton Square
Warren, OH 44484
(216)856-2907

Family Services of Summit County
212 East Exchange Street
Akron, OH 44304
(216)376-9494

HARAMBEE, Services to Black Families
1466-68 East 55th Street
Cleveland, OH 44103
(216)391-7044

Jewish Children's Bureau
22001 Fairmount Boulevard
Shaker Heights, OH 44118
(216)932-2800

Jewish Family and Children's Service
of the Youngstown Area Jewish Federation

505 Gypsy Lane
Youngstown, OH 44501
(216)746-3251

Jewish Family Services
3085 West Market Street
Akron, OH 44320
(216)867-3388

Jewish Family Service
1710 Section Road
Cincinnati, OH 45237
(513)351-3680

Jewish Family Services
1175 South College Avenue
Columbus, OH 43209
(614)231-1890

Jewish Family Service
4501 Denlinger Road
Dayton, OH 45426
(513)854-2944

Jewish Family Service of Toledo
6525 Sylvania Avenue
Sylvania, OH 43560
(419)885-2561

Latter Day Saints Social Services
4431 Marketing Place
P.O. Box 367
Groveport, OH 43125
(614)836-2466

Lutheran Children's Aid and Family
Services
4100 Franklin Boulevard
Cleveland, OH 44113
(216)281-2500

Lutheran Social Services of Central
Ohio
57 East Main Street
P.O. Box 15877
Columbus, OH 43215
(614)228-5209

The Lutheran Social Service of the
Miami Valley
3304 North Main Street
Dayton, OH
(513)433-2140

Lutheran Social Services of North-
western Ohio, Inc.
2149 Collingwood Boulevard
Toledo, OH 43620
(419)243-9178

The Mid-Western Children's Home
4581 Long Spurling Road
P.O. Box 48
Pleasant Plain, OH 45162
(513)877-2141

Northeast Ohio Adoption Services
8031 East Market Street
Warren, OH 44484
(216)856-5582

Office of Social Ministries—Diocese of
Steubenville
422 Washington Street
Steubenville, OH 43952
(614)282-6293

The United Methodist Children's
Home
West Ohio Conference of the United
Methodist Church
1045 North High Street
Worthington, OH 43085
(614)885-5020

Oklahoma

State Agency

Department of Human Services, Adoptions
P.O. Box 25352
Oklahoma City, OK 73125
(405)521-2475

Private Agencies

Baptist General Convention
1141 North Robinson
Oklahoma City, OK 73103
(405)236-4341

Catholic Social Services
739 North Denver
Tulsa, OK 74106
(918)585-8167

Dillion International
7615 East 63rd Place South
Tulsa, OK 74133
(918)749-8531

Lutheran Social Services
227 N.W. 23rd
Oklahoma City, OK 73106
(405)528-3124

Oregon

State Agency

Department of Human Resources,
Children's Services Division
198 Commercial Street, S.E.
Salem, OR 97310-0450
(503)378-4452

Private Agencies

Adventist Adoption and Family Services Program
6040 S.E. Belmont Street
Portland, OR 97215
(503)232-1211

Albertina Kerr Center for Children
424 N.E. 22nd Avenue
Portland, OR 97232
(503)239-8101

Boys and Girls Aid Society of Oregon
2301 N.W. Glisan Street
Portland, OR 97210
(503)222-9661

Catholic Services for Children
814 Oregon Bank Building
319 S.W. Washington Street
Portland, OR 97204
(503)228-6531

Children's Services Division
198 Commercial Street, S.E.
Salem, OR 97310
(503)378-4452

Global Adoptions
1885 Commercial Street, S.E.
Salem, OR 97302
(503)362-6836

Holt International Children's Services
P.O. Box 2880
Eugene, OR 97402
(503)687-2202

Jewish Family and Child Service
316 Mayer Building
1130 S.W. Morrison Street
Portland, OR 97205
(503)226-7079

Latter Day Saints–Oregon Agency
3000 Market Street, N.E., Suite 268
Salem, OR 97303
(503)581-7483

PLAN
P.O. Box 667
McMinnville, OR 97128
(503)472-8452

Pennsylvania

State Agency

Department of Public Welfare
Office of Children, Youth and Families
P.O. Box 2675
Harrisburg, PA 17105-2675
(717)787-5010

Private Agencies

The Adoption Agency
34 Wellington Road
Ardmore, PA 19003
(215)879-4217

Aid for Children International
1516 Ridge Road
Lancaster, PA 17603
(717)393-0296

The Bair Foundation
241 High Street
New Wilmington, PA 16142
(412)946-2220

Catholic Charities Agency of the Diocese of Greensburg
115 Vanear Avenue
Greensburg, PA 15601
(412)837-1840

Catholic Charities Agency of the Diocese of Greensburg
Theatre Building
635 Philadelphia Street
Indiana, PA 15701
(412)463-8806

Catholic Charities of the Diocese of Greensburg
Kiski Park Plaza, RD #2
P.O. Box 224
Leechburg, PA 15656
(412)845-6038

Catholic Charities Agency of the Diocese of Greensburg
Mon-Valley Community Health Center
Eastgate #8

Monessen, PA 15602
(412)684-7800, (412)684-9000

Catholic Charities Agency of the Diocese of Greensburg
Room 20, Bortz Law Building
92 East Main Street
Uniontown, PA 15401
(412)439-3531

Catholic Social Agency of the Diocese of Allentown
928 Union Boulevard
Allentown, PA 18102
(215)435-1541

Catholic Social Services
20 South Mercer Street
New Castle, PA 16101
(412)658-5526

Catholic Social Services of the Archdiocese of Philadelphia
222 North 17th Street
Philadelphia, PA 19103
(215)587-3900

Catholic Social Services of the Diocese of Altoona–Johnstown
1300 12th Avenue
P.O. Box 1349
Altoona, PA 16601
(814)944-9388

Catholic Social Services of the Diocese of Erie
329 West Tenth Street
Erie, PA 16502
(814)456-2978

Catholic Social Services of the Diocese of Harrisburg
4800 Union Deposit Road
P.O. Box 3551
Harrisburg, PA 17105
(717)657-4804

Catholic Social Services of the Diocese of Scranton
300 Wyoming Avenue
Scranton, PA 18503
(717)346-8936

Catholic Social Services of Luzerne County
15 South Franklin Street
Wilkes-Barre, PA 18701
(717)822-7118

Catholic Social Services of Shenango
Valley
318 West State Street
Sharon, PA 16146
(412)346-4142

Catholic Social Services of Washington
and Greene Counties
12 West Pike Street, Room 12
Pittsburgh National Bank Building
Canonsburg, PA 15317
(412)745-4800

Child and Home Study Associates
31 East Franklin Street
Media, PA 19063
(215)565-1544

Children's Aid Society of Mercer
County
350 West Market Street
Mercer, PA 16137
(412)662-4730

Children's Aid Society of Montgomery
County
1314 DeKalb Street
Norristown, PA 19401
(215)279-2755

Children's Aid Society of Pennsylvania
311 South Juniper Street
Philadelphia, PA 19107
(215)546-2990

Children's Aid Society of Somerset
County
574 East Main Street
Somerset, PA 15501
(814)445-2009

Children's Home of Pittsburgh
5618 Kentucky Avenue
Pittsburgh, PA 15232
(412)441-4884

Concern
1 East Main Street
Fleetwood, PA 19522
(215)944-0445

Day Break Children's Services
P.O. Box 17416
12 Federal Drive, Suite 302
Pittsburgh, PA 15416
(412)247-5890

Eckels Adoption Agency
915 Fifth Avenue (Rear)

Williamsport, PA 17701
(717)323-2520

Family and Child Service
110 Tenth Street
Erie, PA 16501
(814)455-2725

Family and Children's Service of Lancaster County
630 Janet Avenue
Lancaster, PA 17601
(717)397-5241

Family Service and Children's Aid Society
716 East Second Street
Oil City, PA 16301
(814)677-4005

Homes for Black Children
1610-14 North Broad Street
Philadelphia, PA 19121
(215)236-9911

Jewish Family and Children's Agency
1301 Spencer Street
Philadelphia, PA 19141
(215)549-9000

Love the Children
221 West Broad Street
Quakertown, PA 18951
(215)536-4180

Lutheran Children and Family Service
2900 Queen Lane
Philadelphia, PA 19129
(215)951-6850

Lutheran Home at Topton
Topton, PA 19562
(215)682-2145

Lutheran Service Society of Western
Pennsylvania
Westmoreland District Office
11 Garden Center Drive
Greensburg, PA 15601
(412)837-9385

Native American Adoption Resource
Exchange
200 Charles Street
Pittsburgh, PA 15238
(412)782-4457

Pearl S. Buck Foundation
Green Hill Farms
Box 181

Perkasie, PA 18944
(215)249-0100

Philadelphia Society for Services
to Children
419 South 15th Street
Philadelphia, PA 19103
(215)875-3400

Social and Community Services,
Beaver County Unit
1445 Market Street, West Bridgewater
Beaver, PA 15009
(412)775-1109

Social and Community Services,
Butler County Unit
140 East Jefferson Street
Butler, PA 16001
(412)287-4011

Social and Community Services of the
Diocese of Pittsburgh, Inc.
307 Fourth Avenue, Bank Tower
Pittsburgh, PA 15222
(412)281-4343

Tabor Home for Children
601 New Britain Road
Doylestown, PA 18901
(215)348-4071

Tressler-Lutheran Service Associates
2331 Market Street
Camp Hill, PA 17011
(717)761-6920

Tressler-Lutheran Service Associates
25 West Springettsbury Avenue
York, PA 17403
(717)845-9113

Tressler-Lutheran Service Associates
435 West Fourth Street
Williamsport, PA 17701
(717)322-7873

Welcome House
Route 202 and Beulah Road
P.O. Box 836
Doylestown, PA 18901
(215)345-0430

Welcome House
P.O. Box 505
Shippensburg, PA 17257
(717)532-8931

Women's Christian Alliance
1610-14 North Broad Street

Philadelphia, PA 19121
(215)236-9911

Rhode Island

State Agency

Department for Children and Their
Families
Division of Direct Services
610 Mount Pleasant Avenue
Providence, RI 02908
(401)457-4500

Private Agencies

Catholic Social Services
433 Elmwood Avenue
Providence, RI 02907
(401)467-7200

Children's Friend and Service
2 Richmond Street
Providence, RI 02903
(401)331-2900

Jewish Family Services
229 Waterman Street
Providence, RI 02906
(401)331-1244

South Carolina

State Agency

Department of Social Services
P.O. Box 1520
Columbia, SC 29202-9988
(803)758-8740

Public Agency

The Children's Bureau of South Carolina
Suite 225, 1001 Harden Street
Columbia, SC 29205
(803)758-2702

Private Agencies

Agage Homes
P.O. Box 643
Lexington, SC 29072
(803)791-5972

Bethany Christian Services
300 University Ridge, Suite 114
Greenville, SC 29601
(803)235-2273

Boys' Home of the South
Route #3, Box 115
Belton, SC 29627
(803)243-3443

Catholic Charities of Charleston
119 Broad Street
Charleston, SC 29401
(803)722-8318

Children Unlimited, Inc.
P.O. 11463
Columbia, SC 29211-1463
(803)799-8311

Connie Maxwell Children's Home
P.O. Box 1178
Greenwood, SC 29646
(803)223-8321

Epworth Children's Home
2900 Millwood Avenue
Columbia, SC 29205
(803)256-7394

Southeastern Children's Home
3506 Edwards Road
Taylors, SC 29687
(803)292-3309

South Dakota

State Agency

Department of Social Services
Office of Children, Youth and Family
  Services
Kneip Building, 700 North Illinois
  Street
Pierre, SD 57501-2291
(605)773-3227

Private Agencies

Catholic Family Services
3200 West 41st Street
Sioux Falls, SD 57105
(605)336-3326

Catholic Social Services
918 5th Avenue
Rapid City, SD 57701
(605)348-6086

Christian Counseling Service
1620 South Minnesota Avenue
Sioux Falls, SD 57105
(605)336-6999

Holt International, Tere Berkland
1003 Burleigh
Yankton, SD 57078
(605)665-2036

Latter Day Saints Social Services
2525 West Main
Rapid City, SD 57701
(605)342-3500

Lutheran Social Services
600 West 12th Street
Sioux Falls, SD 57104
(605)336-3347

Tennessee

State Agency

Department of Human Services
111-19 Seventh Avenue N.
Nashville, TN 37203
(615)741-5936

Private Agencies

AGAPE
2702 Nolenville Road
Nashville, TN 37211
(615)385-0190

Associate Catholic Charities of the
  Diocese of Memphis—St. Peter
  Home
1805 Poplar Avenue
Memphis, TN 38104
(901)725-8240

Bachman Memorial Home, Inc.
P.O. Box 849
Brymer Creek Road
Cleveland, TN 37311
(615)479-4523

Bethany Christian Services
4719 Brainerd Road
Chattanooga, TN 37411
(615)622-7360

Bethel Bible Village
3001 Hamill Road
P.O. Box 500

Hixson, TN 37343
(615)842-5757

Camelot Care Center
Route #3, Poplar Springs Road
Box 267-C
Kingston, TN 37763
(615)376-2296

Catholic Charities of Tennessee, Inc.
30 White Bridge Road
Nashville, TN 37205
(615)383-6393

Child and Family Services of Knox
  County
114 Dameron Avenue
Knoxville, TN 37917
(615)524-7483

Children's Home
315 Gillespie Road
Chattanooga, TN 37411
(615)698-2456

Christian Counseling Services
515 Woodland Street
P.O. Box 60383
Nashville, TN 37206
(615)254-8341

Church of God Home for Children
P.O. Box 391
Park Road
Sevierville, TN 37862
(615)453-4644

Columbus Home, Inc.
114 Hinton Street
Knoxville, TN 37917
(615)524-9896

Crisis Pregnancy Support Center
1915 Church Street
Nashville, TN 37203
(615)321-0005

E.S. Inc.
Oasis House, 1219-16 Avenue, S.
Nashville, TN 37212
(615)327-4455

East Tennessee Christian Services, Inc.
P.O. Box 22816
Knoxville, TN 37933-0816
(615)966-4088

Family and Children's Services
201 23rd Avenue, N.

Nashville, TN 37203
(615)327-0833

Family and Children's Services of
  Chattanooga, Inc.
300 East 8th Street
Chattanooga, TN 37403
(615)755-2800

Family and Educational Advisory
  Associates, Inc.
Serendipity House, 2500 White Avenue
Nashville, TN 37204
(615)283-5972

The Family Link, Inc.
1203-07 Peabody
P.O. Box 40437
Memphis, TN 38174-0437
(901)725-6911

Goodwill Homes Community Services,
  Inc.
P.O. Box 16244
Memphis, TN 38186-0244
(901)785-6790

Greater Chattanooga Christian Services and Children's Home
8 North Tuxedo Avenue
Chattanooga, TN 37411
(615)267-1114

Holson United Methodist Home for
  Children, Inc.
P.O. Box 188
Holson Drive
Greeneville, TN 37743
(615)638-4171

Jewish Family Services, Inc.
P.O. Box 38268
6560 Poplar Drive
Memphis, TN 38138
(901)767-8511

Madison County Juvenile Court Services
224 Lexington Avenue
Jackson, TN 38301
(901)422-2202

Memphis and Shelby County Mental
  Health Center
(Northeast Community Mental Health
  Center)
5515 Shelby Oaks Drive
Memphis, TN 38134
(901)382-3880

Mur-Ci Homes for Retarded, Inc.
P.O. Box 17026
2120 Murfreesboro Road
Nashville, TN 37217
(615)361-6446

Porter-Leath Children's Center
850 North Manassas Street
P.O. Box 7231
Memphis, TN 38107
(901)529-8078

Residential Services, Inc.
1451 Elm Hill Pike, Suite 161
Nashville, TN 37210
(615)367-4333

Sertoma Learning Center
2335 Danridge Avenue
Knoxville, TN 37915
(615)524-5553, (615)525-9080

Tennessee Baptist Children's Homes,
  Inc.
P.O. Box 347
107 Franklin Road
Brentwood, TN 37027
(615)373-5707

Tennessee Children's Home
P.O. Box 10
Main Street
Spring Hill, TN 37174
(615)486-2274

West Tennessee AGAPE
2406 Parkway Place
P.O. Box 11411
Memphis, TN 38112
(901)327-7339

West Tennessee Children's Home
P.O. Box 3261
Jackson, TN 38301
(901)423-4850

Texas

State Agency

Department of Human Resources,
  Adoption Unit
1616 Headway Circle
P.O. Box 15995
Austin, TX 78761
(512)834-0034

Private Agencies

Buckner Baptist Benevolences
P.O. Box 271189
Dallas, TX 75227
(214)328-3141

Catholic Charities, Adoption Service
Matz Building, Suite 225
513 East Jackson
Harlingen, TX 78550
(512)425-3422

Catholic Charities of the Diocese of
  Galveston–Houston
1111 Lovet Boulevard
Houston, TX 77066
(713)526-4611

Catholic Counseling Services, Diocese
  of Dallas
3845 Oak Lawn
Dallas, TX 75219
(214)528-4870

Catholic Family and Children's Service, Inc.
2903 West Salinas
San Antonio, TX 78207
(512)433-3256

Catholic Family Service, Inc.
1522 South Van Buren
Amarillo, TX 79102
(806)376-4571

Catholic Social Service
1404 Hemphill Street
Fort Worth, TX 76104
(817)921-5381

Child Placement Center of Texas
P.O. Box 239
408 North Fourth Street
Killeen, TX 76541
(817)526-8872, (817)526-8884

Children's Home of Lubbock
P.O. Box 2824
Lubbock, TX 79413
(806)762-0481

Children's Service Bureau
625 North Alamo
San Antonio, TX 78215
(512)223-6281

Christian Child Help Foundation
3605 North MacGregor Way

Houston, TX 77004
(713)522-2708

Christian Homes of Abilene, Inc.
242 Beech Street
Abilene, TX 79604
(915)677-2205

Christian Services of the Southwest
3330 Walnut Hill Lane
Dallas, TX 75229
(214)351-9946

Christ's Haven for Children
P.O. Box 467
Keller, TX 76248
(817)431-1544

The Depelchin Faith Home
100 Sandman Street
Houston, TX 77007
(713)861-8136

The Edna Gladney Home
2110 Hemphill
Fort Worth, TX 76110
(817)926-3304

Family Counseling and Children's Services
201 West Waco Drive, Room 213
P.O. Box 464
Waco, TX 76703
(817)753-1509

High Plains Children's Home, Inc.
Box 7448
Amarillo, TX 79109
(806)355-6588

Homes of Saint Mark
1302 Marshall
Houston, TX 77006
(713)797-1791

Hope Cottage Children's Bureau, Inc.
4209 McKinney Avenue
Dallas, TX 75205
(214)526-8721

Jewish Family Service
7800 Northaven
Dallas, TX 75230
(214)696-6400

Jewish Family Service
4131 South Braeswood
Houston, TX 77025
(713)667-9336

Latter Day Saints Social Services—
Texas
1100 West Jackson Road
Carrollton, TX 75006
(214)242-2182

Lee and Buelah Moor Children's Home
1100 East Cliff Drive
El Paso, TX 79902
(915)544-8777

Los Niños International Adoption Center
3200 South Congress
Austin, TX 78704
(512)443-2833

Lutheran Social Service of Texas, Inc.
(Central Texas Office)
1000 East 32nd, Suite 7
Austin, TX 78705
(512)474-9156

Lutheran Social Service of Texas, Inc.
(Coastal Bend–South Texas Office)
1201 Morgan
Corpus Christi, TX 78404
(512)882-7922

Lutheran Social Service of Texas, Inc.
(North Central Texas Office)
6202 East Mockingbird Lane
Dallas, TX 75214
(214)821-5472

Lutheran Social Service of Texas, Inc.
(Panhandle–South Plains Office)
2412 13th Street
Lubbock, TX 79401
(806)763-7051

Lutheran Social Service of Texas, Inc.
(Permian Basin Office)
2705A West Michigan
Midland, TX 79701
(915)563-1883

Lutheran Social Service of Texas, Inc.
(Southeast Texas Office)
161 West Road
Houston, TX 77037
(713)445-1544

Lutheran Social Service of Texas, Inc.
(Southwest Texas Office)
615 Elm at McCullough
San Antonio, TX 78202
(512)227-8142

Lutheran Social Service of Texas, Inc.
(West Texas Office)
9301 Diana
El Paso, TX 79924
(915)751-2377

Marywood Maternity and Adoption
Services
510 West 26 Street
Austin, TX 78705
(512)472-9251

Methodist Home
1111 Herring Avenue
Waco, TX 76708
(817)753-0181

Methodist Mission Home of Texas
6487 Whitby Road
San Antonio, TX 78240
(512)696-2410

Pleasant Hills Children's Home
Route 2, Box 770
Fairfield, TX 75840
(214)389-2641

Presbyterian Children's Home and Service Agency
400 South Zang, Suite 1210
Dallas, TX 75208
(214)942-8674

Presbyterian Home for Children
3400 South Bowie
Amarillo, TX 79109
(806)352-5771

Sherwood-Myrtie Foster Home for
Children
P.O. Box 978
Stephenville, TX 76401
(817)968-2143

Smithlawn Maternity Home and Adoption Agency
Box 6451
711 76th Street
Lubbock, TX 79413
(806)745-2574

South Texas Children's Home
P.O. Box 1210
Beeville, TX 78102
(512)375-2101

Spaulding Southwest, Division of
Christian Child Help Foundation
4219 Richmond, Suite 100

Houston, TX 77027
(713)850-9707

Texas Baptist Children's Home
Drawer 7
Round Rock, TX 78664
(512)255-3668

Texas Cradle Society
8222 Wurzbach Road
San Antonio, TX 78229
(512)696-7700

Therapeikos, Inc.
2817 North Second
Abilene, TX 79603
(915)677-2216

Utah

State Agency

Department of Social Services
Division of Family Services
P.O. Box 45500
Salt Lake City, UT 84145-0500
(801)533-7123

Private Agencies

Catholic Community Services of
Utah
333 East South Temple
Salt Lake City, UT 84111
(801)328-8641

Children's Aid Society of Utah
652 26th Street
Odgen, UT 84401
(801)393-8671

Children's House International
2007 South 1200 East
Bountiful, UT 84010
(801)355-5805

Children's Services Society
576 East South Temple
Salt Lake City, UT 84102
(801)355-7444

Latter Day Saints Social Services—
Cedar City
718 South Main, Suite B
Cedar City, UT 84720
(801)586-4470

Latter Day Saints Social Services—
Granger Agency
3540 South 4000 West
West Valley City, UT 84120
(801)531-4900

Latter Day Saints Social Services—
Logan Agency
95 West 100 South
Logan, UT 84321
(801)752-5302

Latter Day Saints Social Services—
Midvale Agency
101 East 7200 South
Midvale, UT 84047
(801)531-2556

Latter Day Saints Social Services—
Ogden Agency
349 12th Street
Ogden, UT 84401
(801)621-6510

Latter Day Saints Services—Provo
Agency
1190 North 900 East
Provo, UT 84601
(801)378-7620

Latter Day Saints Social Services—
Richfield
55 West 100 North
P.O. Box 827
Richfield, UT 84107
(801)896-6446

Utah Women's Adoption Service
515 South 400 East
Salt Lake City, UT 84111
(801)531-9192

WACAP Adoption Services of Utah
1496 West 2320 South
Salt Lake City, UT 84119
(801)973-6706

Vermont

State Agency

Department of Social and Rehabilitation Services, Adoption Unit
103 South Main Street
Waterbury, VT 05676
(802)241-2150

Private Agencies

The Elizabeth Lind Home, Inc.
Box 45
Burlington, VT 05401
(802)864-7467

International Adoptions
P.O. Box 3115
Burlington, VT 05402
(802)658-0249

Vermont Catholic Charities
311 North Avenue
Burlington, VT 05401
(802)658-6110

The Vermont Children's Aid Society
72 Hungerford Terrace
Burlington, VT 05401
(802)864-9883

Virginia

State Agency

Commonwealth of Virginia
Department of Social Services, Blair
Building
8007 Discovery Drive
Richmond, VA 23229-8699
(804)281-9205

Private Agencies

Bethany Christian Services
10720 Main Street
Fairfax, VA 22030
(703)359-6565

Bethany Christian Services
8215 Centreville Road
Manassas, VA 22111
(703)368-7881

Catholic Charities of the Diocese of
Arlington, Inc.
3838 North Cathedral Lane
Arlington, VA 22203
(703)841-2531

Catholic Charities of the Diocese of
Arlington, Inc.
10604 Warick Avenue, Suite 200
Fairfax, VA 22030
(703)591-5921

Catholic Charities of the Diocese of
Arlington, Inc.

10 West Boscawen Street, Room 25
Winchester, VA 22601
(703)667-7940

Catholic Charities of Richmond,
Inc.
4206 Chamberlayne Avenue
Richmond, VA 23227
(804)264-2778

Catholic Family and Children's
Services of Roanoke Valley and
Western Virginia, Inc.
820 Campbell Avenue, S.W.
Roanoke, VA 24016
(703)344-5107

Catholic Family and Children's
Services Inc. of Tidewater
1520 Aberdeen Road, Suite 109
Hampton, VA 23666
(804)827-0510

Catholic Family and Children's
Services Inc. of Tidewater
1301 Colonial Avenue
Norfolk, VA 23517
(804)625-2568

Catholic Family and Children's
Services Inc. of Tidewater
5347 Virginia Beach Boulevard
Virginia Beach, VA 23462
(804)499-5919

Catholic Family Services
1809 Airline Boulevard
Portsmouth, VA 23701
(804)393-0043

Chabad Lubavitch
372 South Independence Boulevard
Virginia Beach, VA 23462
(804)497-1761

Children's Home Society of Virginia
1620 Fifth Street, S.W.
Roanoke, VA 24016
(703)344-9281

Children's Home Society of Virginia
4200 Fitzhugh Avenue
Richmond, VA 23230
(804)353-0191

DePaul Children's Services, Inc.
4502 Starkey Road, S.W., Suite 200
Roanoke, VA 24015
(703)989-7355

Family Life Services
520 Eldon Street
Lynchburg, VA 24502
(804)847-6846

Family Services of Tidewater, Inc.
T/A Family Services
222 19th Street, W.
Norfolk, VA 23517
(804)622-7017

Holson Methodist Home, Inc.
P.O. Box 186
102 Wall Street, Suite 28
Abingdon, VA 24210
(703)628-8604

Jewish Family Service of Tidewater,
Inc.
7300 Newport Avenue
Norfolk, VA 23517
(804)489-3111

Jewish Family Services, Inc.
7027 Three Chopt Road, 2nd Floor
Richmond, VA 23226
(804)282-5644

Latter Day Saints Social Services of
Virginia, Inc.
8110 Virginia Pine Court
P.O. Box 34361
Richmond, VA 23234
(804)743-0727

Pan American Adoption Agency
12604 Kahns Road
Manassas, VA 22111
(703)791-3260

Rainbow Christian Services
P.O. Box 9
6400 Artemus Road
Gainesville, VA 22065
(703)754-8516

United Jewish Community Center of
the Virginia Peninsula
2700 Spring Road
Newport News, VA 23606
(804)595-6215

United Methodist Family Services of
Virginia, Inc.
3900 West Broad Street
Richmond, VA 23230
(804)353-4461

United Methodist Family Services of
Virginia, Inc.

5560 Virginia Beach Boulevard
Virginia Beach, VA 23462
(804)490-9791

Virginia Baptist Children's Home, Inc.
7100 Columbia Pike
Annandale, VA 22003
(703)750-3660

Virginia Baptist Children's Home,
   Inc.
8309 Orcutt Avenue
Newport News, VA 23605
(804)826-3477

Virginia Baptist Children's Home, Inc.
700 East Belt Boulevard
Richmond, VA 23224
(804)231-4466

Virginia Baptist Children's Home,
   Inc.,
Mount Vernon Avenue
Box 849
Salem, VA 24153
(703)389-5468

Welcome House, Inc.
P.O. Box 596
Christiansburg, VA 24073
(703)382-5975

Welcome House, Inc.
5905 West Broad Street, Suite 300
Richmond, VA 23230

Washington

State Agency

Department of Social and Health
   Services, Adoption Program
OB 41-C
Olympia, WA 98504
(206)753-0965

Private Agencies

Adoption Services of WACAP
P.O. Box 88948
Seattle, WA 98188
(206)575-4550

Adventist Adoption and Family
   Services
1207 East Reserve Street

Vancouver, WA 98661
(206)693-2110

Americans for International Aid and
   Adoption (AIAA)
P.O. Box 6051
Spokane, WA 99207
(509)489-2015, (206)782-4251

Black Child Adoption Program
123 16th Avenue
P.O. Box 22638
Seattle, WA 98122
(206)329-3933, (206)324-9470

Catholic Children and Family Service
   of Pasco
611 West Columbia
Pasco, WA 99301
(206)547-0521

Catholic Children and Family Services
   of Walla Walla
418 Drumheller Building
Walla Walla, WA 99362
(206)525-0572

Catholic Children's Services, Skagit
   Island, San Juan and Whatcom
   Counties
207 Kentucky
Bellingham, WA 98225
(206)733-5800

Catholic Children's Services of Tacoma
5410 North 44th
Tacoma, WA 98407
(206)752-2455

Catholic Community Service, King
   County
1715 East Cherry Street
Seattle, WA 98122
(206)323-6336

Catholic Community Services of
   Seattle
P.O. Box 22608
Seattle, WA 98122
(206)323-6336

Catholic Community Service, Snoho-
   mish County
Room 510, Commerce Building
Everett, WA 98201
(206)259-9188, (206)622-8905

Catholic Family and Child Service of
   Ephrata, Columbia Basin Branch
121 Basin N.W.

P.O. Box 191
Ephrata, WA 98823
(206)754-2211

Catholic Family and Child Services of
Grandview
302 Division
P.O. Box 22
Grandview, WA 98930
(206)882-3050

Catholic Family and Child Service of
Richland
1329 George Washington Way
Richland, WA 99352
(206)946-4645

Catholic Family and Child Service of
Wenatchee
425 Savings and Loan Building
5 North Wenatchee Avenue
Wenatchee, WA 98801
(206)662-6761

Catholic Family and Child Service of
Yakima
916 Larson Building
6 South 2nd Street
Yakima, WA 98901
(206)453-8264

Catholic Family Counseling Center
404 Medical Arts Building
1104 Main
Vancouver, WA 98660
(206)694-2631

Children's Home Society of Washington, Central Area
321 East Yakima Avenue, Room 204
Yakima, WA 98901
(206)457-8139

Children's Home Society of Washington, Northeast Area
4315 Scott Street
P.O. Box 8244, Manito Station
Spokane, WA 99203
(206)747-4174

Children's Home Society of Washington, Northwest Area
3300 N.E. 65th
Box 15190, Wedgwood Station
Seattle, WA 98115
(206)524-6020

Children's Home Society of Washington, Northwest Branch
3300 Northeast 65th

Seattle, WA 98115
(206)524-6020

Children's Home Society of Washington, Southeast Area
405 Denny Building
6 West Alder
Walla Walla, WA 99362
(206)459-2130

Children's Home Society of Washington, Southwest Area
1105 Broadway
Vancouver, WA 98660
(206)695-1325

Children's Home Society of Washington, West Central Area
201 South 34th
Tacoma, WA 98408
(206)472-3355

Church of Christ Homes for Children
30012 South Military Road
Auburn, WA 98003
(206)839-2755

Hope Services
424 North 130th
Seattle, WA 98133
(206)367-4600

International Children's Services of
Washington, Inc.
3251-107th, S.E.
Bellevue, WA 98004
(206)451-9370

Jewish Family Services
1214 Boylston Avenue
Seattle, WA 98101
(206)447-3240

Latter Day Saints Social Services
220 South Third Place
Renton, WA 98055
(206)624-3393

Lutheran Social Services
19230 Forest Park Drive N.E.
Seattle, WA 98155
(206)365-2700

Lutheran Social Services of Washington (Administration Office)
4040 South 188th
Seattle, WA 98188
(206)246-7650

Lutheran Social Services of Washington, Southwest Area
223 North Yakima
Tacoma, WA 98403
(206)272-8433

Lutheran Social Services of Washington, Northeast Area
1226 North Howard
Spokane, WA 99201
(206)327-7761

Lutheran Social Services of Washington, Southeast Area
Plaza I, Suite 700
320 North Johnson Street
Kennewick, WA 99336
(206)783-7446

Medina Children's Services
P.O. Box 22638
Seattle, WA 98111
(206)324-9470

Northwest Adoption Exchange
909 Northeast 43rd, #208
Seattle, WA 98105
(206)632-1480

Northwest Resource Center for Children, Youth and Families
University of Washington School of Social Work
JM-30 4101 15th Avenue, N.E.
Seattle, WA 98195
(206)543-1517

OPT, Options for Pregnancy through Adoption Services of WACAP
130 South Third Street
Sheldon, WA 98584
(206)426-9999

Regular Baptist Child Placement Agency
P.O. Box 16353
Seattle, WA 98116
(206)938-1487

Seattle Indian Center
121 Stewart Street
Seattle, WA 98101
(206)447-9191

TASC, The Adoption of Special Children
123 16th Avenue
Seattle, WA 98122
(206)324-9473, (206)324-9470

Travelers Aid Adoption Service
909 Fourth Avenue, Room 630
Seattle, WA 98104
(206)447-3888

West Virginia

State Agency

Department of Human Services
1900 Washington Street, E.
Charleston, WV 25305
(304)348-2400

Private Agencies

Children's Home Society of West Virginia
1118 Kanawha Boulevard, E.
Charleston, WV 25301
(304)346-0795

United Methodist Child Placement Services
P.O. Box 2515
Fairmont, WV 26554
(304)366-0694

Wisconsin

State Agency

Department of Health and Social Services
Office for Children, Youth and Families
Bureau of Human Resources, Division of Community Services
1 West Wilson Street
P.O. Box 7851
Madison, WI 53707-7851
(608) 266-0690

Public Agencies

Ashland District:
Division of Community Services, City Hall
601 West Second Street
P.O. Box 72
Ashland, WI 54806
(715)682-3405

Eastern Region:
Division of Community Services,
Green Bay

Suite 411, 200 North Jefferson
Green Bay, WI 54301
(414)497-4423

Fond du Lac District:
Division of Community Services
485 South Military Road
P.O. Box 1069
Fond du Lac, WI 54935
(414)929-3046

La Crosse District:
Division of Community Services
3550 Mormon Coulee Road
P.O. Box 743
LaCrosse, WI 54601
(608)785-9459

Northern Region:
Division of Community Services, Rhinelander
1853 North Stevens
P.O. Box 697
Rhinelander, WI 54501
(715)362-7800

Southeastern Region:
Division of Community Services, Waukesha
141 N.W. Barstow Street, Room 209
P.O. Box 1258
Waukesha, WI 53187-1258
(414)521-5085

Southern Region:
Division of Community Services, Madison
3601 Memorial Drive
Madison, WI 53704
(608)249-0441

Western Region:
Division of Community Services, Eau
   Claire
718 West Clairemont Avenue
P.O. Box 228
Eau Claire, WI 54701
(715)836-2634

Wisconsin Rapids District:
Division of Community Services
1691 Second Avenue, S.
P.O. Box 636
Wisconsin Rapids, WI 54494
(715)423-4305

Private Agencies

Adoption Services of Green Bay
130 East Walnut Street

Green Bay, WI 54301
(414)433-9071

Bethany Christian Services of Wisconsin
W255 N499 Grandview Boulevard
Waukesha, WI 53186
(414)547-6557

Catholic Charities, Inc.
128 South 6th Street
P.O. Box 266
La Crosse, WI 54601
(608)782-0704

Catholic Social Services, Green Bay
P.O. Box 1825
Green Bay, WI 54305-5825
(414)437-6541

Catholic Social Services, Madison
2702 International Lane
Madison, WI 53704
(608)256-2358

Catholic Social Services, Milwaukee
2021 North 60th Street
Milwaukee, WI 53208
(414)771-2881

Children's Service Society of Wisconsin
1212 South 70th Street
West Allis, WI 53214
(414)453-1400

Evangelical Child and Family Agency
2401 North Mayfair Road
Milwaukee, WI 53226
(414)476-9550

The Human Element, Inc.
2701 North 56th Street
Milwaukee, WI 53210
(414)445-9111

Latter Day Saints Social Services
4864 South 10th Street
Milwaukee, WI 53211
(414)483-1352

Lutheran Children's Friend Society
3515 North 124th Street
Brookfield, WI
(414)783-4564
Mail: P.O. Box 13367
   Wauwatosa, WI 53213

Lutheran Social Services of Wisconsin
   and Upper Michigan

3200 West Highland Boulevard
Milwaukee, WI 53208
(414)342-7175

Northern Family Services
1835 Stevens Street
P.O. Box 237
Rhinelander, WI 54501
(715)369-1554

Pauquette Children's Services, Inc.
304 West Cook Street
Portage, WI 53901
(608)742-5510

Seven Sorrows Infant Home
Route 1, Box 905
Necedah, WI 54646
(608)565-2417

Wisconsin Association of Family and
    Children's Agencies
30 West Mifflin
Madison, WI 53703
(608)257-5939

Wisconsin Lutheran Child and Family
    Services

6800 North 67th Street
Milwaukee, WI 53219
(414)353-5000

Wyoming

State Agency

Department of Social Services
Hathaway Building
Cheyenne, WY 82002
(307)777-6075

Private Agencies

Catholic Social Services
504 South Durbin
Casper, WY 82600
(307)442-3278

Wyoming Children's Society
P.O. Box 105
716 Randall Avenue
Cheyenne, WY 82002
(307)632-7619

ADOPTIVE-PARENT GROUPS

The following list of adoptive-parent groups was pulled together through several sources, including information provided by the North American Council on Adoptable Children in Washington, D.C.

Adoptive-parent groups are an excellent source of information on all facets of adoption. Be patient if the name, address, or phone number for a particular group turns out to be incorrect. Because most of these groups are run by volunteers, turnover is inevitable and it may take several attempts before the right person is reached. Keep trying; the effort will pay off.

Alabama

Adoptive-Parent Support Groups

Advocates for Global Adoption, Parenting and Education, Inc., (AGAPE)
Rt. 1, Box 266-A
Fairhope, AL 36532
Contact: Dorothy Threadgill, (205)928-9729

Alabama Friends of Adoption
4968 Springrock Road
Birmingham, AL 35223
Contact: Pat Baldwin, (205)871-8799
Focus of Group: Emphasis on American special-needs children

DeKalb County Family for Adoption
507 7th Street, N.W.
Fort Payne, AL 35967
Contact: Patricia Moody

Wiregrass Adoption Association
P.O. Box 6203
Dothan, AL 36302
Contact: Philip E. Paulk

Alaska

Adoptive-Parent Support Groups

Anchorage Adoptive Parents Association
P.O. Box 41685

203

Anchorage, AK 99509
Contact: Jean Bhagatram, (907)279-2780, or Becky Weil (907)344-5660

Valley Adoptive Parents Association
P.O. Box 931
Palmer, AK 99645
Contact: Karen Flagan, (907)745-4611

Arizona

Adoptive-Parent Support Groups

Advocate for Single Adoptive Parenting (ASAP)
P.O. Box 5288
Phoenix, AZ 85010

Arizona Families for Children
P.O. Box 17951
Tucson, AZ 85710
Contact: Anne Keefe, (602)298-1322

Black Child Advocate
P.O. Box 39615
Phoenix, AZ 85069
Contact: Adele Sims, (602)864-1133

Hispanic Support Group, Phoenix
1829 West Elm
Phoenix, AZ 85015

Hispanic Support Group, Tucson
5426 South Aleppo Drive
Tucson, AZ 85706

Open Door Society Adoptive Parents
Group
1332 East Bayview Drive
Phoenix, AZ 85283

Open Door Society of Arizona
2413 North 76th Place
Scottsdale, AZ 85257
Contact: Karen Baugn, (602)247-3038

Open Door Society, Cochise County
RR 1, Box 2402
Sierra Vista, AZ 85635

Tucson Open Door Society, Inc.
9421 East Creek Street
Tucson, AZ 85730
Contact: Penny Lyman, (602)886-8430

Arkansas

Adoptive-Parent Support Groups

Arkansas Special Needs Adoption
Council, Inc.
2200 Gaines
Little Rock, AR 72206
Contact: Rev. Richard Lancaster

Black Family Outreach
1512 Izard
Little Rock, AR 72202
Contact: Gloria Aboagye

California

Adoptive-Parent Support Groups

Adoptaids, Inc.
2550 West Olympic Boulevard
Los Angeles, CA 90006
Contact: Sharon Wright

Adoptive Family Association (AFA)
P.O. Box 5231
San Bernardino, CA 92412
Contact: Carol Wilms, (714)792-6854

Adoptive Parent Group of Calabasa
53 23401 Park Sorrento Drive
Calabasas, CA 91302
Contact: L. R. Tinsley, M.D., (213)999-1425

Adoptive Support Association
6013 Garnet
Alta Loma, CA 91701
Contact: Joyce Thun, (714)989-5390

Aid to Adoption
11167 East Ashland
Sanger, CA 93657
Contact: Patricia Lawrence

Aid to the Adoption of Special Kids
(AASK)
3530 Grand Avenue
Oakland, CA 94610

Aid to the Adoption of Special Kids,
Inc. (AASK), Devocion Chapter
2061 Carolewood Drive
Arcadia, CA 91006
Contact: Mrs. Stanton Davies,
(213)355-7313

Aid to the Adoption of Special Kids
(AASK), Hayward Chapter
817 Webster, Apt. 401
Hayward, CA 94544
Contact: Nancy Weinberg

Aid to the Adoption of Special Kids
(AASK), Huntington Beach Chapter
16391 Lakemont Lane
Huntington Beach, CA 92646
Contact: Mrs. Ron Harris

Aid to the Adoption of Special Kids
(AASK), Romoland Chapter
33041 Briggs Road
Romoland, CA 92380
Contact: Al Hartman, (714)926-2400

Aid to the Adoption of Special Kids
(AASK), West Covina Chapter
3408 Jodee Drive
West Covina, CA 91791
Contact: Ethel Sheffer

Association for the Adoption of Black
Children, Inc. (AABC)
P.O. Box 6643
San Bernardino, CA 92142
Contact: Fred Adams, (714)885-1657

Bay Area Black Adoptive Parents
Council, Inc.
P.O. Box 10495
Oakland, CA 94610
Contact: Jesse Sanders, (415)569-0874

Bay Area Organization for a United
Response (OURS)
1526 Grant Street
Berkeley, CA 94703
Contact: Holly Boss

Bay Area Single Adoptive Parent
Group
4008 Haines Avenue
San Jose, CA 95136
Contact: Jim Forderer, (408)448-4449

Black Linkage for Adoptive Children,
Inc. (BLAC)
4549 Don Tomaso
Los Angeles, CA 90008
Contact: Temple Beaman

California Citizen's Adoption Coalition,
Inc. (South)
1182 Tennyson
Manhatten Beach, CA 90266
Contact: Sheila Anderson, (213)372-
9039

California State Foster Parent Association, Inc.
3168 Gloria Terrace
Lafayette, CA 94549
Contact: Marian Love, (413)934-7118

Central Coast Adoption Support Group
P.O. Box 1937
Santa Maria, CA 93456

Chosen Ones
511 Squires Court
Sacramento, CA 95822
Contact: Midora Ito, (916)443-3794

Christian Home for Orphans of the
World, Inc. (CHOW)
1636 Kathleen Avenue
Sacramento, CA 95815
Contact: Mr. and Mrs. Scott Smith,
(916)482-0936
Focus of Group: Adoption of older chil-
dren

Concillo Hispanic Parents Support
Group
2737 Pleasant Street
Riverdale, CA 92507
Contact: Jose Rivera

Down's Syndrome Parents Group, Inc.
2468 Lyric Avenue
Los Angeles, CA 90027
Contact: Nancy F. Hall, (213)368-4209

East Bay Single Adoptive Parents
1761 Hopkins Street
Berkeley, CA 94797

Families Adopting Inter-Racially, Inc.
(FAIR)
5122 Glentree Court
San Jose, CA 95129
Contact: Linda Thornton, (408)252-
7364

Families By Choice
3538 Torino Way
Concord, CA 94518
Contact: Judy Hernbier

Families Ministries Adoption Support
215 North Marie
Fullerton, CA 92633

Families United Through Adoption
(FUTA)
P.O. Box 2033
Idyllwild, CA 92349
Contact: Alice Regan, (714)659-4165

Friends of Holt/Korea Organization for a United Response (OURS)
2236 Carta Blanca
Cupertino, CA 95014
Contact: Jinny Fruin

Friends of the World's Children/Organization for a United Response (OURS)
7605 Dos Rios Way
Bakersfield, CA 93309
Contact: Karen Dull, (805)833-2684

Holy Family Adoptive Parents
9473 Siskin
Fountain Valley, CA 92708

Humboldt County Council on Adoptable Children, Inc. (COAC)
P.O. Box 4767
Arcata, CA 95521
Contact: Cindy Humphrey, (707)822-2229

JAMAA, Inc.
P.O. Box 552
Seaside, CA 93955
Contact: Eugen Douglas, (408)384-0130

Kings County Adoptive Parents Group
1173 Hanson Court
Hanford, CA 93230
Contact: Sharon Behren, (209)582-4103

League of Mexican American Women
P.O. Box 686
Fresno, CA 93712
Contact: Angie Cisneros, (207)222-6482

Mothers for Intercountry Adoption (MICA)
1753 Glenview Avenue
Simi Valley, CA 93063
Contact: Bobbi Monsue, (805)522-1463

Nevada County Adoptive Parents Group, Inc.
P.O. Box 361
Nevada City, CA 95959
Contact: Bobbi Rowlands, (916)265-3314

North County Adoptive Families Association (AFA)
1433 Kurtz Street
Oceanside, CA 92054
Contact: Kathy Cornwall, (714)433-3863

North Valley Adoptive Families Association
Rt. 2, Box 805
Chico, CA 95926
Contact: Susan Elliott

Open Door Society (ODS) of Gabriel and Pomona Valley
P.O. Box 30
Glendura, CA 91740
Contact: Randy Scharff

Open Door Society (ODS) of Los Angeles, Inc.
12235 Silva Place
Cerritos, CA 90701
Contact: Donna Salisbury, (213)860-8349
Focus of Group: Special-needs adoption; older child; transracial; physical, mental, or emotional problems

Open Door Society (ODS) of Orange County
16783 Beach Boulevard
Huntington Beach, CA 92647
Contact: Deborah Silverstein, (714)848-7549

Open Door Society (ODS) of Riverside and San Bernardino Counties
24424 Tierra De Oro
Sunnymead, CA 92388
Contact: Jean Sovern, (714)653-7364

Open Door Society (ODS) of Ventura County
2157 Basswood Court
Westlake Village, CA 91361
Contact: Susan Heyman, (213)991-2810

Orange County Adoptive Parents Association (OCAPA)
P.O. Box 11371
Santa Ana, CA 92711
Contact: Karen Shea, (714)998-8338

Organization for a United Response (OURS) of Solano County
166 Weymouth Court
Vacaville, CA 95688
Contact: Debbie Rutte, (707)448-4558

Organization for a United Response (OURS) of Southern California, Inc.
2350 Teton Circle
Placentia, CA 92670
Contact: Fred Adams, (714)528-8298

Padres Por Los Ninos, Inc.
3832 West Feemster
Visalia, CA 93277
Contact: Frances Holguin

Parents Adopting Challenging Children
714 Ramona Avenue
Spring Valley, CA 92077

Parents League for Adoptive Youngsters (PLAY)
44758 North Elm Street
Lancaster, CA 93534
Contact: Cheryl Johnson, (805)942-2852

Pleasant Hill Adoptive Parents Group
141 Pleasant View Drive
Pleasant Hill, CA 94523

Room For One More
5342 Keystone Drive
Fremont, CA 94536

San Diego Association of Adoptive Families, Inc.
5604 Galloping Way
San Diego, CA 92129
Contact: Gail Silverhorn, (714)267-4750

Shasta County Adoptive Parents Group
5061 Scheer Drive
Redding, CA 96001

Single Adoptive Parents Association of Los Angeles
26928 Pacific Coast Highway
Malibu, CA 90265
Contact: Michael Blanda

Sonoma County Organization for a United Response (OURS), Inc.
4754 Hidden Oaks Road
Santa Rosa, CA 95404
Contact: Ann Giles, (707)544-1540, or Marcy Clausen, (707)433-6461

Stanislaus Families for Adoption
3113 Laramie Drive
Modesto, CA 95355
Contact: Marilyn Schmidt, (209)524-5697

Tayari Adoptive Parents
884 Banneker Drive
San Diego, CA 92077
Contact: Deanna Taylor

United Native Indian Tribes Adoptive Parent Group, Inc.

3148 Cascade Boulevard
Redding, CA 96003
(916)275-3625

Ward Parent Adoptive Group, Inc.
10920 Jamie Avenue
Pacoima, CA 91331
Contact: Betty Witherspoon, (213)899-3330

Colorado

Adoptive-Parent Support Groups

Adams County Adoptive Parents Association
1640 West 106th Avenue
Northglen, CO 80234
Contact: Frank Kogovek, (303)457-1883

Adoption Awareness Group
1707 Avian Drive
Fort Collins, CO 80525
Contact: Sue Chilcott, (303)484-2238

Colorado Parents For All Children (CPFAC)
6925 West 35th Street
Wheatridge, CO 80033
Contact: Leslie Coffman, (303)423-9502

Colorado Parents For All Children (CPFAC), Boulder Chapter
911 Cypress Drive
Boulder, CO 80303
Contact: Anna Marie Merrill, (303)494-8333

Colorado Parents For All Children (CPFAC), Colorado Springs Chapter
18020 Granite Circle
Monument, CO 80132
Contact: Deborah Ferguson, (303)481-3421

Colorado Parents For All Children (CPFAC), Western Slope Chapter
2821 Hall Drive
Grand Junction, CO 81501
Contact: Deborah Hage, (303)245-1449

Denver Minority Parents for Adoption
1747 Marion
Denver, CO 80205
Contact: Joshua Appo, (303)534-0841

Foreign Adoption Resources
911 Cypress Drive

Boulder, CO 80303
Contact: Anna Marie Merrill, (303)494-8333

Organization for a United Response
(OURS), Denver Chapter
6776 South Bellaire Way
Littleton, CO 80122
Contact: Judy Aronson
Focus of Group: Family recruitment
for special-needs children

Single Adoptive Families Everywhere
(SAFE)
4217 C. Monroe Drive
Boulder, CO 80302
Contact: Joan Sargent

Connecticut

Adoptive-Parent Support Groups

Concerned Parents for Black Adoptions
742 Kennedy Road
Windsor, CT 06095

Friends of the Adopted Child
P.O. Box 1269
Groton, CT 06340
Contact: Maureen Lyman, (203)536-9263

Graney Adoptive Parents
182 West Mountain Road
West Simmsbury, CT 06092
Contact: Beth Delnegro

Manchester Adoptive Parents
143 Trout Stream Road
Vernon, CT 06033
Contact: Marilyn Newton, (203)872-4023

North East Regional Adoption Council
(NERAC)
73 Mather Street
Manchester, CT 06040
Contact: Linda or Jack Cotter,
(203)649-8115

Open Door Society of Connecticut
(ODS)
P.O. Box 478
Hartford, CT 06541
Contact: Linda Cotter, (203)649-8115
Focus of Group: Personal experiences
in adopting internationally

Welcome House Adoptive Parents
Group (WHAPG), Connecticut Chapter
315 Old Lane Road
Chesire, CT 06410
Contact: Roberta Getnan, (203)288-8268

Delaware

Adoptive-Parent Support Groups

Adoptive Coalition for Children
Box 426-D, RD 1
Hockessin, DE 19707
Contact: Maureen Piper, (302)366-8286, or Nancy McKenna, (302)239-7340

Adoptive Families with Information
and Support
2610 Northgate Road, Channin
Wilmington, DE 19810

District of Columbia

Adoptive-Parent Support Groups

Black Caucus
1039 Evarts Street, N.E.
Washington, D.C., 20018
Contact: Wilfred Hamm, (202)526-5200

Committee for Single Adoptive Parents
P.O. Box 4074
Washington, D.C., 20015
Contact: Hope Marindin, (202)966-6367

Concerned Citizens for Black Adoption
P.O. Box 24040
Washington, D.C., 20024
Contact: Karen Pittman

Council on Adoptable Children of D.C.
1813 Glendora Drive
District Heights, MD 20028
Contact: Gary Shapiro

Florida

Adoptive-Parent Support Groups

Council on Adoptable Children (COAC)
Inc. of Mid-Florida

P.O. Box 1263
Winter Park, FL 32790
Contact: Mary Pillmear, (305)678-0664

Holt Families of Florida
P.O. Box 1121
Titusville, FL 32780
Contact: Clyde Maggard, (305)269-4596

Lifeline for Children, Inc.
P.O. Box 17184
Plantation, FL 33318
Contact: Wilma Dorsey, (305)584-5957

North Florida Council on Adoptable
    Children
Rt. 2, Box 24
Newberry, FL 32669
Contact: Kent Brand, (904)472-3817

Northeast Florida Adoption Advocacy
    Council (NEFAAC)
3614 St. Augustine Road
Jacksonville, FL 32207
Contact: Judi Hines, (904)246-9603
Focus of Group: Parent support; moni-
toring of legislation; recruitment on
behalf of special-needs children

Suncoast Organization for a United
    Response (OURS)
2091 Burnice Drive
Clearwater, FL 33516
Contact: Hank and Ann Steffens

Tampa Bay Council on Adoptable Children (COAC), Inc.
7002 Forestview Court
Tampa, FL 33614
Contact: Ken Milligan, (813)884-5182

Universal Aid for Children, Inc.
1175 N.E. 125th Avenue, Suite 202
North Miami, FL 33161
Contact: Lorri Kellogg

Georgia

Adoptive-Parent Support Groups

Adoptive Parents Organization
P.O. Box 164
Lawrenceville, GA 30245
Contact: Patricia F. Brown, (404)963-
5815

Adoptive Parents Organization
2671 Falcon Ridge Drive

Grayson, GA 30221
Contact: Sandra Barber, (404)972-0417
Focus of Group: Foreign child placing
resources; group support; personal
experiences in adopting internationally

Albany Adoptive Parents Association
P.O. Box 3983
Albany, Ga 31706
Contact: Gail Prather, (912)435-9526,
or Janis Burch, (912)432-6579

Gainesville Adoptive Parents Organiza-
tion
Rt. 1, Box 487
Oakwood, GA 30507
Contact: Jo Ann Manning, (404)536-
5901

Georgia Adoptive Parents of Douglas
    County, Inc.
6199 John West Road
Douglasville, GA 30134
Contact: Norman Brazed, (404)949-
4053

Georgia Adoptive Parents of Northeast
    Metro Atlanta
1041 Oakdale Road
Atlanta, GA 30307
Contact: Elizabeth Rowe, (404)378-
5358

Macon Adoptive Parents Organization
2140 Ingleside, Apt. K-7
Macon, GA 31204
Contact: Phil Clark, (912)744-7462

Newton-Rockdale Adoptive Parents
311 Bonnell Street
Oxford, GA 30267
Contact: Jean Williams, (404)483-0027

Hawaii

Adoptive-Parent Support Groups

Adoptive Parent Groups, Hawaii Inter-
national Child Placement
P.O. Box 263
Hawi, HI 96719
Contact: Monroe Woollard

Adoptive Parents League of Hawaii
P.O. Box 1426
Kaneohe, HI 96744

Contact: Cathy Schmier, (808)642-4374
or (808)524-6190

Idaho

Adoptive-Parent Support Groups

Adoptive Families of Idaho
P.O. Box 183
Caldwell, ID 83605
Contact: Jeri Pugh, (208)257-3877

Families Thru Adoption
554 Garfield
Pocatello, ID 83201
Contact: Becky Erickson Black,
(208)232-8929

Forever Families
P.O. Box 7824
Boise, ID 83707
Contact: Susan Dufenhorst, (208)345-
9493

Interracial Families of America Adoption Unit
Route 1, Box 116-A
McCall, ID 83638
Contact: Joy Weller Miller, (208)634-
2775

North Idaho Adoptive Families
P.O. Box 729
Post Falls, ID 83854
Contact: Susan A. Smith, (208)773-
5629

North Idaho Adoptive Families, Kellogg Chapter
Contact: Ann Hamilton, (208)783-5441

North Idaho Adoptive Families, Sandpoint Chapter
Rt. 3, Box 465-A
Sandpoint, ID 83864
Contact: Ginney Libbey, (208)263-5391

North Idaho Adoptive Families, Silver Valley Chapter
111 Woodland Drive
Wallace, ID 83873
Contact: Jeanne Brown, (208)556-6171,
or Ann Hamilton, (208)783-5441

Southern Idaho Parents for Children
Rt. 1, Box 129
Hansen, ID 83334
Contact: Linda Medley, (208)634-2775

Illinois

Adoptive-Parent Support Groups

Adoption Triangle
c/o Children's Home
Suite 4238, 113 North Neil Street
Champaign, IL 61820
Contact: Cathy Colbert, (217)359-8815,
or Ray Murphy, (217)384-5097

Adoptive and Foster Parent Organization
1033 Oxford Court
Charleston, IL 61701
Contact: Betty Thomason, (217)345-
7550

Adoptive Parents Support Group
c/o Lutheran Child and Family Services
2408 Lebanon Avenue
Belleville, IL 62236
Contact: Alfred Armstead, (618)234-
8904

Adoptive Parents Together
822 Kenmore Avenue
Elmhurst, IL 60126
Contact: Mary Gravengaard, (312)834-
1542

Bensenville Reach-Out Group
4415 Blackhawk, Apt. 101
Lisle, IL 60532
Contact: LuAnn Williams

Bloomington/Normal Adoptive Parents
Group
1609 North Roosevelt
Bloomington, IL 61701
Contact: Cheryl McIntire, (309)828-
6138

The Children's Advocate, Inc.
142 Wood Street
West Chicago, IL 60185
Contact: Karen Link, (312)231-8155

Council on Adoptable Children
(COAC), Quincy Area
P.O. Box 19
Sutter, IL 62373
Contact: Sandy Meyer, (217)985-5985

Families Adopting Children of Every
Skin (FACES)
627 Lake Avenue

Wilmette, IL 60091
Contact: Joan Sargent, (312)251-0591

Greater Quad Cities Organization for a
  United Response (OURS)
2929 27th Avenue A
Moline, IL 61265
Contact: Joseph and Ann Vermeire

Heart of Illinois Organization for a
  United Response (OURS)
1117 Summit Boulevard
Peoria, IL 61606
Contact: Sharon Childs

Holt International Mothers Club
36 East Brookdale
Palatine, IL 60067
Contact: Judy McCaskey, (312)397-
  4410

Illinois Council on Adoptable Children
  (COAC), Inc.
P.O. Box 7
Oak Park, IL 60308
Contact: Andy Anderson, (312)359-4467

Illinois Parents for Minority Adoptions
7930 South Colfax
Chicago, IL 60617
Contact: Drucills Fair, (312)734-2305

The Melting Pot
2517 Whitehall Circle
Rockford, IL 61105
Contact: Roberta Flaherty, (815)226-
  8117

Organization for a United Response
  (OURS), South Suburban Chicago
4501 West 117th Street
Country Club Hills, IL 60477
Contact: Michaelyn Sloan, (312)957-
  2866

Organization for a United Response
  (OURS), West Suburban Chicago
1410 Golden Bell
Downers Grove, IL 60515
Contact: Toni Carter, (312)852-4631

Parents of Adopted Children Together
  (PACT)
1 North 740 Route 59
West Chicago, IL 60185
Contact: Mrs. R. Bowie, (312)231-9023

Parents of Adopted Children Together
  (PACT), North
430 North Crystal

Elgin, IL 60120
Contact: Mr. and Mrs. H. Simmons

Pekin Adoptive and Foster Parent
  Group
814 North 4th Street
Pekin, IL 61554
Contact: Sue Wittfield, (309)353-1092

Southern Illinois Adoptive Families
  Association
33 Grainey
Edwardsville, IL 62025
Contact: Kathryn Benatson, (618)288-
  9778

Springfield Council on Adoptable Children (COAC)
2336 South 10th Street
Springfield, IL 62703
Contact: Beverly Reynolds, (217)628-
  1786

Indiana

Adoptive-Parent Support Groups

Adoptive and Foster Parent Support
  Group, Delaware County
R.R. #1, Box 60A
Daleville, IN 46334
Contact: Miss Cindy Michael

Adoptive Parents Together (APT)
3312 Ivory Way
Indianapolis, IN 46227
Contact: Roberta Decker

Adoptive Parents Together
3624 Grand
Connersville, IN 47331
Contact: Mr. and Mrs. Frank Neu

Association for the Rights of Children
  (ARC)
3223 Bass Road
Fort Wayne, IN 46808
Contact: Rebecca Dirig

Association for the Rights of Children
  (ARC)
P.O. Box 509
Notre Dame, IN 46556

Association for the Rights of Children
  (ARC) of Indiana, South Bend Chapter

921 Adams
South Bend, IN 46628

Association for the Rights of Children/
Council on Adoptable Children
(ARC/COAC)
10514 East 25th Street
Indianapolis, IN 46229
Contact: Mrs. Marty Miller

Black Adoption Committee
P.O. Box 1221
Indianapolis, IN 46204
Contact: Nanette Sechrest

Council on Adoptable Children (COAC)
of Grant County
503 East Washington Street
Fairmount, IN 46928
Contact: Tane Templin

Council on Adoptable Children (COAC)
of Lafayette
1021 Holly Drive
Lafayette, IN 47905
Contact: Peg Hurt

Delaware County Foster Parent Association
227 South Mississinewa
Albany, IN 47320
Contact: Helen Medaris

Families Adopting Children Today
819 North Renesselaer
Griffith, IN 46319
Contact: Karen Scheeringa

Families United Our Way
6114 O'Hara Drive
Evansville, IN 47711
Contact: Mr. J. Douglas Lechleiter

Indiana Foster Care Association
R. 1, Box 63
Waveland, IN 47989
Contact: Ruby B. Smith

Indiana Foster Care Association of
Floyd County
Rt. 1, Box 102
Pekin, IN 47166
Contact: Cynthia Miller

Organization for a United Response
(OURS) of Indianapolis
5728 Somers Drive
Indianapolis, IN 46203
Contact: Steve and Mary Dreier

Rainbow Families of Ours
61529, C.R. 127
Goshen, IN 46526
Contact: Jan Parrish

Room For One More
516 East 400 South
LaPorte, IN 46350
Contact: Bonnie Henson

Iowa

Adoptive-Parent Support Groups

Cedar Rapids Organization for a
United Response (OURS)
2925 Bever Avenue, S.E.
Cedar Rapids, IA 52403
Contact: Michael and Jennine Robinson

Council on Adoptable Children
(COAC), Ames Chapter
254 Village Drive
Ames, IA 50010

Council on Adoptable Children
(COAC), Davenport Chapter
2518 West 43rd
Davenport, IA 52806
Contact: Jane Becker

Families for Asian Children, Oxford
Chapter
RR 1, Box 53-A1
Oxford, IA 52322
Contact: Mrs. Lon Drake

For Love of Children (FLOC)
c/o Becci Kelley
Route 1
New Market, IA 51646

Friends of Holtap
1219 Caroline
Burlington, IA 52601
Contact: Pamela Peterson

International Adoptive Parents, Inc.
3809 Elwood Drive, N.E.
Cedar Rapids, IA 52402

Iowa State Association of Foster Parents
Route 1
Spencer, IA 51301
Contact: Bob Tolle

Iowans for International Adoption
403 North K Street
Indianola, IA 50125
Contact: Joanne Walton, (515)961-5573

Open Door Society (ODS) of Cedar
Rapids
Route 4
Iowa City, IA 52240
Contact: Jerry Musser

Open Door Society (ODS), Tri-State
489 South Grandview
Dubuque, IA 52001
Contact: Nancy Long

Parents By Choice
Rural Route #1
Prole, IA 50229
Contact: Beverly Charier, (515)462-3428

Kansas

Adoptive-Parent Support Groups

Adoptive Mother's Club, 1206 High
Topeka, KS 66604
Contact: Nancee Price

Adoptive and Interracial Living
1653 Indiana Street
Lawrence, KS 66044
Contact: Carole Boulton

Council on Adoptable Children (COAC)
of Kansas
644 North Bluff
Wichita, KS 67208
Contact: Evelyn Middlestadt

Council on Adoptable Children (COAC)
of Kansas
Route #5
Abilene, KS 67410
Contact: Ed Hoover

Parents By Choice
6100 West 58th Street
Mission, KS 66202
Contact: Jean Fields

Parents Organized to Support Black
Adoptive Children
7138 Lafayette Avenue
Kansas City, KS 66109
Contact: Shakura Sabur, (913)299-1142

Kentucky

Adoptive-Parent Support Groups

Citizens for Adoption, Inc.
1774 Gettsburg Drive
Lexington, KY 40504
Contact: Burke Anderson, (606)276-2133

Kentuckiana Families for Children
2700 Brownsboro Road
Louisville, KY 40206
Contact: Alice DeVries, (502)895-5145

Organization for a United Response
(OURS), Hopkins County Chapter
P.O. Box 46
Earlington, KY 42410
Contact: Vernon Gipson, (502)383-5772

Louisiana

Adoptive-Parent Support Groups

Adoptive Couples Together, Inc.
5908 Parkforest Drive
Baton Rouge, LA 70815

Adoptive Couples Together, Inc.
P.O. Box 1321
Kenner, LA 70063

Adoptive Couples Together, Inc.
9500 Abie Lane
River Ridge, LA 70123
Contact: Ashton and Royann Avegno,
(504)737-2008

Maine

Adoptive-Parent Support Groups

Adoptive Families of Maine
21 Glenwood Avenue
Augusta, ME 04330
Contact: Sharon Pierce, (207)622-0062

Adoptive Families of Maine
44 Shepley Street
Auburn, ME 04210
Contact: Kathy Novick, (207)784-6022

Adoptive Families of Maine
P.O. Box 87

Hampden, ME 04444
Contact: Dr. Patrick Kamm, (207)862-
4390

Adoptive Families of Maine
20 Day Street
Kennebunk, ME 04043
Contact: Jean Chace, (207)985-7548

Adoptive Families of Maine
RFD 1
Lisbon Falls, ME 04252
Contact: Susan Sayer, (207)353-6479

Adoptive Families of Maine, Bangor
   Chapter
Star Route 38
Hancock, ME 04640
Contact: Lindley Harmon, (207)422-
3084

Council on Adoptable Children (COAC)
56 Court Street
Houlton, ME 04730
Contact: Sandra Bell, (207)532-3300
Focus of Group: Foreign child-placing

Families for Adopted Children (FAC)
P.O. Box 2004
Portland, ME 04104

Growing Through Adoption Parent
   Group
460 Main Street
Lewiston, ME 04240
Contact: Margery Goldberg, (207)786-
2597

Maine Adoption Placement Services
P.O. Box 772
Houlton, ME 04738
Contact: Dawn Degenhardt, (207)532-
9800

Northern Aroostook County Council on
   Adoption
45 Burleigh Street
Limestone, ME 04750
Contact: Frances Costa, (207)328-7204,
   or Kathleen Vargas, (207)328-6870

Maryland

Adoptive-Parent Support Groups

Black Adoptive Parents of Greater Baltimore
1516 North Montford Avenue

Baltimore, MD 21213
Contact: Jackie Garner, (301)563-0793

Concerned Citizens for Black Adoption
10009 Reddick Drive
Silver Spring, MD 20901
Contact: Karen J. Pittman

Council on Adoptable Children (COAC)
1813 Glendora Drive
District Heights, MD 20028
Contact: Gary Shapiro, (703)620-2180

Families Adopting Children Every-
   where (FACE)
P.O. Box 102
Bel Air, MD 21014
Contact: Barbara Holtan, (301)836-
1128

Families Adopting Children Everywhere, Metro Chapter
8108 Phirne Road East
Glen Burnie, MD 21061
Contact: Linda Heriehy, (301)969-7782

Families Adopting Children Everywhere, Southern Chapter
6902 Nashville Road
Lanham, MD 20801
Contact: Sherry Simas, (301)552-1888

International Families by Adoption
P.O. Box 1
Woodsboro, MD 21798
Contact: Kathy Jenkins, (301)271-4163

Latin American Parents Association
   (LAPA), Inc., Maryland Chapter
P.O. Box 4403
Silver Spring, MD 20904
Contact: Pat Buchanan, (301)572-4755

Open Door Society (ODS) of Maryland
219 Altamont Avenue
Baltimore, MD 21228

Massachusetts

Adoptive-Parent Support Groups

Adopt Me Please
154 Elm Street
P.O. Box 1422
Pittsfield, MA 01201
Contact: Alice R. Marshall, (413)443-
2400

Adoption Counsellors, Inc.
95 Dorset Road
Waban, MA 02168
Contact: Louise Lazare, (617)969-1915

Extended Family Institute, Inc.
P.O. Box 1040, Astor Station
Boston, MA 02123
Contact: Jacqui LeBeau, (617)451-1472

Legislative Committee–Open Door Society of Massachusetts
48 Elm Street
Canton, MA 02021
Contact: Deyne Meadow, (617)828-1434

Massachusetts Adoptive Family Association
P.O. Box 1542
Westfield, MA 01086
Contact: Jo Ann Moore

Open Door Society of Massachusetts
25–31 West Street
Boston, MA 02111
Contact: Kathy Metager, (617)366-1724

Open Door Society of Massachusetts, Acton Chapter
15 Knowlton Drive
Acton, MA 01720
Contact: Juliette Weiland, (617)263-1274, or Sue Rosen, (617)263-0857

Open Door Society of Massachusetts, Inc., North Shore Chapter
10 Collins Street
Danvers, MA 01923
Contact: Sarah Macquarrie

Open Door Society of Massachusetts, Inc., South Shore Chapter
53 Brook Terrace
Weymouth, MA 02188
Contact: Judy Baker

Organization for a United Response (OURS), Massachusetts Chapter
P.O. Box 128
East Longmeadow, MA 01028
Contact: Barb and Jacques Begin, (413)566-8929

Parents Adopting Children Together (PACT)
10 Dean R.R.
Ashland, MA 01721

Single Parents Adopt Children Everywhere (SPACE)
86 Edwin Street
North Quincy, MA 02171
Contact: Betsy Burch, (617)655-5426, or Mary Ilacqua, (617)328-0871

Worcester Aid to Children
Contact: Jenny Bedell, (617)839-2864

Michigan

Adoptive-Parent Support Groups

Adoption by Addition/CISCO, Inc.
1424 11 Mile Road
Royal Oak, MI 48067
Contact: Carol Cole, (313)548-4044

Adoptive Family Groups
427 West College
Marquette, MI 49855
Contact: Rita Palomaki

Aid to Adoption of Special Kids (AASK)
6514 Carriage Hills Drive
Canton, MI 48187
Contact: Judith Prince, (313)455-7395

Ann Arbor Friends for International Adoption and Assistance
1213 Olivia Street
Ann Arbor, MI 48104
Contact: Shirley Wolfe, (313)668-6835

Colombian–American Friends, Inc.
P.O. Box 553
Ypsilanti, MI 48197
Contact: Barbara Willett, (313)482-0380
Focus of Group: Liaison organization between families and orphanages in Colombia for purpose of adoption

Council on Adoptable Children (COAC) of Lansing
281 North Every Road
Mason, MI 48854
Contact: Jane Shapley

Detroit Parent Group of Spaulding for Children
7681 Ellsworth
Detroit, MI 48238
Contact: Elaine Ward, (313)862-0673
Focus of Group: Recruitment of homes for black children

Escanaba Council on Adoptable Children (COAC)
Route 1, Box 430A
Gladstone, MI 49837
Contact: Nancy McIntyre

Families for Children, Inc.
19100 West 10 Mile Road, Suite 104
Southfield, MI 48075
Contact: Jan Adler, (313)398-2447

Families for International Adoption Association
254 Ann Street
Plymount, MI 48170
Contact: Diane Dicks, (313)455-8882

Families for International Children
1307 Philadelphia, S.E.
Grand Rapids, MI 49506
Contact: Kris Lee, (616)452-0750

For the Love of Children (FLOC)
1634 Clements
Detroit, MI 48238
Contact: Ann Brown

Friends of Homes for Black Children
1140 Calvert
Detroit, MI 48404
Contact: Bertha Scott

Grand Traverse Council on Adoptable Children (COAC)
Route 1, Box 469
Rapid City, MI 49676
Contact: Pat Wolcott

International Adoptive Families
509 East Grand River
Laningsburg, MI 48848
Contact: Jo Wong, (517)651-5284

Macomb County Association of Adoptive Families
c/o Catholic Social Service
235 South Gratiot Avenue
Mount Clemens, MI 48083
Contact: Sharon Gioia, (313)293-4189

Michigan Association of Single Adoptive Parents
P.O. Box 601
Southfield, MI 48037
Contact: Peggy Coltrin, (313)435-0816

Organization for a United Response (OURS) of Flint
4338 Crosby Road
Flint, MI 48506

Contact: Nancy and Rodney Keisey, (313)736-8891

Organization for a United Response (OURS) of Macon County
204 North Gaylord Avenue
Ludington, MI 49431
Contact: Leeann Clapper, (616)843-8564

Organization for a United Response (OURS) of North Oakland County
2640 Hatton Road
Pontiac, MI 48057
Contact: Sherri Arnold

Spaulding for Children Adoptive Parents Group
18754 Fruitport Road
Spring Lake, MI 49456
Contact: Sandy Bee, (616)846-6578
Focus of Group: Support and advise single people on adoption procedures

Minnesota

Adoptive-Parent Support Groups

Adoption Today, Inc.
P.O. Box 6003
Rochester, MN 55901
Contact: Fletcher A. Miller, Jr., M.D., (507)286-9122

Carver County Adoptive Parent Support Group
c/o Carver County Community Social Services, Courthouse
Chaska, MN 55318
Contact: Becky Varone, (612)448-3661
Focus of Group: Special-needs adoption

Citizens' Coalition on Permanence for Children
17917 Cynthia Drive
Minnetonka, MN 55343
Contact: Patricia L. Teskey, (612)474-7566

Dakota County Adoptive Parent Association
17880 Jaguar Court
Lakeville, MN 55044
Contact: David Fezatte, (612)435-6829

Organization for a United Response
(OURS), Inc.
20140 Pine Ridge Drive
Minneapolis, MN 55303
Contact: Guy and Andrea Wegener,
(612)753-4788 or (612)753-1097

Organization for a United Response
(OURS), Buffalo Chapter
703 8th Street, N.W.
Buffalo, MN 55313
Contact: William and Mary Bemboom

Organization for a United Response
(OURS), Duluth County
183 Beech Street
Duluth, MN 55804
Contact: Dan and Amy Bishop

Organization for a United Response
(OURS), Hastings Chapter
9945 190th Street, E.
Hastings, MN 55033
Contact: Robert and Joanne Schweich

Organization for a United Response
(OURS), Montevideo Area Chapter
Route 4, Box 272
Montevideo, MN 56265
Contact: Larry Danielson

Organization for a United Response
(OURS), New Prague Chapter
Route 3, Box 149
New Prague, MN 56071
Contact: Bob and Colleen Pavek

Organization for a United Response
(OURS), Olivia Area Chapter
Route 2, Box 19A
Olivia, MN 56277
Contact: LeRoy and Jacque Gaub

Organization for a United Response
(OURS), Pine City Chapter
229 11th Street
Pine City, MN 56063
Contact: Jerry and Kay Olson

Organization for a United Response
(OURS), Pine River Chapter
Star Route 60
Pine River, MN 56479
Contact: Paul and Pat Norman

Organization for a United Response
(OURS), Polk County Chapter
c/o Dennis and Carol Hammer
McIntosh, MN 56556

Organization for a United Response
(OURS), Rochester Chapter
318 S.W. Pine Crest Court
Pine Island, MN 55963
Contact: Eldon Skurdahl

Organization for a United Response
(OURS), St. Cloud Area Chapter
Route 4
St. Cloud, MN 56301
Contact: Jerome and Judy Miller

Organization for a United Response
(OURS), South Central Area Chapter
225 East 3rd Street
Blue Earth, MN 56013
Contact: Joseph and Cathy Fox

Organization for a United Response
(OURS), Thief River Falls Chapter
R.R. 1
St. Hilaire, MN 56757
Contact: Gary and Sandra Anderson

Washington County Adoptive Parents
Association
c/o Washington County Social Services
939 West Anderson Street
Stillwater, MN 55082
Contact: Glorian R. Hein, (612)439-
6901

Mississippi

Adoptive-Parent Support Groups

Council on Adoptable Children (COAC)
of Mississippi
P.O. Box 1184
Jackson, MS 39205
Contact: Margrit Garner, (601)355-
7495

Memphis Area Holt Parents
7166 Westbranch Road
Olive Branch, MS 38654
Contact: Marcia Kreunen, (601)895-
2389

Missouri

Adoptive-Parent Support Groups

Adoptive Parents of the Ozarks
345 Brook
Lebanon, MO 65536

Contact: Carolyn Wright, (417)532-3082

Greater Springfield Adoptive Parent Organization
342 Landmark Building
Springfield, MO 65806
Contact: Christine Squibb, (417)865-4506

Group for Adoption Interest Now (GAIN)
4106 West Haverhill Drive
St. Joseph, MO 64506
Contact: Doug and Judy Howard, (816)279-4210

Open Door Society (ODS) of Missouri, Inc.
6199 Waterman
St. Louis, MO 63112
Contact: Sharon Fako, (314)727-9491

Open Door Society (ODS) of Missouri, Kansas City Branch
Route 3
Milo, MO 64767
Contact: Barbara Walker

Open Door Society (ODS) of Missouri, Northeast Missouri Branch
222 East Lafayette
Palmyra, MO 63461

Open Door Society (ODS) of Missouri, West Central Branch
304 Jones Avenue
Warrensburg, MO 64003

Parents Association of the Children's Home Society of Missouri
1028 Terracerock Circle
Ballwin, MO 63011

World Children's Fund, Inc.
P.O. Box 114
O'Fallon, MO 63366
Contact: Jeanne Lang, (314)962-8838

Montana

Adoptive-Parent Support Groups

Citizens Concerned About Adoption (CCAA)
P.O. Box 644
Conrad, MT 59425
Contact Pam Moritz, (406)278-5445

Families for Adoptable Children
P.O. Box 485
Anaconda, MT 59711
Contact: Mel and Lois Ann Jones, (406)563-5077

Nebraska

Adoptive-Parent Support Groups

Child Saving Institute (CSI), NBA Auxiliary
North Star Route, Box 17
Kimball, NE 69145
Contact: Mary J. Larkin, (308)235-2528

Friends of Holt
Route 3, Box 33A
Cozad, NE 69130
Contact: Helen McConnell

Intercultural Families
800 Northborough Lane
Lincoln, NE 68505
Contact: Karen Thiel, (402)466-5183

Intercultural Families, Inc.
1418 South 133rd Street
Omaha, NE 68144
Contact: Janet Schak

Interracial Families
435 South 29
Lincoln, NE 68510

Nebraska Foster and Adoptive Parents Association (NFAPA)
3325 Woolworth Avenue
Omaha, NE 68105
Contact: Penny Winfield, (402)346-9133

Nebraska Foster and Adoptive Parents Association (NFAPA), Blair Chapter
Route 1
Bennington, NE 68007
Contact: Ann Gregerson

Nebraska Foster and Adoptive Parents Association (NFAPA), Central Nebraska Chapter
P.O. Box 117
Sutton, NE 68979
Contact: Mr. and Mrs. Del Stahl

Nebraska Foster and Adoptive Parents Association (NFAPA), Columbus Chapter
2719 19th Street

Columbus, NE 68061
Contact: George Reed

Nebraska Foster and Adoptive Parents
Association (NFAPA), Eastern Ne-
braska Chapter
Route 1
Fremont, NE 68025
Contact: Bill Calta

Nebraska Foster and Adoptive Parents
Association (NFAPA), Fort Kearney
Chapter
Route #1, Box 124
Elm Creek, NE 68836
Contact: Judd and Rena Hagen

Nebraska Foster and Adoptive Parents
Association (NFAPA), Gering Chapter
1445 Gentry Boulevard
Gering, NE 69341
Contact: Ray Richards

Nebraska Foster and Adoptive Parents
Association (NFAPA), Lincoln Chap-
ter
2440 S.W. 18th
Lincoln, NE 68522
Contact: Mr. and Mrs. Ron Malena

Nebraska Foster and Adoptive Parents
Association (NFAPA), Norfolk Chap-
ter
508 South 6th
Norfolk, NE 68701
Contact: Dean Pennington

Nebraska Foster and Adoptive Parents
Association (NFAPA), North Platte
Chapter
Route 1, Box 281
Maywood, NE 69038
Contact: Mr. and Mrs. Carl Yonkers

Nebraska Foster and Adoptive Parents
Association (NFAPA), Omaha Chap-
ter
5625 Pacific
Omaha, NE 68132
Contact: Mr. and Mrs. Tom Matusik

Nebraska Foster and Adoptive Parents
Association (NFAPA), Sarpy County
Chapter
205 Glendale Circle
Gretna, NE 68028
Contact: Mr. and Mrs. Mike Foley

Sharing Through Adoption Club
P.O. Box 772

Winnebago, NE 68071
Contact: Stephan and Lorna Emery,
(402)878-2919

Nevada

Adoptive-Parent Support Groups

Aid to the Adoption of Special Kids
(AASK)
P.O. Box 352
Henderson, NV 89015

Families for Adoption
1858 Citation
Las Vegas, NV 89118
Contact: Karen Gallegos, (702)361-
5615

New Hampshire

Adoptive-Parent Support Groups

Adoption Service League of Greater
Nashua
6 Woodward Road
Merrimack, NH 03054
Contact: Lois Emond, (603)424-6397

Open Door Society
RFD #2, Box 111
Kingston, NH 03848
Contact: Mary Ann Coppola, (603)382-
7060, or Peggy Rees, (603)382-6824

New Jersey

Adoptive-Parent Support Groups

Children of Adoptive Parents, Inc.,
South Jersey
6 Wyndmere Road
Marlton, NJ 08053
Contact: D. S. Erhart, (609)983-4258
Focus of Group: Parents who have
adopted older or handicapped chil-
dren

Children Who Wait
1108 Berkeley Avenue
Ocean, NJ 07712
Contact: Josephine Pohl, (201)531-0761

Concerned Parents for Adoption
200 Parsippany Road
Whippany, NJ 07981
Contact: Julia Brohan, (201)887-9288

Concerned Persons for Adoption,
    Northern New Jersey Chapter
35 Carlisle Road
Wayne, NJ 07470
Contact: Janet Levin, (201)595-6929

Council on Adoptable Children (COAC)
    of New Jersey
55 Stonehenge Terrace
Clark, NJ 07066

Families for Adoption
395 Wyckoff Avenue
Ramsey, NJ 07446
Contact: Sandra Bunger

Latin American Adoptive Parents, Central New Jersey Chapter
P.O. Box 828
Hightstown, NJ 08520
Focus of Group: Latin American adoptions

Organization for a United Response
    (OURS), New Jersey Chapter
1424 Colorado Drive
Toms River, NJ 08753
Contact: Barbara Cenci, (201)270-1838

South Jersey Council of Adoptive Parents
134 Oakdale Road
Cherry Hill, NJ 08034
Contact: Marie Emma, (609)428-8438

Welcome House Adoptive Parent
    Group, Inc. (WHAPG), Central New
    Jersey Chapter
27 Partridge Avenue
Freehold, NJ 07728
Contact: Lawrence Paris

Welcome House Adoptive Parent
    Group, Inc. (WHAPG), Northern
    New Jersey Chapter
37 Wanaque
Hewitt, NJ 07421
Contact: Jim Dougherty

New Mexico

Adoptive-Parent Support Groups
Individuals Making Positive Action/
    Children Today (IMPACT)

4004 Camino de La Sierra N.E.
Albuquerque, NM 87111
Contact: Pat and Judy McDaniel,
    (505)292-1976

Los Escogidos
4374 Ridgeway
Los Alamos, NM 87544
Contact: Sandra B. Luck, (505)662-5424

Otero-Lincoln County Adoptive Parents Group
2041A Hanscom Place
Holloman A.F.B., NM 88330
Contact: Rose Mumbulo, (505)479-4458

New York

Adoptive-Parent Support Groups
Adopt Black Children Association
1027 Harding Street
Uniondale, NY 11553
Contact: Mamie Bouknight

Adoptive Families Association of
    Tompkins County Inc.
220 Eastern Heights Drive
Ithaca, NY 14850
Contact: Judy Hughes, (607)272-1259

Adoptive Families of Cortland County
98 Broadway
Cortland, NY 13045
Contact: Lee Ann Perry

Adoptive Families of Westchester
One Matilda Street
Ossining, NY 10562
Contact: Joan and Bernie McNamara,
    (914)762-6550

Adoptive Families of Westchester/
    Down's Syndrome Program
158 Longview Avenue
White Plains, NY 10605
Contact: Janet Marchese, (914)428-1236

Adoptive Families of Westchester, Putnam Chapter
RFD 3, Whangtown Road
Carmel, NY 10512
Contact: Mary Jo Brett, (914)225-2642

Adoptive Parents Committee, Inc.
210 Fifth Avenue

New York, NY 10010
Contact: Harry Blum, (212)962-0363

Adoptive Parents Committee, Inc.,
Long Island Chapter
P.O. Box 71
Belmore, NY 11710
Contact: Irwin and Susan Wein,
(516)785-6610

Adoptive Parents of Clinton County
76 Beekman
Plattsburgh, NY 12901

American Friends of Children
110 Old Country Road
Deer Park, NY 11729

Black Adoption Recruitment Commit-
tee, Council of Adoptive Parents
P.O. Box 9667
Rochester, NY 14604
Contact: Annie Miller

Catholic Adoptive Parents Association
P.O. Box 893
Harrison, NY 10528
Contact: Howard Fitz-Patrick or Mary
Ellen Havard, (914)723-2204

Central New York Council of Adoptive
Families
168 Chaffee Avenue
Syracuse, NY 13207
Contact: Marge Holt, (315)469-1657

Child
24 Violet Avenue
Mineola, NY 11501
Contact: Rosemary Sullivan, (516)742-
7909

Committed Persons for Black Adoption
271 West 125th Street, Room 414
New York, NY 10027
Contact: Isaac Bembry

Concerned Persons for Adoption
222 Marcus Avenue
New Hyde Park, NY 11040
Contact: Kathe Stojowski, (516)747-
4715

Council of Adoptive Parents (CAP) of
Rochester, Inc.
P.O. Box 9667
Rochester, NY 14604
Contact: Irene and Tom Sinopoli,
(716)352-9638

Families for the Future
P.O. Box 2524
Schenectady, NY 12309
Contact: Randall Fasnacht, (518)463-
2379

Families Interested in Adoption
P.O. Box 932
Williamsville, NY 14221
Contact: David C. Martin, (716)625-
8897

Friends of Children Everywhere (FACE)
415 Madison Avenue
West Hempstead, NY 11552
Contact: Barbara Graffeo, (516)481-
0031

Friends of Children in Need, Inc.
543 Harris Hill Road
Lancaster, NY 14086
Contact: Jackie Peters, (716)685-2580

Holt Families Unlimited
c/o Draper
RD 2
Campbell, NY 14821

Holt Families—Upstate New York
508 4th Street
Liverpool, NY 13088

Hudson Valley Adoptive Families
3 Center Street
Poughkeepsie, NY 12601
(914)417-3336

International Council of Adoptive Parents
56 Daunton Drive
Rochester, NY 14624

International Parents
Box 232, Connell Avenue
Hobart, NY 13788

Latin American Parents Association
(LAPA)
P.O. Box 72
Seaford, NY 11783
Contact: Susan Pignato, (516)433-4168

League of Adoptive Parents Association
44 Bedford Drive
Whitesboro, NY 13492

Love the Children of Long Island, Inc.
P.O. Box 992
Centereach, NY 11720

Contact: Maureen Sullivan, (516)744-1305
Focus of Group: Relief work to overseas orphanages

New York Council on Adoptable Children (COAC)
875 Avenue of the Americas, Room 200
New York, NY 10001
Contact: Clara Vailente-Barksdale, (212)279-4525
Focus of Group: Special-needs children; black and Hispanic advocacy programs

New York State Citizens Coalition for Children
6928 266th Street
Floral Park, NY 11004

Open Door Society of Long Island
P.O. Box 236
Ronkonkoma, NY 11779
Contact: Mary Mayer, (516)724-1665

Orange County Foster and Adoptive Parents
RD 2, Oak Drive
P.O. Box 296
New Windsor, NY 12550

Organization of Foster Families for Equality and Reform (OFFER)
P.O. Box 222
Glen Oaks, NY 11004
Contact: Maris Blechner, (212)343-4981

Organization for a United Response (OURS) of Long Island
P.O. Box 637
Moriches, NY 11955
Contact: Joan and Bob Goetschuer

Organization for a United Response (OURS), Rockland
4 Virginia Street
New City, NY 10956

Parents and Children Together (PACT)
23 Webb Lane
Highland Falls, NY 10928
Contact: Jane Dubuque, (914)446-9444

Parents and Children Together (PACT)
28 Tietjen Avenue
Kingston, NY 12401
Contact: Joan Locke

Parents and Children Together (PACT)
Box 83, RD 3
Red Hook, NY 12571
Contact: Martin and Helene Gershowitz, (914)758-5609

Parents for Adoption
20 Rives Street
Batavia, NY 14020

Parents for All Children (PFAC)
120 Washington Highway
Snyder, NY 14226

Parents for All Children (PFAC) of Western New York
65 Fancher Avenue
Kenmore, NY 14223

Rockland County Council on Adoptable Children (COAC)
108 Union Road
Spring Valley, NY 10977

St. Joseph Children's Service Adoptive Parents Group, Inc.
1707 78th Street
Brooklyn, NY 11214
Contact: Joseph Fisher, (718)643-3060

South Bronx Adoptive Parents Organization
535 East 138th Street
Bronx, NY 10454
Contact: Charles Ruiz

Southern Tier Adoptive Families
R.D. 2
Spencer, NY 14883
Contact: Donna Fitzgerald, (607)589-6172

Tioga County Adoptive Parents
R.R. #2
Spencer, NY 14882
Contact: Ruth Ferrier, (607)589-4905

Welcome House Adoptive Parents Group (WHAPG), Westchester County Chapter
2908 Birch Street
Yorktown Heights, NY 10598

North Carolina

Adoptive-Parent Support Groups

Adoption Awareness
4283 Winnabow Road

Winston-Salem, NC 27105
Contact: Brenda Jarrett, (919)967-8940

Adoptive Parents Together, Inc.
Rt. 1, Box 279
High Point, NC 27260
Contact: Betty S. Lewis, (919)454-3580

Black Adoption Task Force
P.O. Box 6587
Greensboro, NC 27405
Contact: Hunter G. Haith, (919)275-
5064 or (919)273-9451

Cleveland County Council of Adoptive
Parents
2946 College Road
Shelby, NC 28150
Contact: Jerry E. Ellis, (704)482-4828

Council for Adoptive Families, Inc.
6922 Burlwood Road
Charlotte, NC 28211
Contact: Sherrell Godsby, (704)364-
1164

Metrolina Black Adoption Task Force
301 South Brevard Street
Charlotte, NC 28202
Contact: Sandra Yarborough, (704)334-
2854

Parents of Adopted Children Together,
Inc. (PACT)
213 North Crestwood Drive
Wilmington, NC 28401
Contact: Barbara Cook, (919)791-6402

Piedmont Council on Adoptable Children (COAC)
3032 Dillion Road
Jamestown, NC 27282
Contact: Bea Corley, (919)452-4227

Wake Families for Adoptable Children,
Inc.
Rt. 2, P.O. Box 56-A
Apex, NC 27502
Contact: Jan Chadwick, (919)362-7066

North Dakota

Adoptive-Parent Support Groups

Families and Friends of Adoption
1814 Lewis Boulevard
Grand Forks, ND 58201
Contact: Hazel Cartier, (218)773-1029

North Dakota Adoptive Parents
Groups
774 10th Street, East
Dickinson, ND 58601

Southwestern North Dakota (OURS)
540 2nd Avenue S.E.
Dickinson, ND 58601
Contact: Marty Van Velhuizen

Ohio

Adoptive-Parent Support Groups

Action for Children
1293 East Broad Street
Columbus, OH 43205
(614)252-0791

Adopting Older Kids (AOK)
504 West Wenger Road
Englewood, OH 45322
Contact: Janet Weeks, (513)836-7277

Adoptive Family Organization of
Northwest Ohio
P.O. Box 502
Maumee, OH 42537
Contact: Virginia Oravecz, (419)866-
8362

Area Adoptive Parent Association
P.O. Box 311
Wooster, OH 44691
Contact: Gladene Hershberger,
(216)682-0103

Black Adoption Recruitment Committee
1882 Nason Avenue
Columbus, OH 43207
Contact: Victor Ricks

Black Adoptive Parent Outreach
1565 Thurston Street
Akron, OH 44320
Contact: Carolyn Rucker, (216)836-
7175

Caring Families Through Adoption
2255 Rugged Hill Road
Casstown, OH 45312
Contact: Salley Humphrey, (513)355-
3274

Citizens for Children of Hamilton
County

4718 Winton Road
Cincinnati, OH 45232

Concern for Children, Inc.
325 North Scranton Street
Ravenna, OH 44266

Council on Adopting Children Today
(COACT)
925 Woodview Avenue
Cleveland Heights, OH 44121
Contact: Jeanne Kurtz, (216)932-3204

Families for Black Adoptable Children
2044 West 38th Street
Cleveland, OH 44113
Contact: Gloria Mareda, (216)281-0028

Families Thru World Adoption/Organization for a United Response
2933 Lower Bellbrook Road
Spring Valley, OH 45370
Contact: Donna Morris

Forever Families for Kids, Inc.
1670 Meadow Lane Drive, S.E.
North Canton, OH 44709
Contact: Denny and Gail Weisend,
(216)494-2327

Helping Hands for Black Adoption
c/o Loraine County Children Service
Board
226 Middle Avenue
Elyria, OH 44035
Contact: Ruth Palmer, (216)329-5310

Organization for a United Response
(OURS) of North Central Ohio
1144 County Road 175, Route #1
Polk, OH 44866
Contact: Denny and Marilyn Reed

Parents of Adopted Children (PAC)
Route 2, Box 206
Mansfield, OH 44903
Contact: Eleanor Brown, (419)468-7199

Putnam County Parents for Child's
Rights, Inc.
P.O. Box 14
Ottawa, OH 45875
Contact: Tim Calvelage, (419)532-3064

Single Adoptive Parents Group
180 West Kenwood
Columbus, OH 43214
Contact: Odette Blum, (614)262-1541

Oklahoma

Adoptive-Parent Support Groups

Oklahoma Council on Adoptable Children (COAC)
P.O. Box 18
Oklahoma City, OK 73101
Contact: Eva Carter, (405)232-8055 or
(405)721-7243

Oklahoma Council on Adoptable Children (COAC), Bartlesville
Route 1, Box 137
Dewey, OK 74029
Contact: Suzanne Joyce, (918)534-2237

Oklahoma Council on Adoptable Children (COAC), Canadian County
Route 1, Box 43
Union City, OK 73090
Contact: Terri Dries, (405)483-5540

Oklahoma Council on Adoptable Children (COAC), Kay County
1510 Queens
Ponca City, OK 74601
Contact: Terri Monger, (405)762-8168

Oklahoma Council on Adoptable Children (COAC), Oklahoma City Branch
12100 Greystone
Oklahoma City, OK 73120
Contact: Jeane Hartmann, (405)751-5738

Oklahoma Council on Adoptable Children (COAC), Tawhuska
Red Eagle Route, Box 42
Tawhuska, OK 74056
Contact: Barbara Walker, (918)287-3075

Oklahoma Council on Adoptable Children (COAC), Tulsa Branch
8619 Janis Lane
Tulsa, OK 74131
Contact: Terry Yates, (918)224-4776

Oregon

Adoptive-Parent Support Groups

Adoptive Parents Organization
216 Exchange Street
Astoria, OR 97103

Contact: Ernest Atkinson, (503)325-5107

Banks Parent Group
Star Route, Box 76-K
Banks, OR 97106
Contact: Carol Newman, (503)324-7921

Be A Parent
Rt. 3, Box 102
Newberg, OR 97123
Contact: Ellen G. Boyd, (503)538-4786

Bend Adoptive Parent Group
66700 Gerking Road
Bend, OR 97701
Contact: Marlys Coonrod, (503)389-6673

Coos County Parents for Children
Fairview Route, Box 672
Coquille, OR 97423
Contact: Donna Danielson, (503)396-4647

Extended Family Outreach
4524 N.E. 9th Street
Portland, OR 97211
Contact: Maxine Williams, (503)284-8710

Families Adopting Children Together (FACT)
Route 1, Box 41
Summerville, OR 97876

Families Celebrating Individual Differences
8951 S.E. Woodhill Court
Portland, OR 97211
Contact: Vivian Shuri, (503)661-2981

Family Opportunities Unlimited
Box 194
McMinnville, OR 97128
Contact: Harriet Gahr, (503)472-6960

Give Us This Day
Route #3, Box 140-C
Newberg, OR 97132
Contact: Joshua and Virginia Phillips, (503)538-2111
Focus of Group: Special-needs children

Holt Adoption Program
P.O. Box 2440
Eugene, OR 97402
(503)687-2202, for information on parent-support groups

Lane County Open Door for Adoptable Children
3801 Donald
Eugene, OR 97405
Contact: Roz Slovic, (503)344-8484

Lincoln County Adoptive Parents
P.O. Box 362
Siletz, OR 97380
Contact: Di Goodman, (503)444-2631

McMinnville Adoptive Parent Group
2920 Redwood Drive
McMinnville, OR 97128
Contact: Greg and Jan Kerry, (503)472-3379

Open Door Society (ODS)
16801 Webster Road
Gladstone, OR 97202
Contact: Judy Bentley

Organization for a United Response (OURS), Oregon Chapter
P.O. Box 332
Tualatin, OR 97062
Contact: Lyn McDonald, (503)638-9430, or Linda Cordes, (503)658-6195

Salem Area Adoptive Parent Group
407 Browning, S.E.
Salem, OR 97302
Contact: Gary and Kathy Haney, (503)364-4341

South East Portland Adoptive Parent Group
19393 Kapteyns
West Linn, OR 97068
Contact: Clark and Linda Jeli, (503)636-9829

South Oregon Adoptive Parent Group
368 Kent Street
Ashland, OR 97520
Contact: Jim and Sue Goodman, (503)482-9774

Team of Adoptive Parents
322 Arcadia Drive
Roseburg, OR 97470
Contact: Carol Surrency, (503)673-7815

Pennsylvania

Adoptive-Parent Support Groups

Adopted Parents Group of Delaware County

146 Ashley Road
Newtown Square, PA 19073
Contact: Aurora O'Brien, (215)356-
2317

Adoptive Families with Information
and Support
RD #1, Box 23
Landerburg, PA 19350

Black Adoptable Parents Association of
Western Pennsylvania
1020 South Mill Street
New Castle, PA 16101
Contact: Peter Franklin, (412)652-0289

Bucks County Council on Adoptable
Children (COAC)
6365 Powderhorn Court
Cornwells Heights, PA 19020
Contact: Dewain McClees, (215)757-
0476

Child Advocates–Adoptive Parents
15 Public Square
Suite 400, Bicentennial Building
Wilkes-Barre, PA 18701
Contact: Hopkin Rowlands

Council on Adoptable Children (COAC)
of Chester County
125 Glendale Road
Exton, PA 19341
Contact: Susan Beattie

Council on Adoptable Children (COAC)
of Northwest Pennsylvania, Inc.
327 Joliette Avenue
Erie, PA 16511
Contact: Janet Staley, (814)899-3517

Council on Adoptable Children (COAC)
of Southwest Pennsylvania, Inc.
P.O. Box 81044
Pittsburgh, PA 15217
Contact: Linda Jay, (412)367-3667 or
(412)322-5408

Families Adopting Children Everywhere (FACE)
1119 Tidewater Drive
Bethel Park, PA 15102

Families for Black Children
138 Marlyn Avenue
Bryn Mawr, PA 19010
Contact: Virginia Hammond, (215)525-
8205

Friends of Children of Viet Nam/Open
Door Society of Pennsylvania
1835 Troxell Street
Allentown, PA 18103
Contact: Pat Sexton, (215)865-1882

Indaba
114 East 14th Avenue
Homestead, PA 15120
Contact: Joseph T. Moran, (412)462-
2917
Focus of Group: Facilitating adoption
of black children

Latin American Parents Association
(LAPA), Philadelphia Chapter
P.O. Box 18107
Philadelphia, PA 19116

Parents and Adopted Children Organization (PACO)
122 West Springettsbury Avenue
York, PA 17403

Parents and Adopted Children Organization (PACO) of Beaver Valley
764 Blackhawk Road
Beaver Falls, PA 15010
Contact: Debra Elefson, (412)846-8821

Parents and Adopted Children Organi-
zation (PACO) of Lawrence/Mercer
Counties
P.O. Box 5031
New Castle, PA 16105
Contact: Malcena Mooney

Parents and Adopted Children Organization (PACO) of Mercer County
1816 Rambold Road
Hermitage, PA 16148
Contact: Marti and Jim McWilliams,
(412)342-5596

Parents and Adopted Children Organization (PACO) of Midwest Pennsylvania
233 West Fulton Street West
Butler, PA 16001
Contact: Pamela Grabe, (412)283-1971

Parents and Adopted Children Organization (PACO) of North Central
Pennsylvania
1029 Rural Avenue
Williamsport, PA 17701
Contact: Rosemary E. Bailey, (717)326-
3133

Parents and Adopted Children Organization (PACO) of Philadelphia
2900 Queen Lane
Philadelphia, PA 19129

Parents and Adopted Children Organization (PACO) of Westmoreland
12 Madison Avenue
Irwin, PA 15642
Contact: Peg McElhose, (412)795-5912

Parents and Adopted Children Organization (PACO) of Wiliamsport/Lewisburg
RD 1, Box 347
Lewisburg, PA 17837

Parents and Adopted Children Together (PACT)
20 Lansdowne Court
Lansdowne, PA 19050
Contact: Marcia Siegel, (215)259-3934

Pennsylvania Coalition for Children
608 East Edison
New Castle, PA 16101
Contact: Jan Reitnauer, (412)658-5848
Focus of Group: Education of legislators as to needs of waiting children

Together for Adoptive Children (TAC)
904 Lansdale Avenue
Lansdale, PA 19446
Contact: Will and Susan Liegel, (215)368-8913

Welcome House Adoptive Parent Group (WHAPG)
P.O. Box 265
Doylestown, PA 18901
Contact: Kate DeLosso, (215)853-2088

Welcome House Adoptive Parent Group (WHAPG)
P.O. Box 17
Kintnersville, PA 18930
Contact: Jane Brown

Welcome House Adoptive Parent Group (WHAPG), Philadelphia Chapter
8638 Marigold Place
Philadelphia, PA 19136
Contact: Donna Weldon

Welcome House Adoptive Parent Group (WHAPG), Tri-County Chapter
619 West Valley Forge Road

King of Prussia, PA 19406
Contact: Monica Gosling

Rhode Island

Adoptive-Parent Support Groups

Ocean State Adoptive Groups, Inc.
170 Westminster Street, Suite 1200
Providence, RI 02903
Contact: Elaine Cassinelli, (401)789-6243

Parents Adoptees Liberty Movement (PALM)
P.O. Box 3073
Pawtucket, RI 02861
Contact: Betty Angier, (401)847-4773

Rhode Island Families for Interracial Adoption
100 Shelton Street
Providence, RI 02903

South Carolina

Adoptive-Parent Support Groups

Parents Adoption Information Resource (PAIR) of South Carolina
P.O. Box 1383
West Columbia, SC 29169
Contact: Patricia Aimar, (803)796-9447

South Carolina Black Adoption Committee, Inc.
P.O. Box 2516
Columbia, SC 29101
Contact: Beverly Pittman, (803)779-5350

South Carolina Council on Adoptable Children (COAC)
1453 Hammond Pond Road
North Augusta, SC 29841
Contact: Joyce Thompson, (803)776-5658

South Dakota

Adoptive-Parent Support Groups

Pierre Adoptive Parent Group
Part A

Pierre, SD 57501
Contact: Becky Ivers, (605)224-5243

Rapid City Adoptive Parents Group
1120 Farlo
Rapid City, SD 57701
Contact: Jean Montoya, (605)342-4508

South Dakota Foster Care and Adoption Association
P.O. Box 27
Pierre, SD 57501
Contact: David Shisler, (605)224-5027

Tennessee

Adoptive-Parent Support Groups

Adoptive Families of Nashville
6029 Sedberry Road
Nashville, TN 37205
Contact: Betty Miller

Chattanooga Council on Adoptable Children (COAC)
2110 Rambler Lane
Hixson, TN 37343
Contact: Sue Rucker, (615)842-4218

Knoxville Council on Adoptable Children (COAC)
P.O. Box 1787
Knoxville, TN 37901
Contact: Mimi Brody, (615)693-0476, or Ginger Reynolds, (615)693-3053

Memphis Council on Adoptable Children (COAC)
P.O. Box 18951
Memphis, TN 38118
Contact: Alan Miller

Texas

Adoptive-Parent Support Groups

Adopt Black Children Committee
8602 Allwood
Houston, TX 77016
Contact: Odessa Sayles

Adoptive Parents of El Paso, Inc.
P.O. Box 26712
El Paso, TX 79926
Contact: Ann Delaney, (915)591-5224 or (915)778-0158

Council on Adoptable Children (COAC) of Texas, Inc.
P.O. Box 842
Houston, TX 77001
Contact: Sandra Dush, (512)928-0702

Council on Adoptable Children (COAC) of Texas, Amarillo Branch
3306 Ostega
Canyon, TX 79106
Contact: Beverly Groninger, (806)352-0543

Council on Adoptable Children (COAC) of Texas, Austin Branch
P.O. Box 14662
Austin, TX 78761
Contact: Chris Hoelscher, (512)258-6791

Council on Adoptable Children (COAC) of Texas, Corpus Christi Branch
3902 Holly Road, #2
Corpus Christi, TX 78415
Contact: Maureen Burgess, (512)854-3140

Council on Adoptable Children (COAC) of Texas, Dallas Branch
P.O. Box 1691
Richardson, TX 75080
Contact: Phyllis Penny, (214)286-4382

Council on Adoptable Children (COAC) of Texas, East Texas Branch
P.O. Box 737, Avenue A
Huntington, TX 75949
Contact: Dena Rembert, (713)876-4642

Council on Adoptable Children (COAC) of Texas, Galveston County Branch
191 Loch Lomond
League City, TX 77573
Contact: Charles and Judy Hunsucker, (713)332-3649

Council on Adoptable Children (COAC) of Texas, Houston Branch
P.O. Box 2571
Houston, TX 77001
Contact: Sallie Moore, (713)537-1530

Council on Adoptable Children (COAC) of Texas, Montgomery County Branch
Route 4, Box 1110 Dp
New Caney, TX 77357
Contact: Barbara Couture, (713)354-5266

Council on Adoptable Children (COAC) of Texas, Permian Basin Branch
3406 Princeton
Midland, TX 97093
Contact: Mary Dunn, (915)694-9902

Council on Adoptable Children (COAC) of Texas, Rio Grande Branch
2614 Cypress
Harlingen, TX 78550
Contact: Claudio Savio, (512)428-1266

Council on Adoptable Children (COAC) of Texas, San Angelo Branch
P.O. Box 3472
San Angelo, TX 76901
Contact: Ken Mayville, (915)949-1013

Council on Adoptable Children (COAC) of Texas, San Antonio Branch
P.O. Box 11791
San Antonio, TX 78217
Contact: Richard Mogas, (512)494-0141

Council on Adoptable Children (COAC) of Texas, Temple Branch
208 South 27th
Temple, TX 76501
Contact: Randy Weatherford, (817)778-5842

Friends of San Antonio Lutheran Social Services
112 Cotillion
San Antonio, TX 78213
Contact: Patricia Dorner, (512)227-2852

New Hope Advisory Committee
2110 Hemphill
Fort Worth, TX 76110
Contact: Bobbie Matthews, (817)926-3304

San Antonio M.A.P.L.E. (Methodist Mission Home)
1830 Elizabeth
Kingsville, TX 78363
Contact: Stephen and Gaby Hill, (512)592-3284

Utah

Adoptive-Parent Support Groups

Families for Intercultural Adoption
P.O. Box 642

Logan, UT 84321
Contact: Robin Garner, (801)753-5282

HOPE of Utah (Helping Orphans and Parents Everywhere)
P.O. Box 1146
Provo, UT 84601
Contact: Billie Jean Lee, (801)377-HOPE

Utah Families of Intercultural Adoptions (FIA)
P.O. Box 15977
Salt Lake City, UT 84115
Contact: Huntley Thatcher, (801)451-7021

Vermont

Adoptive-Parent Support Groups

Concerned United Birthparents (CUB)
RD #1, Box 716
Bridgeport, VT 05700
Contact: Carol Gile, (802)758-2369

Room For One More, Inc.
RD 3
Williston, VT 05495
Contact: Nancy Van Gulden, (802)878-4558

Room For One More, Southern Chapter
Woodstock Avenue
Rutland, VT 05700
Contact: Bonnie and Christopher Oakman, (802)775-2653

Vermont Adoption Alliance
17 Sibley Place
Montpelier, VT 05602
Contact: Nancy Miller, (802)223-6113

Virginia

Adoptive-Parent Support Groups

Children, Inc.
P.O. Box 5318
Richmond, VA 23220
Contact: Jeanne C. Wood

Christian Adoptive Parents
8518 Calvary Lane

Manassas, VA 22110
Contact: Marianne Nigreville

Council on Adoptable Children (COAC)
2285 Marginella Drive
Reston, VA 22091
Contact: Gary Shapiro, (703)620-2180

Council on Adoptable Children
(COAC), Prince William County
Chapter
13413 Carrageem Drive
Manassas, VA 22110
Contact: Mary Adams

Families Adopting Interracially
Through Faith
726 Myrtle Drive
Salem, VA 24153

People for the Adoption of Children
2604 East Franklin Street
Richmond, VA 23223
Contact: Ruth Finley, (804)643-3231
Focus of Group: Permanent placement
for special-needs children

Reach Out for Black Adoption (ROBA)
c/o Children's Home Society
4200 Fitzhugh Avenue
Richmond, VA 23230
Contact: Nadine Wingfield, (804)284-
1175

Tidewater Council on Adoptable Children (COAC)
512 Lavender Lane
Virginia Beach, VA 23462
Contact: Eleanor Green, (804)499-9934
Focus of Group: Encourage adoption
of special-needs children

Washington

Adoptive-Parent Support Groups

Adoptive Support Group of Kitsap
County
4508 Basswood Lane, S.E.
Port Orchard, WA 98366
Contact: Vicki Butterfield

Colville Area Adoptive Parents
Route 1, Box 657
Evans, WA 99126
Contact: Linda Blandt

Goldendale Adoptive Parents Association, Inc.
421 West Main
Goldendale, WA 98620
Contact: Alice DeHart, (509)773-5737

Interracial Family Association (IFA)
3333 Hunter Boulevard
Seattle, WA 98144
Contact: Margie Patsula, (206)723-5827

Interracial Family Association (IFA),
Whatcomb County Chapter
2631 Walnut Street
Bellingham, WA 98225
Contact: Leslie Neidigh

Kids In Need (KIN)
4229 Thompson Avenue
Everett, WA 98203
Contact: Paula Erickson, (206)334-
7183, or Sharon Thompson,
(206)252-7035

Northwest Adoption Services
2516 Henry Street
Bellingham, WA 98225
Contact: Barbara McHugh, (206)733-
1709

South Puget Sound Adoptive Parents
425 Ramsdell Street
Fircrest, WA 98466

Valley Adoption Services
1425 Mount View Road
Mount Vernon, WA 98273

Washington Association of Christian
Adoptive Parents (WACAP)
P.O. Box 2009
Port Angeles, WA 98362
Contact: Merrily Ripley, (206)452-2308

Washington Association of Christian
Adoptive Parents (WACAP), Bellingham Chapter
2516 Henry Street
Bellingham, WA 98225
Contact: Barbara McHugh, (206)733-
1709

Washington Association of Christian
Adoptive Parents (WACAP), Bremerton Chapter
143 Lebo Street
Bremerton, WA 98310
Contact: Carol and David Wedeven,
(206)377-2441

Washington Association of Christian
Adoptive Parents (WACAP), Chehalis
Chapter
675 N.W. St. Helens Avenue
Chehalis, WA 98532
Contact: Karen Emerson, (206)748-
0985

Washington Association of Christian
Adoptive Parents (WACAP), Cie
Elum Chapter
113 West 4th Street
Cie Elum, WA 98922
Contact: Jo Ann Rowles, (509)952-9752

Washington Association of Christian
Adoptive Parents (WACAP), Everett
Chapter
9425 32nd S.E.
Everett, WA 98205
Contact: Paula Erickson, (206)334-7183

Washington Association of Christian
Adoptive Parents (WACAP), Goldendale Chapter
421 West Main
Goldendale, WA 98620

Washington Association of Christian
Adoptive Parents (WACAP), Long-
view Chapter
#20 Jeffrey Place
Longview, WA 98632
Contact: Karen Penta, (206)577-8244

Washington Association of Christian
Adoptive Parents (WACAP), Mount
Vernon Chapter
1625 Mountainview Road
Mount Vernon, WA 98273
Contact: Madlyn Yarcho, (206)422-
6711

Washington Association of Christian
Adoptive Parents (WACAP), North
King County Chapter
22198 61st Street, S.E.
Bothell, WA 98011
Contact: Lillian Thogersen, (206)481-
8034

Washington Association of Christian
Adoptive Parents (WACAP), Olympia
Chapter
401 West 17th Avenue
Olympia, WA 98501
Contact: Martha Liska, (206)352-0981

Washington Association of Christian
Adoptive Parents (WACAP), Port Angeles Chapter

527 Rose Street
Port Angeles, WA 98362
Contact: Sharon Alton, (206)452-7052

Washington Association of Christian
Adoptive Parents (WACAP), Prosser
Chapter
Rt. 2, Box 3704
Prosser, WA 99350
Contact: Dennis and Lynda Yule,
(509)786-3269

Washington Association of Christian
Adoptive Parents (WACAP), South
King County/North Pierce Chapter
1814 Aberdeen Avenue
Renton, WA 98055
Contact: Donna Copp, (206)266-3129

Washington Association of Christian
Adoptive Parents (WACAP), Spokane
Chapter
North 14915 Glenedon
Spokane, WA 99208
Contact: Elaine Vaugh, (509)466-1109

Washington Association of Christian
Adoptive Parents (WACAP), Tacoma
Chapter
1202 West Pioneer
Puyallup, WA 98371
Contact: Donna Pierson, (206)848-5189

Washington Association of Christian
Adoptive Parents (WACAP), Tri-
Cities Chapter
3902 South Dennis
Kennewick, WA 99336
Contact: Jaki Sievers, (509)586-0239

Washington Association of Christian
Adoptive Parents (WACAP), Vancou-
ver Chapter
11014 N.E. 202nd Avenue
Brush Prairie, WA 98606
Contact: Judy Nordberg, (206)892-9250

Washington Association of Christian
Adoptive Parents (WACAP), We-
natchee Chapter
2410 1st N.E.
East Wenatchee, WA 98801
Contact: Merry Rou, (509)884-2874

Washington Association of Christian
Adoptive Parents (WACAP), Yakima
Chapter
Rt. 2, Box 625
Yakima, WA 98906
Contact:Anne Anna, (509)966-9326

West Virginia

Adoptive-Parent Support Groups

Adoptive Parent Support Group
112 South High Street
P.O. Box 800
Morgantown, WV 26505
Contact: Kathy Merrill, (304)291-5541
or (304)296-8246

Adoptive Parents Group of West Virginia
1032 Valley Road
Charleston, WV 25302
Sally Preston, (304)345-1958

Parkersburg Area Parents by Adoption
Route 1, Box 252
Williamstown, WV 26817

Wisconsin

Adoptive-Parent Support Groups

Adoptive Mother's Club of Greater Milwaukee
1408 Cottonwood Drive
Waukesha, WI 53186
Contact: Elaine Cori, (414)549-5861

Adoptive Parent Group of Southern Wisconsin
1408 Vilsa Avenue
Madison, WI 53711
Contact: Marilyn Holshuh

Brown County Adoptive Parents
1251 Doblon Street
Green Bay, WI 54302
Contact: Connie Thirion

Fox Valley Adoptive Parent Support Group
1231 Jackson Street
Oshkosh, WI 54901
Contact: William Christianson,
(414)223-4535

International Families
6917 5th Avenue
Kenosha, WI 53140
Contact: Berge and Mary Jane Whitmore

Namaste
511 Highway 153
Mosinee, WI 54455
Contact: Kathy and Dave Zimmerman

Open Door Society (ODS)
865 North 11th Street
Manitowac, WI 54220
Contact: Bob and Janice Jump,
(414)682-8050

Open Door Society (ODS) of Milwaukee, Inc.
P.O. Box 1352
Milwaukee, WI 53202
Contact: Jackie Omdahl, (414)442-3924, or Jay and Kathlyn Kirk,
(414)964-2516

Open Door Society (ODS) of Northwest Wisconsin
225 Hudson Street
Eau Claire, WI 54701
Contact: Sue Gambrell, (715)834-8688

Open Door Society (ODS), Tri-County
P.O. Box 193
Ashippun, WI 53003
Contact: Marie Capps, (414)474-4562

Organization for a United Response
(OURS) of Central Wisconsin
1010 Parcher Street
Wausau, WI 54401
Contact: Lee and Donna Kitchens,
(715)842-9213

Organization for a United Response
(OURS), Coulee Region
216 North Water
Sparta, WI 54656
Contact: Mrs. Sue Shockley

Organization for a United Response
(OURS) of Greater Milwaukee
2536 North 90th Street
Wauwatosa, WI 53226
Contact: Diane Beck

Organization for a United Response
(OURS) of North Central Wisconsin
Route 2, Box 155
Hatley, WI 54440
Contact: Warren and Virginia Heckert

Organization for a United Response
(OURS) of Northeastern Wisconsin
133 Appletree Court
Green Bay, WI 54302
Contact: Mike and Linda Troyer,
(414)465-0818

Organization for a United Response
(OURS) of South Central Wisconsin
1801 Kenneth Street
Madison, WI 53711
Contact: Mary Ann Fix

Organization for a United Response
(OURS) of Western Wisconsin
212 South 8th Street
River Falls, WI 54022
Contact: Ellie Richards, (715)425-7467

Wisconsin Federation of Foster Parents
1405 Madison Avenue
South Milwaukee, WI 53172
Contact: Rudy Czapiewski

Wisconsin Single Parents of Adopted
Children
3433 Solaris Lane
LaCrosse, WI 54601
Contact: Barbara Zakrajsek

Wyoming

Adoptive-Parent Support Group

Adoptive Parent Group
636 Bridger
Rock Springs, WY 82901
Contact: John and Mary Jo Gregg,
(307)362-2685

INTERNATIONAL ADOPTIONS

I f you are interested in adopting an infant or older child from outside the United States, you should first check with an adoption agency in your area for help and information. It is possible a local agency has a foreign program.

If not, the following list includes agencies that serve all parts of the United States.

Agape Social Services
Box 471
Carrollton, TX 75006
(214)245-8603
(Hard-to-place children from Latin America)

American Adoption Agency
1611 Connecticut Avenue, N.W.
Washington, D.C., 20009
(202)797-3756
(Chile, India)

Americans for International Aid and Adoption
877 South Adams, Suite 106
Birmingham, MI 48011
(313)645-2211
(Guatemala, India, Korea)

Catholic Social Services
222 North 17th Street
Philadelphia, PA 19103
(215)587-3873
(Korea, Hong Kong, Philippines, Peru)

Children's Home Society of Minnesota
2230 Como Avenue

St. Paul, MN 55108
(612)646-6393
(Hard-to-place children from Korea, Guatemala, Colombia)

Family Adoption and Counseling Service
2 Bon Price Terrace
St. Louis, MO 63122
(314)567-0707
(India and various countries in Latin America)

Friends of Children of North Vietnam
600 Gilpin Street
Denver, CO 80218
(303)321-8251

Globe International Adoptions Inc.
6220 West Monte Vista Road
Phoenix, AZ 85035
(602)247-3038
(Asia and Latin America)

Hand in Hand International
4965 Barnes Road
Colorado Springs, CO

(303)596-1588
(Philippines)

Holt Adoption Program
P.O. Box 2880
Eugene, OR 97402
(503)687-2202
(Korea, Philippines, Thailand)

Illien Adoptions International Ltd.
1254 Piedmont Avenue, N.E.
Atlanta, GA 30309
(404)872-6787
(El Salvador, India)

International Mission of Hope
10734 Tancred
Denver, CO 80234
(303)457-4206
(India)

International Social Service, American
  Branch
20 West 40th Street
New York, NY 10018
(212)398-9142
(Hong Kong)

Love the Children
221 West Broad Street

Quakertown, PA 18951
(215)536-4180
(Korea)

Thursday's Child Inc.
227 Tunxis Avenue
Bloomfield, CT 06002
(203)242-5941
(India, Latin America)

Universal Aid for Children
P.O. Box 610246
North Miami, FL 33161
(305)893-1535
(Central America and the Caribbean)

Welcome House
P.O. Box 836
Doylestown, PA 18901
(215)345-0430
(Hard-to-place children from Korea,
  Hong Kong, India)

World Child Inc.
2025 I Street, N.W.
Washington, D.C., 20006
(202)429-8885
(Latin America)

SINGLE-PARENT INFORMATION

Many adoptive-parent groups also have chapters made up of singles who have adopted. For other help and information on single-parent adoptions, check the following.

Committee for Single Adoptive Parents
P.O. Box 15084
Chevy Chase, MD 20815
(This group publishes a newsletter
that costs ten dollars for two years
and includes updates.)

Latin America Parent Association Singles
Contact: Barbara Breusley (212)410-4586

Michigan Association of Single Adoptive Parents
P.O. Box 601
Southfield, MI 48039
Contact: Jody Munday

Minnesota Single Adoptive Parents
1290 Englewood
St. Paul, MN 55104
Contact: Judy Dahlberg (612)646-9481

Single Adoptive Families Everywhere
11003 West 41st Avenue
Wheatridge, CO 80033
Contact: Judy Stewart (303)431-7171

Single Parents Adopting Children
Everywhere
6 Sunshine Avenue
Natick, MA 01760

Single Parents for Adoptions
1013-91st Street
Niagara Falls, NY 14304
Contact: Maggie Schultz (716)283-8827
or (716)837-1360

Single Parents for Adoption of Children Everywhere
95 Poplar
Roslindale, MA 02131

ADOPTION EXCHANGES

A nyone interested in adopting an older or special-needs child can receive help by approaching one of the adoption exchanges located throughout the United States. These exchanges keep files on waiting children and work to match these children with adoptive parents. Often their lists are computerized so that the searches can be done quickly.

Aid to Adoption of Special Kids
3530 Grand Avenue
Oakland, CA 94610
(415)451-1748

Child Care Association of Illinois
300 East Monroe Street, Suite 106
Springfield, IL 62704
(217)528-4409

Council of Adoptive Parents
700 Exchange Street
Rochester, NY 14608
(715)232-5110

Delaware Valley Adoption Resource
    Exchange/National Adoption Ex-
    change
1218 Chestnut Street, Suite 204
Philadelphia, PA 19107
(215)925-0200

Exchange of Mid-America
Kansas Children's Service League
P.O. Box 517
Wichita, KS 67201
(316)942-4261

Maine–Vermont Exchange
Maine Department of Human Services
Bureau of Social Services

221 State Street
Augusta, ME 04333
(207)289-2971

Northwest Adoption Exchange
909 N.E. 43rd Street, Suite 208
Seattle, WA 98105
(206)632-1480

Rocky Mountain Adoption Exchange
3705 East Colfax, Suite 105
Denver, CO 80206
(303)333-0845

Southeastern Exchange of the United
    States
P.O. Box 11181
Columbia, SC 29211
(803)799-1234

Southwest Regional Adoption Ex-
    change
227 North 23rd Street
Oklahoma City, OK 73103
(405)525-2451

Three Rivers Adoption Council
239 Fourth Avenue
Pittsburgh, PA 15222
(412)471-8722

INDEX